NATURE ~~VS~~ *Meets* NURTURE

STACEY N. DOAN, PHD *&* JESSICA L. BORELLI, PHD

NATURE

Meets

NURTURE

SCIENCE-BASED STRATEGIES
for RAISING RESILIENT KIDS

 AMERICAN PSYCHOLOGICAL ASSOCIATION

This project was funded in part by NSF BCS: 2027694 to SND

Published by
American Psychological Association
750 First Street, NE
Washington, DC 20002
https://www.apa.org

Order Department
https://www.apa.org/pubs/books
order@apa.org

In the U.K., Europe, Africa, and the Middle East, copies may be ordered from Eurospan
https://www.eurospanbookstore.com/apa
info@eurospangroup.com

Typeset in Sabon by Circle Graphics, Inc., Reisterstown, MD

Printer: Gasch Printing, Odenton, MD
Cover Designer: Mark Karis

Library of Congress Cataloging-in-Publication Data

Names: Doan, Stacey N., author. | Borelli, Jessica L., author. | American
  Psychological Association.
Title: Nature meets nurture : science-based strategies for raising
  resilient kids / by Stacey N. Doan and Jessica L. Borelli.
Description: Washington, DC : American Psychological Association, [2022] |
  Includes bibliographical references and index.
Identifiers: LCCN 2021047279 (print) | LCCN 2021047280 (ebook) |
  ISBN 9781433833106 (paperback) | ISBN 9781433833359 (ebook)
Subjects: LCSH: Parenting. | Parent and child. | Child
  development--Environmental aspects. | Resilience (Personality trait) in
  children.
Classification: LCC HQ755.8 .D597 2022 (print) | LCC HQ755.8 (ebook) |
  DDC 649/.1—dc23/eng/20211110
LC record available at https://lccn.loc.gov/2021047279
LC ebook record available at https://lccn.loc.gov/2021047280

https://doi.org/10.1037/0000284-000

Printed in the United States of America

10 9 8 7 6 5 4 3 2 1

For Eliana, my answer, Samara, my morning sun,
and always, Daniel, my blessing.
But, most of all, for my mother, Tien Dang,
who will never be able to read this book
but will recognize her name, here, and these words:
cảm ơn mẹ đã hy sinh tất cả cho con.

—Stacey

To all of the people who have taught me what a family is,
starting with my own.

—Jessie

CONTENTS

Contents

ACKNOWLEDGMENTS

We wrote this book in the middle of the COVID-19 pandemic when millions of women were considering leaving the workforce. I remember one night, at 3 a.m., holding my daughter, Samara, and nursing her in one arm while typing on my laptop with the other hand. On the cover of this book, you will see only Jessie's name and mine as authors, but this is certainly a falsehood. This book would not exist without the support of our partners, colleagues, friends, and family—and our children's teachers and child care providers. Just as importantly, our research was built on the work of so many other scientists, the parents who shared their stories with us, and the children who played along. To all of you, I express my profound gratitude for allowing me to make this journey.

At the same time, I would be remiss not to single out "dan dan noodles," who does the laundry, changes all the diapers, parents like a pro, goes along with every crazy idea, puts up with my moodiness, and single-handedly proved to me that love is not a fairy tale. I am grateful for my mother, Tien, and my daughters, Samara and Eliana, who taught me the critical distinction between "theory" and "application" when it comes to parenting—in other words, they showed me how to be a better mother. I give special thanks to my dear friend and mentor, Stefan Hofmann, who would have long discussions with me over Indian food about book writing, relationships, and parenting long before I ever wrote a book, had a grown-up relationship, or had raised kids. Pat Smiley, thank you for your friendship; for the free therapy; and for your compassionate, empathetic words of support. To Peter, I really do appreciate your last-minute perspectives, Schubert, and patience with me at the piano! I am grateful to my colleagues, Dan Krauss, Wei-Chin Hwang, Shana Levin, and Cathy Reed who advocated for me and created a work context that normalized parenting and, importantly, allowed me to explore and take risks. And, of course, Jessie, I am in awe of all that you have done and am floored by your brilliance and bravery. But mostly, I am simply befuddled by how you manage to write so fast and parent so well. You do it all beautifully.

—*Stacey*

A heartfelt thanks goes to my partner in this parenthood adventure, Dale, who has taught me more about how to love and be loved and from whom I have learned the importance of trust, unconditional support, and creativity. Nothing has made me love you more than watching the way you parent our kids (and, trust me—there was already a high bar in place). To Sam, Charlie, and Talia, thank you for allowing me to write about your experiences in this book and, more generally, for letting me share your hearts, cuddles, laughs, and tears. I would just like to set the record straight on one count here and now—I love you more than you love me! To Mom and Dad, thank you for being there for me through thick and thin. To Sarah, Adam, Daniel, Stephanie, and Ray, I thank you for encouraging me to pursue my goals and loving my family always.

To my clients and to the families that have participated in my studies, thank you for allowing me into your life, letting me learn from you, and permitting me to advocate for you. It has been an honor to step into the trenches with you and stand by your side. Thanks to the people who have inspired me to reach higher and dig deeper—my mentors in this field: Ann Kring, Alicia Lieberman, Linda Mayes, Arietta Slade, Nancy Suchman, and Dave Sbarra. Wanting to be like you made me a better person, and seeking to learn from you made me a better scholar. To my closest colleague, Pat Smiley, thank you for your friendship, partnership, and brilliance. And to my students, thank you for asking tough questions, keeping me engaged, and helping me grow alongside you. I couldn't ask for more. And, finally, thanks to Stacey for being a wonderful leader and teammate in this adventure. Your wit, vast knowledge of the field, humility, and humanity made you such a wonderful writing partner. I always knew you were a brilliant scientist, but now, I also know you are a wonderful storyteller.

—Jessie

INTRODUCTION

The idea for writing this book began germinating in our heads a couple of years after we had both received tenure. Now comfortable that we would have jobs for the foreseeable future, we were free to think more broadly about the kind of work we wanted to do. At this point in our lives, we had written dozens of scientific papers, but our children were still young. We were waking up in the middle of the night to face nightmarish monsters, fetch cups of water, and pat our younger children back to sleep. Our older kids were starting school, encountering new challenges with learning and with peers. We had years of training in developmental science at our fingertips, and after reading dozens of books on parenting—how to get children to sleep, what to do to help children be successful—we realized that there was a lack of parenting books focused on the basics of how children thrive emotionally with the goal of building *resilience*.

More specifically, our research and dozens of new studies over the past several decades have identified strategies and parenting behaviors that help children navigate challenges, bounce back from failures, and to thrive. We were interested in writing a back-to-basics books that would provide concrete techniques and tips to help parents with the goal of raising happy and healthy children. We firmly believe that a happy, healthy childhood is what all parents want and that it is the foundation for all goals and aspirations. We could have waited to write this book, but something about having the early childhood years fresh in our memory motivated us and added a sense of urgency to the story we wanted to tell.

Then the COVID-19 pandemic hit. All the supports we had put in place to make our careers feasible collapsed overnight. The precarious arrangement we had previously struck with work–life balance suddenly became a joke and gave us even more reason to wait to write our book. At the same time, though, the need for the book was becoming increasingly apparent. In this world of change, of rapid technological advances, societal upheavals, and natural disasters, what are the most essential aspects of parenting? What matters for children's happiness and well-being? Parents everywhere struggle with these same challenges of how to navigate this complex world in which we have so much information at our fingertips and so much pressure to invest in our children, all of which creates tremendous pressure to know the right thing to do—as if there were a single "right" way to parent. The pandemic took a pot of water that was already at a boiling point and turned it up 50 degrees because, suddenly, the pressure was on to be everything your child needed all at the same time (while also being everything your profession needed). Moreover, evidence was coming out showing an increase in stress, anxiety, and depression in children from toddlers to college students. We decided to write our book.

Becoming a parent may be the single most life-changing event a human being experiences. Despite having 9 months to prepare for this shift (longer, if you've been trying to get pregnant, less if it was a surprise), nothing can truly prepare you for this life change. No amount of babysitting, reading parenting books, or watching other parents as they parent prepares you to understand the gravity of having the sole responsibility for keeping a human being alive; for inculcating them with the values you wish a person to grow into adulthood with; for being the person your child looks to for guidance, for comfort, and for the answer to all of their woes. And nothing prepares you to turn into the kind of parent you want to be when you bring this person, who is to be your child, into the world. What if you don't have the answer to all of your own woes, let alone all of theirs? Well, of course you don't, because that's what being human is all about: None of us has the answer to our own pains. We travel this path of life not knowing where it ends, or where the path will wind, or where the bumps lie, and the transition to becoming a parent is no exception to this rule.

We, Stacey and Jessie, the authors, come to this book with overlapping and distinct expertise and intentions. One of us (Stacey) is a developmental psychologist by training with expertise on stress and children's biology. The other (Jessie) is a clinical psychologist, an academic and a practicing clinician who specializes in parenting, children, and relationships. This book has been a journey for us and a challenging one in many ways. We wanted to distill the voluminous body of research into something that parents can read and appreciate. We very much wanted to take a "whole person" approach to parenting. When we say, *whole person*, we mean we wanted to explain how biology, the mind, emotions, and thoughts all relate and play out in the context of parenting research. Parents are smart, and they want to know and understand their child. We also understand that parenting is complex and that children's development is influenced by a myriad of factors. We wanted to acknowledge this complexity.

This book, in many ways, is my (Stacey's) own therapy session. I am the first to admit I am not the greatest parent. Compared to my husband, I am impatient and can be harsh. My parenting behavior is likely very much influenced by my father, your stereotypical strict, authoritarian dad. I have spent years in therapy trying to understand his actions and trying to undo some of the harm he did. As an adult, I do understand and am more empathetic to his intentions. Yet, at the same time, I rarely write about my mother. She does not occupy my mind in the same way my father does. My mother knew how to love unconditionally. It is because of her love that I am here today. This book, then, is very much a book about her.

This experience of being hit over the head by the reality of parenthood cannot be any more humbling than having a PhD in child development and clinical psychology like I (Jessie) do. I spent years studying parent–child relationships and the importance of healthy emotional development in laying the foundation for a lifetime of health before I had my first child. Imagine what you might expect of yourself if you had earned a doctorate in parenting (effectively speaking) only then to become a parent and realize that the academic study of parenting is a far cry from the reality! I had also spent years working clinically with parents and children—hearing their stories, catching their tears, and weeping alongside them for their struggles—but even this could not prepare me for what it felt like to step into a parent's shoes.

Early in my (Jessie's) clinical training, the parent of one of my clients told me this:

> I would never fully trust a psychologist who hadn't been a parent before. If you haven't held a baby who wouldn't stop crying at four in the morning and had no idea what to do, how to soothe that baby—really experienced what it is like when there is nobody to call but you—then I just don't buy that you get what it's like to be me.

I remember thinking (in my naive therapist voice) that this might be the client's lens but that my lack of firsthand experience was made up for by my objectivity and ability see the situation clearly, unclouded by my own experience of parenting. Now, standing on the other side of 11½ years of being a parent, I see things completely differently. I know what it's like to be up in the middle of the night unable to soothe my crying baby, having nobody to rely on (or blame) but myself. I know that feeling of desperation and pain and fear. I know the questions that emerge: Will this ever end? Do I have what it takes to see this through? What can I possibly try next? In addition to these challenges of parenting an infant, I also know firsthand the deeper scars that come from parenting an older child, the gut-wrenching sadness that comes from watching your child experience something unkind in the outside world (like teasing or bullying) and knowing there's nothing you can do to shield your child from such pain. Parents of children who have qualities that likely will lead to teasing, bullying, or discrimination and racism know this kind of pain all too well. We release our children into this big world, knowing that the world isn't a safe place for them.

I (Jessie) wish I could go back to that parent and tell her that I now understand—and that I couldn't possibly have been as good of a therapist to her child then as I could now—or to her. There is no way I could have ever understood what it's like to have your child's heart sewn into your own in such a way that there is no mine and theirs. There is just an *us* and *ours*.

Our children grow and change in ways that surprise, delight, and dismay us, and we may similarly grow and change as parents. Our job is to shift alongside them, to adapt in the ways they need us to adapt so that we can be there with them. Where, though, are we to look for guidance about parenting? The amount of information out there in the media and our daily lives about parenting is dizzying. Now, more than ever, we are inundated with advice! Everyone from your grandmother to *The Economist* to Kim Kardashian has an opinion on everything related to parenting. The advice churns out unsolicited; it begins from the moment a pregnancy is announced, and it ends—well, it never really seems to end. The one thing that seems to be universal about parenting advice is that everyone is certain they've got it right, and people are quite dogmatic about their advice. And yet the advice given is completely conflicting, so one self-proclaimed expert may tell you that exclusively breastfeeding is the only way to go, and another one will tell you that formula feeding is absolutely guaranteed to help your baby.

The problem with all of these messages, too, is that somehow what is implied is that if you don't follow the given advice, you will have made a terrible mistake, taken a wrong turn, and have done something that will somehow exact irrevocable harm on your child. The other important corollary from these messages is that parents are incredibly powerful creatures: They have the power to exert tremendous influence over their children's future. Specifically, parents have the power to make horrible mistakes that could mess up their children's ability to realize their potential. Such pressure! You receive no training before you get there, and yet you somehow have all the pressure in the world to do it the right way the first time out of the gate!

Then there is an upsurge in the public discussion of biological and genetic underpinnings of personality and behavior, which often leaves parents feeling as though their children's struggles boil down to their fault because of (a) their genetics or (b) their parenting practices. The end result is that parents' anxiety has spiraled out of control. Worries—about one's own ability to parent, the extent to which parenting matters, and the thousands of ways the things we do (or don't do) can inadvertently hurt our kids—abound in social media and popular writings. At the same time, recent data suggest that parents and children are more stressed than ever. Rates of depression are rising with the most rapid increase seen in young people. Something has gone very wrong here. We aren't helping parents cope with the challenges of parenthood, and we might just be harming them. How are you, as a parent, to sort through this mess when all of these messages are coming at you from every which way?

All of this provided the motivation for this book. We felt the need for some sound, science-based, practical guidance for parents who do not want to be talked down to and don't want to be judged while parenting. The overarching goal of this book is to provide a science-based framework for best parenting practices that foster children's social-emotional development and adaptive stress-regulation strategies. Furthermore, in writing this book, we are seeking to balance equally the need to promote mental health within the whole family based on the understanding that children will suffer if parents' emotional needs are unmet. Thus, in our writing, you will feel us moving back and forth between considering the emotional needs of children and the emotional needs of parents, and advocating for approaches that optimize whole family health and well-being in the service of moving closer to open communication regarding everyone's rights and needs within the family system.

This book accomplishes these goals by reviewing and translating cutting-edge research on parenting in pursuit of the thesis that biology and parenting behavior are integrally intertwined. We make complex scientific insights regarding child development understandable for readers and underscore the practical implications of such understanding. We focus on best parenting practices that foster children's social-emotional development and adaptive stress-regulation strategies, and we offer concrete strategies parents can use to enhance their parenting in the service of promoting children's emotional well-being.

To make our points more concrete, we use examples from real parents and children, including from our own children's lives, and from our friends and colleagues. We also use examples from the families we have worked with in our research laboratories or clinical practice. When quoting our sources, we have made changes to preserve their confidentiality while remaining true to their stories. We often find that using examples helps us make our points more effectively, and we hope you will agree.

One thing you'll notice: We frequently try to illustrate how to use a parenting strategy effectively. Showing this means that we are probably talking about our parenting successes more than we are talking about our parenting struggles (although we do some of that, too). However, we don't want to give the impression that our parenting is full of successes and devoid of struggles. Like every parent, we find the experience of parenting to be one of ups and downs, trials and tribulations, frustration and reward. Oftentimes we present advice from experts in a way that is simplified to make it clear, but we know (from our own experiences) that parenting is *anything* but simple. Please keep this in mind as you go through the book and know that we are in this adventure alongside you—and that we strongly believe that being "in it" with your child is what matters more than arriving at a certain place.

INTENDED AUDIENCE

Who did we write this book for, you may be wondering? We wrote it for any parent or caregiver who is interested in joining this conversation about the impact of parenting on their child's development. The intention of this book is to help parents consider their parenting from different vantage points, to open up new ways of thinking and viewing their relationship with their child. As such, much of what we do in this book is invite you to engage in reflective practices and to consider information and how it pertains to your relationship with your child, rather than offer prescriptive or one-size-fits-all advice.

We wrote this book for parents who do not have any background in science, statistics, psychology, or medicine, so the terms we use and the way we describe the research studies used as examples throughout the book are designed to be accessible. Most importantly, we wrote this book for parents or caregivers of any gender or from any racial, ethnic, cultural, or religious background. Parenting practices undoubtedly vary across these demographic dimensions, however, and much of the research we have to draw on will, unfortunately, not feature people from all demographic backgrounds equally. Nonetheless, we intend for this book to be inclusive and for the messages we offer to be open to all parents and caregivers of children.

We believe this book will be most useful to parents of children under age 12 years; parents of children at this age have a stronger influence on their day-to-day lives. However, it's never too late to be reflective and intentional about your parenting, and even parents of late adolescents may find some of the topics we discuss to have relevance to their parenting experiences.

A SELF-GUIDED TOUR

Consider this book a self-guided tour through some of the latest ideas in the field of developmental psychology. You can think of it as something of a conversation with me (Stacey), a developmental health psychologist who designs laboratory-based studies on children's responses to stress, and with me (Jessie), a developmental clinical psychologist who sees clients and does research. As academics, we believe in the power of evidence and research. As parents, we also understand the importance of practical advice and the application of science. We cover a lot in this book and recommend you read the chapters in order—but take your time! At the end of each chapter, we also have a "Too Long, Didn't Read" box (with the heading "TL, DR") in which we quickly summarize the chapter's key points. We understand that, as a parent, sometimes the only free time available is the walk from the car seat to the driver's seat!

In Chapter 1, we lay out the complexities of the nature versus nurture debate in light of the recent work on *epigenetics*, the discipline devoted to understanding the influence of the environment on gene expression. We also make the case that parenting matters much more than we could have ever realized. Parenting behaviors can shape biology; they can also shape your children's genes. In Chapter 2, we discuss the nature of contemporary parenting with particular emphasis on the increased levels of stress and anxiety. We put forth the critical premise that, to be good parents, we need to be able take care of ourselves. In Chapter 3, we review the literature on love with an emphasis on why it is essential for resilience. We also seek to demystify "love" by being explicit about what it means. Chapter 4 focuses on prenatal development. The reality of the matter is that what "good parenting" looks like varies a lot as a child ages. Young children are unique, and in this chapter, we discuss strategies for helping very young children to develop into happy and healthy adults. Chapter 5 focuses on parenting during the early years of children's lives. Chapters 6 through 8 discuss concrete strategies that parents should nurture in themselves (e.g., empathy, mentalizing) and strategies for parents to try to regulate children's negative affect and also to capitalize on their positive emotions. In Chapter 9, we discuss the idea that your child's personality plays a role in how you parent (sometimes called an "individual differences approach"). In Chapter 10, we discuss the dynamics of coparenting and focus on how the complex interactions between parents can influence children's development. We round out the book with an epilogue.

On the whole, you can view this book as a user-friendly tour of the latest science out there on the ways in which parenting influences children's development. This tour focuses in particular on helping you raise children who will be resilient in the face of stress.

We thank you for going on this journey with us. Let's start, shall we?

CHAPTER I

PARENTING, STRESS, AND THE SHAPING OF CHILDREN'S BIOLOGY

Like many jokes, the story we are about to tell starts in a bar. But, unlike many jokes, this chance encounter led to one of the most astounding scientific discoveries in the past decade, with implications for parenting that have reverberated to this day.

It was 1992, the largest mall in America was just about to open its doors, Hurricane Andrew hit South Florida that summer, and Bill Clinton became the next president of the United States. The bar was on a street corner in Madrid, Spain, home to that country's oldest academic center for the study of neurobiology: the Cajal Institute. The institute was named after Santiago Ramón y Cajal, who won the Nobel Prize in Physiology and Medicine in 1906.

The Cajal Institute was hosting a conference that summer. At the meeting was Moshe Szyf, a molecular biologist and geneticist. At the time, he was not particularly interested in psychology or neurology, but a colleague had convinced him to attend the conference. Similarly, Michael Meaney, a professor of psychiatry, was also at the conference. Both were professors at McGill University, but, like most academics, they spent the majority of their time working in their silos and never interacting with one another. The two met up that fateful summer at a corner bar to discuss one of the oldest debates in psychology: Nature versus Nurture.

Meaney and Szyf's conversation that evening led to a series of studies that would profoundly influence how we think about the role of parents in shaping children's development. Moreover, their seminal studies would lay the foundation for some of the most groundbreaking work in the field of developmental psychology today, work that pointed at the immense influence of parents on a vast array of outcomes from mental to physical health. This work has even gone so far as to demonstrate that parental behavior can influence DNA and that these changes can be transmitted to the next generation. That's right: The simplistic nature versus nurture dichotomy—one that is so widely discussed in popular culture and the news media—is simply false. Thanks to Meaney and Szyf and the generations of researchers they inspired, we now know that parental nurture shapes the expression and influence of genes.

Just as important, by assessing the underlying biological mecha-nisms, researchers have started to understand *how* parenting behaviors get "underneath the skin," so to speak, to affect health and well-being. And guess what? The body's stress response system is the likely culprit. Biological imprinting is occurring during a time of immense change and stress. As we were writing this book, the world was experiencing a worldwide pandemic. While COVID-19 is affecting a broad swath of the population, parents are reporting more significant levels of anxiety, stress, and depression than their peers without young chil-dren.[1,2] In addition, despite increased investments in our children, in a report provocatively titled *The Kids Aren't All Right*, the American Psychological Association reported sky-high rates of stress and anxiety in children with findings showing that one out of five chil-dren reported that they worry a great deal.[3] Just as troubling, the report demonstrated that parents did not seem aware of the stress that children were feeling.

Given the intensity and importance of parenting young children, not to mention the heightened levels of stress associated with parenting in a time of rapid technological changes and societal upheavals, what does the new science of parenting tell us? Fortunately for us, the past decade of parenting research has looked precisely at the interactions among parenting, biology, and children's adaptation in the context of stress. If you decide to put this book down and not read beyond this first chapter, we have one important message that we would like you to leave with: Children's biological and behavioral stress responses are profoundly shaped by their social experiences. And, yes, there's more: The most important of all these relationships is the relationship with their primary caregiver. This is particularly true of young children. As a parent, *you* have the power to nurture your child to be resilient in the face of stress, to give them strategies to turn challenges into opportunities, and to empower them to face the real and imaginary dragons they will encounter. When people talk about grit, perseverance, and resilience in the face of stress, this is the stuff they are referring to. By gently encouraging your child to take on challenges and by equipping them with the skills to do so, you have the power to help your child become this superhero. Similarly, by modeling this type of behavior in your own life—facing your fears, believing in yourself, and challenging yourself to do better—your child will observe an example of this type of behavior in their most important role models.

OF RAT PUPS AND PARENTING

In 1957, a psychiatrist named Seymour Levine found that baby rats that were taken away from their mother for 15 minutes each day had lower levels of stress hormones.[4,5] This finding was somewhat surprising because being taken away from one's mother is a stressor, so you would think these rat pups would have higher levels of stress hormones, not lower. In looking closer at the data, it became clear that the rat pups that were taken away received extra licking and grooming when they were returned to their anxious mothers. The extra attention these rat pups received might not be very different from when a human baby cries in the arms of a stranger, and when the baby is handed back to the mother, the mother shushes, soothes, and pats her crying baby. Or it may not be so different from the working mother who eagerly rushes to day care at the end of each day and spends a few minutes kissing and caressing her children (sound familiar?). Levine thought that the extra licking and grooming these rat pups received might be somehow associated with their lower levels of stress later on.

Meaney had been conducting a series of experiments with rodents to test Levine's hypothesis that this extra licking and grooming were responsible for the reduction in stress hormones when he met Szyf at the bar that summer. In the course of his work observing hours and hours of video feed of licking and grooming, Meaney found that this behavior varied tremendously across individual rat mothers. Some engaged in a lot of this type of behavior, whereas others did so only minimally.

Meaney and his team followed the offspring of these rat mothers until the offspring were adults and then looked at these adult offspring's behaviors when encountering stressful situations. They found that, as adults, the offspring of the mothers who engaged in high amounts of licking and grooming behaviors appeared to behave more adaptively when encountering novel situations and facing scary or strange stimuli. They spent more time exploring new surroundings and were quicker to begin eating in a novel environment (a behavior suggesting that they were quicker to recover from the stress of a new environment). In addition to these overt behaviors, Meaney and his team also examined receptors in the brain systems associated with the expression of fearfulness and found that receptors for benzodiazepine (think Valium) were elevated in the amygdala, the area of the brain often associated with fear processing.[6] They also found decreased corticotropin-releasing factor (CRF) mRNA in the hypothalamus.[7] The CRF is responsible for activating hormonal and behavioral responses to a variety of stressors.

In follow-up work using a cross-fostering design, Meaney ruled out genetic effects and demonstrated that it was *who* the rat pups were reared by—and not who they were biologically related to—that influenced their fear responses. In other words, it was the adoptive mother and her behaviors that matter, not the biological mother's genes. That fateful night in the bar, Meaney and Szyf were not just having a conversation about genes *versus* the environment but the new science of epigenetics. The word *epigenetics* is Greek in origin and means "above" the genome. It is a field of science that focuses on heritable changes that are caused by the activation and deactivation of genes—that is, epigenetics focuses on gene expression. These changes occur without any underlying change to the DNA sequence. *Gene expression* is when the instructions in our DNA get used and interpreted usually into proteins. It is considered the most basic level at which our genes give rise to our different characteristics. This process, however, can be changed along with the way such that the timing and even the amount of protein that is being created can be altered. For example, one can consider DNA the recipe that sits in a box (or, these days, on a webpage somewhere). Unfortunately, or maybe fortunately, for my (Stacey's) waistline, one has to actively look up the recipe, gather the ingredients, and follow a series of steps before chocolate appears! The process of baking the cake is the gene being expressed.

One way to think of epigenetics is to consider genes as instructions, maybe a screenplay, and epigenetic markers as the director. The director significantly determines the sense, feel, and even meaning of the story by interpreting and editing the script, deciding what scenes to cut or keep, and directing the actors and camera. Through all these facets, the director shapes the end product, which would look different if the film had been directed by, say, Steven Spielberg, Spike Lee, or Ridley Scott. In the rat pups, the biological mother provided the genes or the instructions, but the adoptive mother influenced the gene expression, that is, how much fear they actually ended up feeling. How your DNA is going to affect you, and even whether it will, depend on epigenetic processes.

Researchers have long known that epigenetics is the process by which a cell's specialization (whether it will be a skin cell or blood cell) occurs during development. Moreover, an already growing body of research has suggested that exposure to chemicals, such as bisphenol A[8] (you might have noticed the sign "BPA free" on many plastics), and nutrition[9] exert epigenetic effects. Chemicals in the environment can turn off and on genes and, in the process, increase or decrease the risks for certain types of disease. But the idea that the social environment or parenting behavior can act as a lever, turning genes on and off in this way, was much more novel. What Meaney and Szyf considered together in this corner bar was whether maternal behavior could actually be exerting epigenetic effects—turning off and on the genes of these rat pups. As a parent, can we tinker with our child's DNA? Spoiler alert: Yes, we can.

In a seminal paper, Meaney and Szyf rocked the world by determining that this specific behavior of the mother rat, the high licking and grooming, led to a cascade of cellular and molecular changes. In scientific terms, that behavior reverses the methylation state of the glucocorticoid receptor gene in the hippocampus, resulting in higher numbers of glucocorticoid receptors in the brain of the rat as an adult.[10] The number of glucocorticoid receptors is essential because those receptors help to effectively regulate the amount of cortisol, a prominent stress hormone, circulating in the brain and body. To put it simply, the licking and grooming behavior in the rat mothers changed how genes were expressed in the rat pups, resulting in more effective regulation of the physiological stress response and leading to a much happier and healthier rat pup. These changes stuck around into adulthood to influence both their behaviors in a stressful situation and how their bodies responded. Moreover, the rat pups who were raised by the high licking and grooming behavior grew up and became high lickers and groomers themselves, thereby passing on this trait to the next generation. And just like that, Meaney and Szyf developed this beautiful model of intergenerational transmission of caregiving, at least insofar as it applied to rodents.

In essence, what this body of work tells us is that Nature is hedging her bets. Because it is unclear what the environment will be like after the child is born, it doesn't make sense to have a DNA program that is fixed. Essentially, the prenatal period (as we discuss in Chapter 4) and early childhood are periods during development when signals that come from the environment tell the child what kind of world the child will grow up in. If the world is a dangerous place, it might be important to be hypervigilant and wary so that one can be prepared for danger. To illustrate, research has demonstrated that hunger and malnutrition can program the genes of offspring to influence metabolism.[11] In particular, higher levels of malnutrition or undernutrition lead to a slower metabolism, thus urging the body to hold on to each calorie. This programming might be adaptive if the child were born into an environment in which food is scarce, but that could lead to a host of metabolic health problems if the child were born into a nutrient-rich environment, that is, an environment with easy access to high-sugar, high-caloric foods. It is important to understand that these programming effects are not inherently positive or negative in and of themselves, but they can cause problems in the case of a mismatch between what our bodies are programmed to do and the environment we live in.

I (Stacey) had the honor of hearing Dr. Meaney talk about his work in Boston when I was in graduate school studying child development. After hearing his talk, I asked him, "What does licking and grooming look like in humans? Do you think variations in human maternal behavior have such profound impacts on our children?" I will never forget his answer: "You're the psychologist. Why don't you figure it out?" In some ways, this book *is* a response to those questions. Although epigenetics studies allow us to determine links between genes and parenting in rodents, establishing causality of human parental behavior is much more challenging than studies with rats. But a growing host of research in our labs and in the labs of our mentors, collaborators, and other developmental psychologists have definitively demonstrated that parental behavior can profoundly influence the shaping of children's psychological, behavioral and biological development.

Before we get into the nitty-gritty details of specific parenting behaviors that matter for children, we provide you with biology basics drilled down to be intelligible. In this first chapter, we describe some of the latest research in psychobiology and epigenetics. *Psychobiology* is the science that focuses on how biology and behavior relate to one another. Epigenetics, on the other hand, provides a framework for understanding how experiences in the world shape the expression of genes. Because so much of how parenting affects children's health and well-being is thought to be mediated through the stress response system, we start with this topic. If you are stressed out, up late at night, and just want to know why parenting matters, you can always skip this section!

STRESS AND THE BIOLOGICAL STRESS RESPONSE

To understand the profound effect of parenting on children, we need to understand both stress and the biological stress response system as well as how children experience stress. When I (Jessie) asked my children if they knew what "stress" was, Talia responded, "It's a feeling, worried, or mad, or a combination of all of those. [Stress is] when you are tired of something—or if you have lot of stuff to do, or if you are late for something." Sam, my oldest child, added, "Kids can *definitely* feel stressed for a number of reasons. Like for school and homework, mean teachers, parents getting into an argument." Similarly, when stress researchers talk about stress, they can be referring to multiple things. For example, they can be talking about stressful events, also known as stressors, such as the loss of a beloved pet or an upsetting interaction at work. Alternatively, stress can refer to the subjectively felt emotions that a stressful event elicits (e.g., feeling stressed out by an impending deadline). Stressors, though, don't in and of themselves have to be negative to cause stress. Even events inspiring a great deal of excitement and joy can also cause stress. You can ask any bride planning a wedding, a parent about to embark on a vacation with their toddler, or a student moving to a new state to go to college, and chances are they feel stressed! Broadly, stress is essentially any threat to homeostasis or, to put it bluntly, change. Change, whether good or bad, requires us to mobilize our cognitive, emotional, and bodily systems to respond. When we have the right coping strategies, the right support systems, we experience stressors as exhilarating challenges or even as fun, engaging, and motivating activities (e.g., the thrill of a roller-coaster ride or, for actors, the opening night of a play).

There's more about how researchers characterize stressors. When we think about stressors, we can often (although, not always) distinguish between acute and chronic stress. *Acute stress* is time limited; it is often short lived and has a concrete beginning and end. Almost getting hit by a car or getting a vaccination (or seeing your child get the shot!) can be considered acute stressors. In contrast to these acute stressors with their discrete stop and start times, *chronic stressors* and daily hassles are events that occur over long periods. Experiencing poverty or never knowing where your next meal will come, living near a loud airport, or dealing with traffic every day all constitute chronic stressors. Note that the distinction between chronic and acute is not always clear. Receiving the diagnosis of cancer can be an acute stressor (you may remember the details of the event down to the minute), but the consequences after that can be long lasting. Of the two, research suggests that chronic stress is more detrimental to health and well-being.[12] This finding is important to keep in mind when we are raising children. Inevitably, there will be times when children feel stress, scared, or sad. The key to whether this stressor is dangerous is its dosage, that is, how long it lasts.

When facing a stressor, we also experience a range of emotions: We can feel scared, defeated, or simply a little worried. Like the story of "Goldilocks and the Three Bears," there is such a thing as an optimal amount of stress. As professors, we are worried when a student proclaims, "Nah, I am not stressed about taking this upcoming exam at all." While one might think that this student is overprepared and merely ready for the exam, it is often more likely the case that they are not engaging with the material or that they don't feel invested in the course. If you care about something, it makes sense to be a little bit stressed about being evaluated. And a little bit of stress is motivating. Even though we both have given hundreds, if not thousands, of talks and lectures during our careers, the night before we step in front of the classroom, go on stage, or walk into our workshops, the rise in blood pressure and increased sweating motivate us to review our lecture materials one more time, to check our notes, and to make sure we are capable of rising to meet the challenge.

We get stressed because the event matters to us—in this case, our emotion tells us that an important occasion is ahead and we must devote some attention and resources toward it for it to be successful. There is even a name for this phenomenon. The Yerkes–Dodson Law states that the relationship between arousal (or stress) and performance is an inverted *U* shape. If you plot stress on the horizontal axis and performance on the vertical axis, at low levels of arousal, performance is poor—we aren't motivated to perform. In other words, we don't have that excited energy. As arousal starts to go up, we see performance go up, eventually getting to an optimal level, or peak, at the top of the inverted *U* shape. This is the sweet spot where we have the perfect amount of arousal to influence our best performance. However, if you reach high levels of stress, you start feeling the pressure and anxiety, which negatively affects performance. We see this in athletes all the time. When the competition is fun and engaging, they're feeling the good stress of motivation, they can get in the zone, but if they start to feel immense pressure with a coach and fans yelling in their ears, they can't focus as much on the game. They're too stressed out.

While both stressors and the subjective experience of stress are concepts that most of us can understand and relate to, fewer of

Talia 7

us think about the third facet of stress that researchers often discuss: the physiological or biological stress response. Consider, for example, that when we are stressed, our heart rate tends to speed up, our eyes dilate, and our skin becomes a tad bit clammier. This physiological or biological stress response enables the body to "rise to the challenge" and deal with the threat. This physiological stress response is evolutionarily adaptive and likely enhanced our chances of survival.[13] In our evolutionary past, when we were being chased by a lion, the mobilization of these systems—the rush of sugar to the bloodstream, the increased vigilance—helped us to fight or flee. This is why the stress response system is often called the fight-or-flight system. The cascade of physiological changes is also likely the reason why chronic stress is much more damaging to our bodies. Even though activating the stress response system helps us to handle stressors, repeated mobilizations lead to wear and tear on the body, with consequences for health.[14]

The two most crucial stress systems are the autonomic nervous system and the hypothalamic–pituitary–adrenal axis (HPA).[15] These two systems act in coordinated ways to mobilize the body's ability to respond to stress but also to recover from stress. Under stress, the peripheral nervous system takes a break, and the sympathetic nervous system (SNS) pushes down the gas pedal, leading to the release of hormones that increase heart rate, trigger the release of sugar into the blood, and increase blood flow to the muscles. In the central nervous system, it leads to alertness and speeds up our ability to act. This process is incredibly fast and can occur even outside of our awareness! For example, we might jump out of the way of a flying ball before we even realize what's happening. If the stress continues, the brain then activates the HPA, which, in turn, triggers the adrenal glands to release cortisol. Cortisol amplifies and sustains the activity of the SNS and has wide-ranging effects with implications for our weight, how our immune system functions, and for our risk for heart disease![16] These systems are intricately intertwined and sophisticatedly coordinated, and the balance of these systems helps maintain our health and well-being.

Importantly for contemporary society, the stress response system is a "general adaptation system."[17] What this means is that a similar stress response is activated across a range of stressors whether that stressor is physiological, such as when we step into a cold winter night, or social, like when we are tasked with giving a speech to a loud, unsupportive audience. In his influential book on stress, *Why Zebras Don't Get Ulcers*, Robert Sapolsky, a professor at Stanford University, argues for the idea that although the stress response system is similar across species, what humans do with it makes us significantly different from other animals.[18] Unlike, say, a zebra, humans get stressed not only by actual events but also by merely thinking and imagining past events, future events, or possible future events. We get stressed thinking about an interview tomorrow or about the time we made that stupid comment in front of our boss. We worry about climate change and feel empathy for the refugee child on the other side of the world. This ability to abstract and consider the past, future, and possible scenarios is powerful. The feelings that we associate with these abstractions are also motivating. At the same time, however, these worries have the potential to overwhelm us. When we are up at night ruminating about things we can't change, we activate this stress response. These daily ruminations become a chronic stressor that can, over time, make us sick. Our bodies simply weren't designed for this type of overactivation of the stress system over long periods. Evolution designed our stress response to cope with stressors like lions, but, instead, we have brains that make us worry about theoretical or looming long-term threats like climate change, the next presidential election, and the next pandemic.

THE SOCIAL SHAPING OF THE STRESS RESPONSE

It should come as no surprise that other people help us deal with stress. What exactly this social support looks like in our daily lives varies. Other people can provide instrumental and material support, providing us with basic needs, such as food and shelter. That this type of support helps us to survive is nothing new, but what is striking is that the emotional sustenance that other people can provide is just as necessary for our health and well-being. Emotional sustenance might look like visits to a therapist to help us deal with our emotions or receiving a hug after a long and stressful day at work—or, for children, "It makes me feel better to be able to talk with my mommy and to make a plan to solve the issue," says Sam, my (Jessie's) child. Sam adds, "I think it's harmful to just be upset and not do anything about it. It will just build up and get worst. It makes you feel a lot better if you tell someone."

When stressed, say, when we are on stage, a simple smile from a supportive audience member can go a long way. Indeed, the mere presence of someone sitting and holding our hand can influence how our brain responds to threat.[19] "I really like it when people just say, 'It's okay,' or when Mommy rubs my back," my (Jessie's) 7-year-old Talia states. Decades of research have demonstrated that people with high levels of social support live longer and are generally happier and healthier.[20] Analogously, loneliness and social isolation have the opposite effects and are detrimental for psychological and physical health.[21] Among those who are married, the quality of the relationship predicts a wide range of health factors, including faster recovery, lower risk of getting sick, and even a lower rate of death following a life-threatening illness.[22,23] Some researchers have argued that "humanity's greatest strength is other humans."[24]

Human children are no different in that the bond they build with those who love them is pivotally important for their health and well-being. At the same time, human children are significantly different from adults: Because of their immaturity, they are much more susceptible to outside influences. Notably, the HPA axis that we discussed earlier is shaped by social experiences even before the child is born (more on this in a later chapter on parenting before birth). Supportive early relationships train the HPA to respond in adaptive ways to stress. Importantly, loving relationships are powerful buffers against stressful events in children's lives.[25]

One of the giants in the field of developmental psychobiology, Megan Gunnar at the University of Minnesota, pioneered some of the earliest work examining children's stress response. In particular, she focused on the hormone cortisol. Cortisol, as you remember, is the end product of the HPA axis, one of the body's primary stress response systems. There is robust research on cortisol in children compared with other hormones, and this is partly because of how it's extracted. In the past, getting hormone data in children required drawing blood. As any parent would tell you, enrolling your child in a stress study in which they will be pricked and prodded is not most parents' idea of a good time. However, advances in science have now allowed researchers to measure cortisol in children's spit. Fortunately, for us, children don't mind, and many even enjoy spitting!

In stress studies, researchers either bring kids to the lab or they capitalize on naturalistic everyday stressors, such as doctor visits. Gunnar and her students realized again and again that children who had responsive, warm caregivers produced lower levels of stress hormones than their peers. Repeatedly, across different types of stressors, whether that meant getting their immunizations, seeing a scary toy spider, or meeting a clown (who wouldn't be scared of that?), if a parent were there, cortisol levels simply did not rise to the degree that they would if the children were not with a parent. At the same time, if the quality of the relationship was not warm and nurturing, the parent's presence did not protect the children from increases in cortisol.[26] So, by regulating children's stress response, parents help children to confront novel and new situations. And, for children, almost everything is new and novel from the neighbor's dog to the moving escalator. However, parents' presence is only protective for children (in terms of their cortisol response to a stressor) when they have previously proven themselves to be supportive of their children. Without a supportive presence, elevated stress hormones could shape a more fearful, anxious brain.[25] Moreover, repeated activations of the system can lead to dysregulation that may cause the stress response to go awry. For example, it may become more hyperactive, responding too intensely to novel or fearful situations. Alternatively, it may be hypoactive (where it doesn't respond when it should), or, perhaps, the system responds but simply doesn't recover and remains revved up when it should calm down.

These sustained levels of cortisol and other stress hormones have long-lasting effects. In one study, researchers found that older adults who reported that they had warm, supportive relationships with their parents during childhood had a larger hippocampus and also lower cortisol in response to a stressor.[27] The effect of warm, supportive parents cannot be underestimated!

ADVERSE CHILDHOOD EXPERIENCES

Fortunately, or unfortunately, parenting does not occur in a vacuum. And unfortunately, early events, particularly stressful events in the lives of children, can also profoundly alter their DNA and biological functioning. While Meaney and Szyf were tinkering around with the genes of mice, evidence was emerging that stressful experiences during childhood could have long-term effects on health and disease in adulthood. The first adverse childhood experiences (ACEs) study came out of Kaiser Permanente, a managed care consortium based in Oakland, California.[28] In this watershed study that would forever change the way the world thinks about early experiences, this group of investigators asked more than 17,000 patients receiving physical exams to fill out questionnaires regarding their childhood experiences, current health status, and health behaviors.

Results of this study demonstrated several key findings. First, almost two thirds reported experiencing at least one ACE. Just as significantly, the more ACEs the individual experienced as a child, the higher the risk of negative health and negative health behaviors in adulthood. ACEs have been linked to autoimmune disease,[29] cancer,[30] disability,[31] depressive disorders,[32] and increases in drug and alcohol use during adolescence.[33] Some of these effects were found decades after the occurrence of the adversity.[34]

Studies have also demonstrated that ACEs exposure is associated with epigenetic changes.[35] In a sample of 215 participants, one study found that the severity, frequency, and type of ACE exposure was related to higher levels of methylation of the *NRC31* gene, the gene that codes for glucocorticoid receptors.[36] This finding was replicated in another study in which the researchers found that early life adversity was associated with methylation profiles associated with the stress response.[37] In follow-up work, Meaney and Szyf demonstrated that similar epigenetic regulation processes were likely at play when looking at the brains of victims with a history of childhood abuse.[38]

In addition to ACEs exposure, researchers have also looked at exposure to natural disasters. In one rare longitudinal study, researchers studied mothers who were pregnant at the time of a major natural disaster in Canada. In the Quebec ice storm of 1998, Suzanne King, a professor in the department of psychiatry at McGill University, like hundreds of thousands of others, lost power and was without heat for weeks. After her power was restored, King had her blood pressure checked; it was far higher than normal. That was when she realized the ice storm could serve as a natural, albeit tragic, experiment to examine the effects of stress on outcomes. She recruited mothers who were pregnant at the time and followed them and their children for nearly 20 years. King published a series of papers from this cohort demonstrating that self-reported stress in mothers at this time predicted anxiety, depression, and aggression in their children.[39] Objective, but not subjective, experiences of stress were associated with IQ and language[40] and physical health outcomes, including obesity, at age 5.[41] King and her colleagues also found relations between objective indicators of hardship at the time of the ice storm and methylation levels associated with 957 genes in the children.[42] As King has said,

> You cannot change a person's DNA, but along the DNA there are these little spots that are a little bit like little switches that turn different genes on and off according to the environment. So it's a little bit like a piano. You can't change the keys on the piano, but you can play a different tune.[43]

Other studies have also found evidence for this intergenerational transmission of trauma. Holocaust survivors and their children have epigenetics markers on the *FKBP* gene linked to posttraumatic stress disorder, depression, and anxiety.[44] This paper had a small sample, and it did not look at third or fourth generations. Still, it is consistent with work that showed a significant increase in generalized anxiety disorder among adult children of Holocaust survivors as compared with the general population.[45]

It is clear that both objective stressful experiences and everyday, loving interactions (or the lack thereof) in the home can have profound, long-lasting effects—all the way down to the genetic level.

PUTTING IT ALL TOGETHER

Our goal in this first chapter is to be explicit about the thesis of our book. We argue that parents not only contribute their genetic makeup to their children but also continue to profoundly shape their children's lives in how they react and respond to those children. Genetics do not determine who a child becomes. Instead, children's experiences in their environment interact with their genetic background to influence who they become. And their most important early environment is you, the parent! Importantly, there are clear underlying biological mechanisms for how these types of early experiences "get underneath the skin" to affect health and well-being. However, we cannot underscore enough that being an "effective regulator" of our children does not mean that we should always protect our children from stress.

As psychologists, we are often asked, "What do I need to do not to mess up my kid?" Many parents may hear this message about epigenetics and get really stressed out. We get it; we know it can feel like pressure to think that you are going to have a profound influence on your child's development. It is clear to us that parenting can engender tremendous anxiety. Most often, parents think that the way to help their children live good lives is to help them avoid pain and only experience good feelings, and to provide them with as many resources as possible so that they can compete in this harsh-seeming world. If every day in your child's life were like that perfect sun-dappled day of summer vacation, untarnished by a skinned knee or sunburn, life would be peachy keen for your child. And if you could give them all the extra dance class, tutors, and skill in sports, then they would be successful. We try so hard to protect our children from negative emotions and from stressful events, and we to give them every advantage in the world. We are here to tell you that this philosophy is neither practical nor even beneficial. Rather, this "all in" mentality can emotionally cripple our children. Our aim in this book is to demystify what really matters when it comes to parenting, to arm you with tools that empower you in your parenting so that you feel equipped to parent with purpose. Our hope is that this book will anchor you in your parenting values so that you are standing solidly in this position feeling empowered, knowing what really matters for children.

In this chapter, we presented the literature on stress and how parents shape the process in their children. But we want to make sure that parents also understand that their role in "shaping" children's biology is simply not about removing all stress. Stress is not all bad. Our role as parents is not to protect our children against all stress and negative emotions but to create contexts in which they can practice facing challenges. By experimenting dealing with stress in the presence of a loving parent, children will be able to effectively deal all by themselves with the stressors that life will inevitably throw at them in the future. Allowing children to practice managing moderate levels of stress is good for them, and it is a skill that can be taught. It's through handling stress that our children get the opportunity to develop coping strategies, overcome their fears, and experience themselves as being strong and powerful. Those are important lessons to learn and ones you don't want your child to miss out on. And, if we are good at helping children manage moderate levels of stress so they can handle challenges early in life, they will get better and better at handling challenges on their own, and we will become redundant.

Let's illustrate these ideas with some examples. One Saturday, I (Stacey) took my daughter, Eliana, to a rock climbing wall when she was 5. Eliana is a very emotional child. Physical exercise and sleep are both essential for Eliana to get rid of her angst and to moderate her emotions. As physical activity and a good night's sleep go hand in hand, finding activities that are engaging and physical is a regular weekend activity in the household.

Eliana had seen pictures of me rock climbing, and she loved to climb on everything (playground equipment, of course, but also furniture and even her father). The *idea* of rock climbing was very exciting for Eliana, but the reality as it presented itself on that day was terrifying. Once we got there and Eliana saw the high walls and the thin ropes, she was absolutely terrified. She adamantly refused to get into her harness and protested all attempts to coax her into going up the wall. I explained, cajoled, and, at later points of desperation, even bribed her. But she refused. She cried loudly and screamed that she wanted to go home. This tantrum went on for approximately 30 minutes, causing quite a bit of embarrassment for my partner and me. Many parents would have gotten up and left, perhaps, telling themselves their child wasn't ready. And these parents may be correct. But I knew my daughter; I knew that Eliana loved to climb, and I had faith this would win out in the end. I also knew Eliana was scared.

So, I repeated the following 20 times (although it feels like a gazillion) and reminded Eliana of her strengths: "Remember, how you climbed the wall at the playground? You can do it again here. Eliana, you will love it." I affirmed Eliana's emotions: "I know it looks scary. I know you want to forget about it and go home." And I explained the situation: "It is very safe. See this harness? It keeps you attached to the rope. You won't fall, I promise." I told Eliana that we would not leave until she tried it (and hoped fervently that we wouldn't get kicked out). Eliana, once realizing I was serious, started to climb the wall while still crying. And lo and behold, through her tears, she started to smile. "Do you want to try it again?" I asked. "Yes, Mama! More!" she yelled. Now she goes rock climbing without me. Ironically, it is now Eliana who causes fear in me at the rock climbing gym because she regularly takes risks that cause a shiver to crawl up my back.

This is a strategy that I (Jessie) recommend my clients use with their children, particularly those who are having trouble managing stress or anxiety. There will never be a safer or more understanding or forgiving "playground" in which to practice managing stress than in their parents' presence. The desire to protect children from pain is powerful in parents—we love our children and don't want to see them suffer—but dealing with manageably hard things can help us learn how to cope with challenges so that we are better able to handle stress over the long term. And it provides opportunities to talk through how your child is feeling, what they are thinking, and ways of coping with stress, so there are lots of teaching moments and opportunities for connection embedded in these experiences. This is one of the most commonly used techniques in cognitive behavior therapy, an empirically validated form of psychotherapy that is used with both children and adults.[46] The main principle behind this form of intervention, which is called *exposure*, is precisely what we just articulated: that by being able to tolerate the feelings and thoughts that come up when confronting a moderately difficult situation and by developing coping skills for managing these situations, the individual grows stronger and is better able to handle these situations in the future.

An example from my (Jessie's) own life is of my eldest daughter, Sam, who is very sensitive to criticism. A few months ago, my daughter was having trouble whenever my partner or I would make critical comments about her behavior. Sam would react strongly to these comments, and I wanted her to work on being less sensitive to criticism because these comments were intended to be constructive, not hurtful. I decided to talk to Sam about the fact that I wanted her to get more comfortable with criticism. Sam is extremely well behaved and rarely, if ever, gets into trouble, so she is probably highly motivated by the praise of her parents and other adults. This is generally a positive quality, but I also wanted Sam to be able to hear moderately critical feedback and not be so hurt by it (after all, getting criticism and encountering failure just means you are taking risks, which is a *good* thing!).

So, I initiated a "game" that we started playing. In this game, I practiced giving Sam silly criticism, pretending I was scolding her for certain actions so that she could get used to hearing me express negative feedback about her behavior. For instance, I would say something to her that I would simply never say: "Sam, what on earth are you wearing? You can't possibly think that your shirt is appropriate!" (Note that I almost never tell Sam what she can and cannot wear, so this is very unusual behavior on my part.) At first, I started out saying it in a way that conveyed to Sam that this was mock criticism (using a very silly, exaggerated, high-pitched, and loud voice). At first, even that criticism was hard for Sam to hear, and she would frown and have hurt feelings. Importantly, though, these were manageable feelings, ones that could be discussed and used as learning experiences.

We talked through how it felt to hear the feedback, what thoughts Sam had about the feedback and why (that she wasn't a good person, that she had to be perfect to be a good person), and why it's important to be able to hear feedback from others. Gradually, I increased the level of difficulty over the criticism so that I was making critical comments that were more believable (i.e., making negative comments about things that I might conceivably make comments about, such Sam's behavior toward her siblings). In doing so, in an increasingly realistic tone of voice (less use of the silly, exaggerated tone), these increases in realism were paired with Sam's growing ability to tolerate the criticism. As her criticism-resistance muscles were strengthening, I made the game more challenging so that Sam was still getting a good workout. Over time, this "game" resulted in lots of laughing and some frustration and also tears, but it did help my daughter become more resilient in the face of criticism, which was the ultimate goal. It was a goal that my partner and I and our daughter pursued over the period of a year, not just through the "game" but through various strategies, all of which involved a combination of exposure and conversation about my daughter's reactions to the criticism.

CONCLUSION

When we started writing our book, the COVID-19 pandemic had just begun, and many psychologists were worried about the long-term impact on children's mental health. Our research as well as that of others was demonstrating significant increases in children's behavioral problems immediately after schools were closed. But as the pandemic continued, and more and more data arrived, we started to see that most children were bouncing back. While not easy, families were adjusting. Indeed, the data suggest that in the face of stressors, resilience is the norm. An abundance of research suggests that this resilience can be attributed to loving, supportive relationships. By providing a safe and nurturing environment for children to face their stress—to risk failure—we are raising children who can later tackle not only their own problems but also the problems of the world.

Our hope in sharing this information with you is that you can feel empowered to help chart and rechart your child's course. We parents will never have complete control of who our children are. They enter this world with their own little personalities, their own quirks, each one different from the next. But know that your daily, small interactions with them will, over time, have an outsize influence. You can have some say on how this little creature will look after they grow up. When we have young children, we have our own lump of clay that we get to shape into a bowl or a cup or a vase. We can't control what size the lump is that we are given or how round or flat it is to begin with, but, to some extent, we can control how much time we spend shaping it and the way in which we massage it. And knowing this gives you the power to do something about it.

TL, DR

- Experiences within the parent–child relationship affect the child's developing stress biology.
- Exposure to moderate levels of stress can help children learn how to cope with stress.
- Exposure to negative, uncontrollable experiences of stress or adversity can have long-lasting effects on children's development.

CHAPTER 2

THE CHALLENGES OF CONTEMPORARY PARENTING

In an increasingly competitive world, parents have greatly increased resources, including the time, money, and, perhaps most important, attention, they put into "cultivating" their children. To quote one mom, "After all this parenting, I think I'll become a hostage negotiator. Seems less stressful." The perception is that parents have it more difficult today than in past generations. To set children up for success, they must be groomed and cultivated. This stands in contrast to the idea that children should simply be provided a safe place to grow and that nature will take its course in directing children's development.

PARENTING IN TODAY'S SOCIETY

Over the past 50 years, we have turned a corner in pop culture's portrayal of parenthood. Long gone are the days of the blissful, stress-free portrayals of parenthood, such as *Leave it to Beaver's*[1] carefree Barbara Billingsley or diaper advertisements with parents joyfully delighting in their children's every coo. No, we no longer expect parents to delight in their child's every milestone and to savor every experience of parenthood. The pop culture representations of parenting have moved toward acknowledging that stress is an inevitable aspect of the experience of parenting children. Barbara Billingsley has been replaced by characters like *Workin' Moms'* Kate Foster,[2] a working mother trying to squeeze parenthood into a life populated by a multifaceted identity; other complex characters deal with post-partum depression and anxiety, grapple with crumbling marriages, cope with infidelity, and experience the painfully real (and sometimes gross) changes and discomforts associated with parenthood. In essence, gone are the rose-colored glasses and in their place are the focus lenses that have allowed us to humanize the experience of parenthood. With this humanizing process, we have acknowledged that stress and the experience of negative emotionality is part and parcel of parenting.

So, you wonder, has the shift to portraying parenting more realistically in the media reduced parents' experience of stress? Meaning, now that it's out in the open that parenting is stressful, and we can more freely talk about the difficulties of parenting, has this relieved some of the pressure from parents and enabled them to become less stressed? Well, you would certainly hope so, and perhaps it is so, but, unfortunately, the data suggest that today's parents are highly stressed. It appears that parenting today is associated with far more stress than it was in prior decades.[3] One study found that compared with mothers assessed in the 1970s, mothers in the early 2000s reported feeling more exhausted from child-rearing even though these same parents reported believing that their children were healthier and lived in higher quality neighborhoods.[4] So, if temporal patterns are any indication, there is not a positive association between media coverage of parenting stress and reductions in stress. Perhaps the correlation goes the other direction: The media is covering parenting stress because parenting stress has become so darn ubiquitous that it just can't be overlooked any longer. In other words, we can't contain it because we're bursting at the seams with the stress of parenting.

Even if we, as parents, weren't worried about our kids' future economic health, this idea of intense cultivation is still pounded into us everywhere we look. We are constantly bombarded with information and advice from medical professionals, family, friends (even those without kids!), the occasional kind stranger, and the ubiquitous World Wide Web. Everyone has an idea and an opinion about how to raise our kids, what gadgets we need, the latest enrichment activity, how much to use technology, or whether to use it at all—and all of this even before the baby is born. "Don't drink coffee, be wary of deli meat," we're told, and, more recently, "Meditate, do yoga, stress is not good for the baby." The rise of social media has also made us even more keenly aware of how others are raising their kids. Social media provides windows into the lives of other people. Unfortunately, these windows are often dressed up to an unnatural degree. As Melanie, a mother of four children, a lawyer, and an advocate for children with special needs, put it,

> Parents post only the successes that their children achieve: "Little Johnny got into Stanford!" and "Emma just placed first in her swim meet!" It makes me feel that I am not doing enough for my own children despite the fact that I know the troubles some of these families are having.

This phenomenon to cultivate and compete is so pervasive in American and other Western societies that it's felt from the most affluent communities to the most disadvantaged, and the disadvantaged communities are having an even harder time keeping up. Take a look at Evan. His parents proudly stated, "In addition to school, Evan is enrolled in Mandarin classes, French classes, and Russian math. He also does swimming, soccer, and piano." Evan's parents are upper middle class and they have two young children and a nanny who helps take care of the kids, drive them around, and do some light cleaning. Yet, the exhaustion on Evan's mother's face is clear when she says,

> It's what everyone in the neighborhood does and Evan enjoys all these activities. We're privileged to be able to afford all of these things, but I am grinding my teeth at night. I am constantly sick. I think I am stressed, but I don't even know it.

On the other side of town, Lila, a single mother of three, is saying, "I am terrified I will be deported. Where will my children go?" Lila lives in a small, one-bedroom apartment. Mattresses line the floor and all five family members sleep in the same room. She has less time and money to ensure her children have a safe and secure home, let alone provide advantages like foreign language classes or nannies. "The people I work for hire coaches, all kinds of coaches, from family coaches to test tutors to coaches who help get their kids into college," she says. "I constantly feel like my kids can never compete. But at the same time, all of the parents are stressed out, we all are."

THE CASE AGAINST INTENSIVE PARENTING

Is it that today's parents today face more pressure than ever before to be more and to do more for their children? How could this be? In some ways, the children of today have far less to worry about because they are growing up with relatively fewer threats of violence and economic instability. However, whereas parents of yesterday were content to allow their children to roam free and spend their time unscheduled in the neighborhood, today's parents experience more pressure to provide enrichment activities scheduled on queue for their children throughout the day. The idea that we need to cultivate our children rather than let them grow wild certainly has some merits. In my (Stacey's) conversations with parents, I have encountered some parents who think there is no need to give kids additional opportunities or training or extracurriculars. We know that the idea that "it's all genetics, so it doesn't matter what school my kid goes to" is inaccurate. But the idea that parenting matters in some ways has gone too far.

The phenomenon of "overparenting" has been referred to using various terms, including "intensive parenting," "helicopter parenting," and "overcontrolling parenting." Most commonly, *overparenting* is used to signify the use of parenting practices that are inappropriately involving or controlling based on the child's or young adult's developmental stage.[5,6] And *intensive parenting* involves intentionally cultivating children's skills, interests, personalities, and proclivities through a highly focused level of attention.[7] Primarily more common among upper middle-class parents, intensive parenting has now been extended to parents across all socioeconomic classes.[8] The pressure felt to engage in wraparound parenting that meets a child's every need appears to fall unevenly on mothers.[9–11] One essential feature of this absorbed state of parenting is that this child-centered parenting ethos is highly demanding of parental resources, such as parents' emotional investment, time, effort, energy, and money.[12,13] This parenting approach is premised on the notion that parents are highly influential in children's developmental outcomes[3,10,12] and that children need be protected from negative environmental influences.

Unsurprisingly, ample evidence shows that these forms of intensive parenting are related to poorer adjustment in both the children and the parents themselves. In terms of the recipients of the parenting practices, studies have shown that children raised by caregivers who engage in these practices are at a greater risk for developing anxiety, depression, behavioral problems, lower academic achievement, and decreased motivation.[14–16] These findings are particularly ironic because parents who engage in these parenting practices are undoubtedly doing so because they have the desire to protect or to support their children and adolescents, to promote their growth and development, and to increase their motivation—in other words, they are trying to help them. However, their strategies are associated with long-term reductions in their children's functioning.

It is not a stretch to link these types of parenting practices—those that parents feel pressured by society to enact—and the types of parenting practices that are known to confer risk for the development of anxiety problems in children.[17] Intensive parenting can be related to clinically significant impairment in children and adolescents, too. For instance, it is not uncommon for me (Jessie) to see a family in my therapy practice caught in a similar type of situation in which the overparenting has contributed to a dynamic that has turned toxic for the child. The child is anxious (e.g., the child has become fearful of spiders), and the parent, in an attempt to help the child, has stepped in to assist the child in some way by accommodating the child's anxiety (e.g., the parent engages in an elaborate routine of checking the child's bedroom each night for spiders). This behavior, which appears helpful on its face, ends up becoming harmful for the anxious child because anxiety is like a gas and will expand to fill whatever space it is given. Before you know it, the child can't fall asleep without the parent engaging in this bedroom-checking behavior because the child has grown dependent on this behavior, and their anxiety has been made all the more powerful as a result of the accommodation. Although the parent intended to be helpful and supportive, this type of behavior has ended up being the opposite of helpful for a child who really needed to be lovingly challenged to face their fear rather than assisted in avoiding their fear.

In one of my (Jessie's) studies on this topic,[18] my colleagues and I were interested in identifying whether controlling parental behavior was associated with a reduction of physiological arousal in the parent. This hypothesis was based on my clinical observation that when parents engaged in controlling behaviors with their anxious children, the parents appeared to be relieved. Naturally, the parents found it upsetting to see their children in distress; efforts to reduce that distress were, therefore, a comfort to the parents. We had begun conceptualizing controlling parental behavior as a way of helping both the parent and the child avoid dealing with a potentially aversive situation. Controlling parenting helps the parent avoid having to deal with a child in distress that they cannot help, and it helps the child avoid having to deal with an anxiety-provoking situation (the situation that caused the distress). However, in both circumstances, the controlling parenting has a negative outcome because both the parent and the child are ultimately deprived of the opportunity to see that they can overcome the obstacles in their way and that they can confront what it is that is frightening them.

Back to the study: We sought to create a situation in which the mothers participating in the study would be highly tempted to intervene in the situation and become controlling because, after all, the goal of the study was to understand more about controlling parenting and the circumstances under which it occurs and the effects it has on both parents and children. We wanted to engineer a situation in which the mothers would feel that their children really needed them to step in to help them and that, without their help, their children would become upset or would be unable to overcome an obstacle. Thus, we relied on the brainchild of our colleague, Pat Smiley, who had designed a brilliant task: a series of impossible puzzles. Neither the child nor the mother was told that the puzzles were impossible.

The puzzle was presented on a computer screen, and the child was told to solve them. We asked the mothers in the study to sit 3 feet behind their child and to watch them work on the puzzles. All of the puzzles were timed, and after each puzzle's time ran out, the child received feedback on the answer they had provided in response to the puzzle. Because all of the puzzles were designed to be impossible, children received the feedback that they had not solved the puzzles correctly. As a result, the majority of the mothers in our study quickly began stepping in and helping their children, some of them by providing supportive comments (e.g., "You can do it. You're doing great!") and others, by becoming controlling in their behavior toward their children (e.g., taking the computer mouse themselves and attempting to solve the puzzles, forcefully moving the child's hand).

Before the beginning of the task, we had hooked mothers and children up to our psychophysiological equipment, so throughout the entire task, we were monitoring their heart rate, which allowed us to have a window into their stress throughout the task. What we learned from this study was intriguing. The mothers with higher anxiety showed reductions in their heart rate after they initiated controlling behavior during the puzzle task. In contrast, the children of these same mothers—the ones with high anxiety and higher control—showed increases in their physiological stress. Thus, our findings seemed to suggest that, in the short term at least, this controlling behavior in the mothers is associated with a physiological trade-off: For higher anxiety mothers, controlling behaviors are associated with reductions in stress physiology for parents but increasing physiological signs of stress in children.

Even though our laboratory findings suggested that controlling parenting was associated with a short-term "gain" in terms of the avoidance of stress physiology, most psychologists agree that avoiding stress in the short term makes things worse over the long term. In support of this rationale, for the mothers who subscribe to these parenting values or who use these parenting practices, there is a cost. Several studies suggest a positive association between intensive parenting and maternal depression, anxiety, stress, and guilt.[19,20]

One of the problems with intensive parenting is that it seems to entail the parent's solving the child's problem or taking away the child's distress. Remember how earlier we discussed the importance of children's encountering manageable levels of stress so that they can gain a sense of mastery in managing stressful experiences? Some theorists argue that intensive parenting places children at risk for anxiety because it deprives them of opportunities to develop strategies for coping with distress, which is an important skill to develop. An alternate explanation for the link between intensive parenting and child anxiety is that this parenting style signals to children that they are inherently vulnerable and in need of protection by their parents.[21] Children internalize the views of themselves that they perceive their parents have of them—that is, when children think their parents perceive them to be vulnerable and likely to crumble from stress, they, too, come to perceive themselves to be vulnerable and likely to crumble from stress.

On the other hand, children can derive tremendous strength when they perceive that their parents believe in them. They may gain confidence from knowing that a parent conceives of them as being capable of confronting challenges and rising above those challenges, of encountering distress and regulating a response to this distress, and of overcoming obstacles. Instead of perceiving the self as vulnerable and likely to crumble under stress, it would behoove children to conceive of themselves as persistent, determined, and willing to put in the effort to confront things that are hard. Thus, coming from a resilience, strengths-based, coping-oriented perspective, it is important that parents project the confidence in their children that they desire their children to have for themselves.

EVERYTHING TO EVERYONE: WORK–FAMILY CONFLICT

One significant source of stress for parents is the pressure to do everything and be everything for one's child. It should be unsurprising, then, that parents report that not spending enough time with their children contributes to their parenting stress in a major way.[22] Indeed, one study conducted in Canada in 2011 found that nearly half of working parents reported they felt they did not spend enough time with their children; these same parents then indicated they themselves were having more psychological and health problems.[22,23] Indeed, consistent with this general ethos of intensive parenting, today's parents have indicated that greater amounts of time spent with children, particularly time spent engaged in focused play activities with children, such as reading, engaging in imaginary play, and singing, is associated with better mental health in parents,[24] and the amount of time parents wish to spend with their children has been increasing.[25] However, as it turns out, this time may not be as rewarding for mothers: Findings from the American Time Use Study, which explored the ways people spend their time, indicated that compared with fathers, mothers are more stressed, more tired, and less happy.[26]

This is a good place to pause a moment to comment on the different responsibilities that parents have that can, at times, conflict with one another and make the task of parenting, well, more complicated. At the time we were writing this book—Spring 2021—the coronavirus pandemic was in full swing: almost exactly a year before the World Health Organization had declared COVID-19 a worldwide pandemic. For a year now, we have been juggling working from home, initiating and enforcing new health habits (e.g., "Stay 6 feet away!") and attempting to homeschool our kids. (For the record, teaching college is much easier than teaching elementary school children!) These times are out of the ordinary, thank goodness, but the pandemic highlights a commonplace condition of contemporary parents: the need to juggle multiple competing demands. And it comes at a cost. Already, the evidence is in: Millions of women are dropping out of the workforce, and the mental health consequences are being felt disproportionately by women.[27,28] Indeed, in some of our preliminary work, we are finding that the challenges of child care

are associated with anxiety and depression, more so than even fears of the pandemic. These challenges have not been born equally by mothers and fathers, setting women back many years.

There is a term to describe this juggling act that parents engage in and the conflicts that erupt when work and family demands are incompatible with one another and the individual is unable to meet the demands in one domain or the other.[29] Sociologists and psychologists refer to this dynamic as *work–family conflict*. These conflicts can be further broken down into *work-interfering-with-family conflict*, such as when meetings prevent us from picking our children up from their after-school program, and *family-interfering-with-work conflict*, such as when one of our children is sick and we have to stay home from work to care for them and end up missing important meetings as a result. One study conducted in Turkey reported that men and women reported statistically indistinguishable levels of family-interfering-with-work conflict, but women reported significantly greater levels of work-interfering-with-family conflict.[30] In contrast, a study we conducted among parents in the United States 10 years later did not reveal gender differences in family-interfering-with-work conflict or work-interfering-with-family conflict.[31] It is possible that the gender roles or time difference between these two contexts were sufficiently different to make the results of the studies pan out differently.

Studies reveal that for mother and fathers who experience higher levels of work–family conflict of either variety (work-interfering-with-family conflict or family-interfering-with-work conflict), both types of conflict are associated with depression; higher alcohol use; poorer physical health; and more negative emotionality, such as worry, frustration, and guilt[32–35] as well as lower job and life satisfaction.[36] Mothers, in particular, may be at risk for experiencing guilt about the negative impact that working has on their children. The results of several of my (Jessie's) studies have found that compared to working fathers, working mothers demonstrate higher levels of guilt about the negative effect of their employment on their children.[31,37] These effects are strongest among mothers who have greater work–family conflict and who work a greater number of hours. A similar line of work has found that new mothers whose values regarding the roles of women in the workplace and their own status as a worker were discordant had higher anxiety levels than new mothers whose values and status were in sync.[38] These findings suggest that gender is an important factor to consider when thinking about parents' stress levels and the factors that predict it.

Juggling Parenting and Work. Sam D. 12

Other contextual factors place significant pressure on parents, too, and should be considered when thinking about parents' overall stress levels. For instance, living in poverty, contending with financial pressures, being a member of an ethnic minority group, being a single parent, living in a household with domestic violence, encountering discrimination, having a physical illness—all of these factors have been linked to higher levels of parenting stress.[39–43] These factors often co-occur within the same individual or family, having multiplicative effects on parenting stress. The effects can be even more dramatic if one's child bears the effect of the parenting stress. Families that have more stress to begin with have more to shoulder, and these families then have fewer resources to enact the ideal parenting practices. Unsurprisingly, children raised in families with higher parenting stress levels have more behavior problems, making them more difficult to parent. This can quickly become a cycle that is difficult to break in which the parents who had more parenting stress to begin with (and therefore less psychological bandwidth) end up with children whose behavior makes them more challenging to parent. This helps to illustrate why getting ahead of the parenting stress curve is so crucial because getting behind the parenting stress curve is a lose–lose for all involved.

THE IMPORTANCE OF REGULATING PARENTS' STRESS

Parents serve multiple roles for children, alternating between caregivers, nurturers, protectors, disciplinarians, mediators of conflict, and teachers. Serving in such a diverse array of roles in and of itself can place significant demands on parents' emotion regulation abilities. In addition, as any parent can tell you, being a parent means being tied to your child's emotions, which can be a bit of a roller-coaster ride. Fluctuating emotion is such a common aspect of parenting that a whole field of study has developed around the notion of understanding parents' *emotion regulation*,[44] the ways in which parents modulate their own emotions as they go about the hard work of helping their children develop their emotion regulation skills. It should be crystal clear from the first part of this chapter that parenting stress is a prevalent and important aspect of the experience of parenting. We now pivot to discuss why it is crucial to have a handle on your stress level as a parent.

Parents' Stress Impacts Children and Makes Them More Stressed

An overwhelming amount of evidence out there suggests that children can pick up on even extremely subtle cues from the people around them that they are distressed. For the purposes of illustration, we review just a few of these studies that demonstrate these effects.

This ability to sense the emotions of others is present from an early age. Some of the most classic studies within psychology tell this story. For instance, in a phenomenon referred to as *social referencing*, Joseph Campos from the University of California, Berkeley, found that from as early as 12 months of age, children can use the facial expressions of their parents as a source of information to guide their behavior.[45] He designed a paradigm in which infants who have not yet learned to walk are placed at the edge of a piece of glass made to look like a visual cliff (because of a drop-off in the wallpaper underneath the glass). Their parent, holding an appealing toy, is placed on the other side of the piece of glass. To reach the parent and the toy, the child needs to cross the apparent drop-off. The parent is asked to either adopt an encouraging, friendly expression or a worried, concerned expression.

Campos found that these children will use their parent's facial expression to guide their behavior: When their parent shows encouragement, the children are significantly more likely to cross the visual cliff despite that their depth perception makes this feel like a risky proposition. Their parent's encouragement is enough to make them override their senses and trust their parent. However, if their parent looks concerned, they will remain on the shallow side of the visual cliff, unable to risk the danger. Campos followed up this study with other studies that demonstrated the same effects with respect to children's responses to strangers, who also elicit fear during this developmental stage.[46,47] Thus, Campos's work demonstrated that even children younger than age 1 year use their parents' facial expressions as sources of information that guide their risk-taking behavior when their depth perception is developing.

The concept of *emotion coregulation* has been introduced to describe the ways in which two or more people's emotions can be yoked or connected to one another in a way that is mutually beneficial or regulating.[48,49] As an example, a parent's and a child's emotions can be linked such that each one's emotional states influences the other's emotions in a way that is mutually beneficial. We might think that a mutually beneficial way of coregulating emotion would be to dampen, or downregulate, negative emotion and to increase, or upregulate, positive emotion. When a child is scared of a monster hiding in their closet, a parent can run into the room, scoop the child up in their arms and cradle the child using a combination of calming phrases, rocking body movements, and touch to bring the child's fear emotion back down to a lower level. This is an example of coregulation in which the parent helps to regulate the child's fear. Similarly, if a child picks up a book and has a look a mild delight on their face, a parent may choose to increase the child's positive emotion by running over to the child, bending down, peering into the child's face, and grinning and letting out a little giggle, which may inspire the child to similarly giggle. This upregulation of positive emotion in which the child's positive emotion is led to build on itself is also a way in which the parent can coregulate the child's emotion.

In addition to coregulation of emotion, pairs can also experience *codysregulation*,[50] which in the context of parent–child relationships, refers to when a parent's and children's negative emotions interact with each other in a way that exacerbates the initial negative emotional experiences. An example of codysregulation is when a child is scared of a monster hiding in their closet, and a parent comes into the child's room. Instead of picking up and comforting the child, the parent yells at them for being frightened, saying they should know better by now than to be afraid of make-believe things. The child reacts by feeling fearful of the monster and fearful of the parent as well as feeling ashamed, thanks to the parent's treatment of the child's fear. The parent is also highly agitated, having become angry and dysregulated in yelling at the child. Both the parent and the child are left upset, and neither achieves a healthy or regulated resolution to the situation. And the key to why this is referred to as codysregulation is that the child's emotional display dysregulated the parent, and the parent's emotional display dysregulated the child.

Importantly, the degree of emotion coregulation of the parent–child pair may also be evident in terms of the physiological synchrony of the parent–child pair. A handful of recent studies examined the degree to which parents and children are synchronized in their physiology based on the argument that physiological interdependence belies a degree of coregulation of arousal. In general, research suggests that the parent–child pair tends to show positive correlations in the parent's and child's cortisol levels, a stress hormone secreted by the adrenal cortex.[51–56] So, when parents have high cortisol streaming throughout their bodies, it is highly likely that children also have high levels of cortisol streaming throughout their bodies. Thus, when parents are stressed, not only might we see evidence of codysregulation in terms of children's felt experience of stress but we also might see evidence of this in their physiology. This means that parents' stress might have physiological ramifications for children's physiology.

The aforementioned studies we reviewed were "correlational," meaning that we do not yet know if parental stress itself causes the effect on children's physiology.

Parents Don't Make Good Parenting Decisions When They're Stressed

You won't make your best parenting moves from a position of stress. This is another important motivation to keep your stress levels down. Calm, level-headed parents make good parents, and frenzied, chaotic, hot-headed parents make, well, not-so-good parents. Studies have found that parents who reported higher traitlike levels of parenting stress also reported poorer parenting behavior. For instance, greater parenting stress is associated with more laxness, more criticism, and more physical discipline.[57–60] The results of another study found that parenting stress predicted less positive parent–child interactions even after controlling for other forms of life stress.[61] The proof, so to speak, is in the pudding. Parents higher in parenting stress are more likely to have children who have more behavior problems, such as internalizing (depression and anxiety) and externalizing (attention-deficit/hyperactivity disorder [ADHD] and aggression) symptoms.[57,59,62]

The results of other research studies have examined these questions: What happens when you put parents into a state that mimics a high and low stress state? Do they parent differently? This might seem like a no-brainer, but from a scientific perspective, until we know the answer, we cannot assume anything. In one study, we (Stacey and colleagues) looked at a common scenario involving mothers and their young children: snack time.[63] We placed a platter of healthy and unhealthy snacks in front of the mothers. One group of mothers was what we called the "high-stress" group. After the snack break, these mothers were told that they would have to give speech and do difficult math problems in front of a panel that would analyze their nonverbal behavior. (Apparently, public speaking is one of America's biggest phobias.) In the low-stress conditions, mothers were told that they would still give a speech and do some math problems but would do so in privacy—alone. In our data, mothers in the stress condition were harsher in how they regulated their children's food intake. They were more likely to make demands on their children's snacking behavior versus inquiring and creating space for children's autonomy. This idea of being less patient and more agitated when we are stressed is a common experience for all parents.

Parents Lose the Ability to Mentalize When They're Stressed

Theorists who discuss the psychological capacities that are essential for sensitive parenting talk extensively about the importance of *mentalizing,* or reflecting on one's own and one's child's mental states (thoughts and feelings) as a psychological process. Peter Fonagy, Mary Target, Arietta Slade, and other theorists who have worked on this issue have focused on the idea that being able to get inside of your child's mind to understand what they might be thinking or feeling in a given moment is an integral part of being able to respond to the child's underlying need in a sensitive way.[64,65] This concept of parental mentalizing is the focus of Chapter 6, but we mention it here because we also know that high levels of stress or arousal can inhibit mentalizing regarding the self or the child.[64–66]

When a parent is flooded with emotion or physiological arousal, the cognitive flexibility needed to mentalize—which requires creativity, attentional bandwidth, and an ability to think through alternative ideas—is elusive. As a result, high levels of anxiety can be incompatible with a mentalizing mode of operating. Thus, finding ways to contain or downregulate physiological arousal is all the more important because regaining the ability to mentalize is crucial from a parenting perspective. We turn now to strategies parents can use to assist in this goal.

TOOLS FOR REGULATING PARENTS' STRESS

There are many tips and tricks for regulating stress in life and as a parent. Some parents rely on exercise; some, on deep breathing; some, on friendships; and some, on wine. The trick is to find the one strategy or multiple strategies that work best for you. Stress is contagious, so being a good parent means being good to yourself. In this next section, we focus on a few tips and tricks that have garnered empirical support as a means of centering and grounding parents and reducing their stress level. Some may not be right for you, and that is okay. You just need to find one that is right for you and use it, use it, use it.

Radical Self-Care

It goes without saying that when we are stressed, we can't be good parents. I (Stacey) acknowledge that "I am never meaner, more impatient, and more angry than when I am stressed." Thus, building a set of habits and tools to use to regulate stress is a key process of good parenting. Just as important is developing your coping strategies before a crisis occurs. It is difficult in the moment to have the capacity to stop, reflect, and decide in a coherent manner. Coping research identifies a series of strategies that people use, including using positive reinterpretation, venting and seeking social support, using humor, relying on spirituality or religion, and actively planning and engaging in problem solving. Reflecting on these strategies and considering whether they are effective for you before a crisis occurs gives you a toolset to draw on when feeling stressed.

In the previous chapter, we discussed the cascade of physiological effects that come about when a stressor does occur. These physiological effects can linger after a stressor has passed, which can have implications for health; thus, it is important to "terminate" the stress response. Being aware of coping strategies and stressful triggers in your life is important, but in addition, being aware of your physical body and how it feels, along with treating it well, are also important for ending the physiological stress response so that it doesn't lead to burnout. On this note, being physically active, whether that means exercise or even play (e.g., wrestling with your kids!) are great strategies for terminating this response. Other coping strategies are venting to a close supportive friend; engaging in physical touch, including a prolonged hug from a loving partner; or getting a massage. Once again, there is no one-size-fits-all approach. The key is being aware of the multitude of strategies and identifying one what works for you.

At the same time, the absence of stress is not the presence of happiness. In addition to strategies for downregulating stress, we want to emphasize the importance of "daily uplifts" or small moments of joy that you create in your life. "For me," says June, a mother of two,

> it's the presence of a good cup of coffee—the routine of making my espresso every morning, packing down the grinds, steaming the milk, and sitting for just a moment with it, enjoying the smell and the taste. The caffeine is revitalizing, but the experience is also key. It's a little thing, and sometimes, on a hectic morning with multiple school drop-offs, I pick up my coffee from Starbucks, but even then, I make sure that I sit in the parking lot for a few minutes, savoring the experience.

Regardless of what your daily uplifts are, whether going for a run, connecting with a friend, or going for a walk, give yourself this gift—if not daily then several times during the week. Positive uplifts can help buffer the effects of stress, so make joy a habit.

Always keep in mind that your health and well-being matter for your children, too. I (Stacey) remember, when sleep training for my firstborn, Eliana, how important this idea was. I come from a culture where cosleeping was the norm and letting your child cry it out was considered cruel and unusual punishment. But the cosleeping was not working for Eliana; she was waking up multiple times a night. The stress was compounded because, that year, my husband and I were living apart. He was finishing his training on the East Coast, and I was starting a new job in California. There was essentially no break. At some point, I was trying to find drugs that would keep me awake and keep the fog of sleep deprivation away. It became untenable. Not only was I completely exhausted, but I also realized that the sleep deprivation made me a really poor parent. I was always irritable and tired. I never wanted to play. I was grumpy and mean all the time because I thought it would be cruel if I let my daughter cry it out. So, I decided to sleep-train.[67] After a few days, Eliana slept through the night for the first time in her entire life. The funny thing is, I let her cry it out, thinking that it was for my own benefit. But I realized that with sleep I was kinder, more giving, and more loving as a mother. Moreover, Eliana became less clingy and moody and was a generally happier baby. I don't know if the change was because she was finally getting a good night's sleep or whether it was because I was a better mom as I was getting a good night's sleep. Taking care of yourself is taking care of your children.

We acknowledge that being able to engage in radical self-care is a privilege. Finding time to take care of yourself might often feel like a luxury we can't afford. But, like many health issues, prevention is often less costly than intervention. By developing effective coping strategies and creating moments of joy, we prevent stressors from overwhelming us.

Mindful Parenting

Mindful parenting is a practice that has as its goal the retraining of parent attention, reducing parent reactivity, increasing awareness of parent stress, and reducing the intergenerational transmission of poor parenting practices.[68,69] Mindfulness in the parenting role enables parents to have a psychologically distanced perspective when they encounter stressful circumstances in the parenting role.[70] There are various conceptualizations of mindful parenting, but all share similar features. According to Susan Bögels, a psychologist in the Netherlands, mindful parenting involves a greater awareness of a child's unique characteristics, a greater ability to be present for the child, a greater ability to accept things as they are, and a greater ability to recognize one's own impulses and respond in more adaptive ways to the child.[71] And according to Larissa Duncan, a psychologist at University of Wisconsin–Madison, mindful parenting entails listening to your child with your complete attention; engaging in nonjudgmental acceptance of self and child; and having emotional awareness of self and child, compassion for self and child, and self-regulation in the relationship.[70]

Mindful parenting results in positive outcomes for parents and children alike. Parents who naturally have a mindful stance in their parenting report less parenting distress, less physiological reactivity, and more positive parent–child relationships, and have children with fewer behavior problems.[72–76] Evidence also exists that this is a trainable skill: Parents who complete a mindful parenting training program have been found to have higher quality interactions with their children,[77] lower levels of stress and anxiety,[76] greater parenting efficacy,[78] higher quality coparenting,[79] and children with fewer internalizing (depression, anxiety) and externalizing (ADHD, aggression) symptoms.[79]

So, what does mindful parenting look like? It looks a lot like mindfulness except as applied specifically to the realm of parenting. Mindful parenting means being present and engaged in the moment with one's child, having a nonjudgmental stance, being attentive to what is happening in the parent–child dynamic, and responding to your child's cues as they emerge in the interaction. Being mindful helps us to respond rather than simply to react, and it is crucial in situations in which we find that our child has made us upset or angry or has triggered us in some personal way. I (Stacey) remember once when Eliana said that the dinner I had made was "gross," and when I told her she still had to try it, she said, "You are so mean! You are such a mean mommy!" I was so angry! I come from a culture in which respect to adults is of utmost importance, and I pride myself on my personal cooking skills. For me, it was really upsetting to have my own child act out in such a way that I felt was terribly rude and ungrateful. My immediate reaction was to yell, "Fine! Then don't eat!" It doesn't help that weekday dinners are often a source of stress, and I was very much preoccupied with an email to my boss that I needed to respond to. This is the type of situation that makes us more likely to get angry and react.

Mindful parenting practices emphasize that, in these moments, we pause before responding. Pausing allows us to create some breathing space; it allows us to be aware of our emotions and even to reflect on why we are so triggered by this event and if our reactions are appropriate to the situation at hand. In addition to noticing our own feelings and pausing, the practice of mindful parenting also asks us to see things from our children's viewpoint—even if we don't agree with them. In reflection, I (Stacey) saw that Eliana had the right to her opinion about the quality of my cooking. In some ways, we don't control what we like and dislike. I was most concerned about how she was expressing that opinion. But in the heat of the moment, I was being rude right back. I was modeling the exact behavior I didn't want to see in my children. Children are not our spitting image. They didn't have our life experiences; they have their own thoughts and ideas that may be very different from ours. Moreover, they are not always able to regulate their emotions (or express their opinions politely), and if we are mindful of their perspectives, we can be more compassionate.

Mindful parenting is all the more necessary in the fast-paced world in which we live—where there are so many other temptations to not be present with one's child. Mindful parenting is a helpful antidote to *technoference*, when technology interferes in our everyday interpersonal interactions 24–7.[80] We are not here to condemn technology or smartphone use. Technology has allowed us many a peaceful meal out and given us the 10-minute reprieve we so often need. But technology has a way of pulling us away from the current moment, making us more distracted in our parenting and more impatient in our interactions. Thus, using it mindfully, and being aware of its impact helps us to be better parents.

Mindful parenting essentially means that, in the midst of a whirling stressor, you keep two feet planted on the ground and focus on what is right in front of you—your child—and to respond without distraction. This state of mindful parenting can be an end goal: Even if it seems unattainable at first, striving for this goal is a worthy pursuit.

Feelings: Acknowledging and Talking About Them

Another strategy is to be open and honest with your children about how you are feeling so that your children don't have to worry about what might be wrong. My (Jessie's) oldest child has started to ask me if I am feeling stressed when she's rushing around the house or appears frenzied (this happens not infrequently). She also tells me when she is feeling stressed. I would like to think (and so I tell myself) that this is because I have done such an admirable job of talking openly about emotions that my daughter feels comfortable talking about her own and her mother's emotions. But, really, it might be that it is because my own stress is so palpable and possibly so frightening for her. At any rate, when my daughter raises the question "Are you stressed?" this simple question snaps me back into parent mode and helps me become more aware of the vibes I'm projecting into my children's atmosphere. The question also acts as an important reminder to slow down and remember that there are other people around who will be affected by my expressions and behavior. So, for us parents, the solution is not so much to stop acting and feeling stressed but to discuss and verbalize these feelings with our children and to strategize coping strategies in front of them, acting as models for how we would want them to respond.

For so long, psychologists advised parents to hold in their feelings around their children, arguing that adult conversations, topics, and feelings should be kept away from children. Although certainly there are topics that should not be discussed in front of children, something that is perhaps more frightening than anything else for children is when they can sense that something is wrong but cannot put their finger on what it is. The half-knowing is often more terrifying than knowing for sure. Sometimes we can visibly see our children relax when they learn what it is that we are worried about. We can strategically prepare a "child-sanitized" version of certain stories to tell them ahead of time so that we can be honest with them about our feelings. For instance, if we are stressed about a situation at work, we can describe the big picture elements of the situation (e.g., "I'm upset because I feel like I have more work than I can accomplish within a certain period of time, and that makes me feel pressured and stressed") without going into all of the details that could be frightening or upsetting to children (e.g., "and if I don't get this done, I could lose my job"). We can also debate and discuss ideas about whether our problem has a solution, and, if so, what might it look like (e.g., "I am trying to think of creative ways to make the work go faster or to get other people to help me with the work so that I can move more quickly on it"). Alternatively, we may be explicit that, in this context, there is no practical solution, so we need to focus on emotions and to work on how we can feel better.

Verbalizing what is stressing us out and discussing how we are coping with it allow our children to know why we might be acting stressed or angry or sad. It gives them a reason for why their parent is behaving differently so that they don't have to wonder and worry. By discussing our strategies for handling big emotions with them, we also give children a sense that we, as adults, do get stressed out but that there are healthy ways in which we can deal with these feelings.

Inevitably, no matter how hard we try, there will be times when we overreact, say something mean, or say something we regret. In those moments, we can acknowledge our own limitations and apologize to our children in appropriate ways. Consider saying something like, "I am really sorry I overreacted and yelled. Next time, it would be better if I asked you calmly first, right? How else can I do better?" By apologizing, you are acknowledging that you were in the wrong and are repairing the relationship. By working with your child to develop solutions, you are modeling how things can change. And if you find that you are frequently unable to manage your emotions and that you need help and support, seek out a therapist.

CONCLUSION

Stress-free parenting? Why, there's no such thing! Stress is part of the human condition, and if you have a pulse, you are going to experience stress from time to time. Part of caring about your parenting and your child means sometimes experiencing stress. The trick is to try to not get overwhelmed by your stress and to be able to channel it effectively.

People get overwhelmed by stress when they are unable to find ways to regulate the stress or when they layer feelings on top of the stress, such as when they feel guilty about feeling stressed (sound familiar? "I should be enjoying this time when he's so little, not being stressed about it," "I feel so bad that I just wasted his first Halloween being stressed!") or anxious about feeling stressed (sound familiar? "Why am I the only one who gets so stressed out by these parenting things?" "There must be something wrong with me that I can't handle these things and everyone else can!"). The best strategy is to accept that stress is a part of the human condition and a part of the experience of being a parent (it's because you love your child and because taking care of another human being is hard!), and to acknowledge that it takes work to learn how to manage that stress. Techniques like mindfulness or deep breathing can help, but what is most important is for you to find what it is that works for you to help you de-stress.

TL, DR

- In a competitive society, an increasing number of parents are overinvolved in children's lives, which leads to increased levels of stress.
- Managing stress in our own lives helps us to be a better parent.
- Be aware of stress reduction strategies that work for you! Develop those strategies.
- The absence of stress is not the presence of joy. Create moments of "daily uplifts" in your life.
- Mindful parenting means to be aware of how the stress situation is serving as a trigger, learning to pause so that you can respond instead of react, and considering your children's viewpoint even if it is different from yours.
- Acknowledge and talk about your feelings with your child. Apologize and repair if you need to.

CHAPTER 3

LOVE AND RESILIENCE

In the popular children's book series *Harry Potter*, the titular character is attacked by the nemesis of the book, the Dark Lord, Voldemort.[1] Harry's mother, Lily Potter, steps in between Voldemort and her infant son, saving Harry's life but losing her own. The power of her love, however, does not end at her death. The power of Lily's love is imprinted in Harry's blood and continues to protect him from Voldemort as he grows up.

The story of Harry Potter is a dramatic rendition of adversity and the power of a mother's love, and the idea of relationships, the mother–child bond in particular, as being protective is pervasive. From our mother-bear metaphors to religious iconography of Mary, the mother of Jesus, there is no imagery more long-lasting and powerful. While it is without a doubt that other caregivers, such as grandmothers and fathers, matter, the sheer amount of time and level of involvement provided by the mother figure in a child's life allow that person to be a formidable force in the developing child's life. We would argue that in the early years of development, the child's environment is the parent's environment. Over time, the child's social circles widen to include others: teachers, siblings, and peers, and, eventually, romantic partners. These relationships are all vitally important, but it is often the first love that lays the foundation for the rest of these relationships.

We devote a whole chapter in this book—a book very much focused on stress and its potentially terrible implications—to the idea of love because we believe that love is the cornerstone of a fundamental concept in human development: resilience. Again and again, the research literature has consistently demonstrated that despite terrible adversity, some children exhibit remarkable *resilience*, defined by psychologists as the ability to successfully adapt despite adversity, to bounce back from difficult experiences and grow and improve even in the face of challenges. Levels of resilience vary across individuals. And one of the most primary predictors of resilience in both adults and children is social bonding or love.

Love is a measure of the positive, affectionate relationship between the individual and their social worlds. Because humans are incredibly social primates, being loved signifies belonging, and the desire to be loved is an essential need that drives us all. Indeed, what sets us apart from other species, what makes us unique, is not language or tool use but our hypersociality, which allows us to work with one another, to cooperate, and to have shared goals and values.[2] It is because humans are hypersocial creatures that the emotional indicator of belongingness, or love, is so crucial to our well-being. Neuroscience and clinical psychology support the idea that the human brain *expects* closeness and human connection.[3] The brain construes intimate, nurturing, social relationships as bioenergetic resources. Put simply, the human brain doesn't just need food and water; it needs and requires energy in the form of social relationships characterized by mutual interdependence. John Bowlby, the theorist who developed attachment theory, argued that this drive for connection is as important to survival as the drive for food, shelter, and protection from prey.[4] This need for and expectation of relationships is the default or baseline state of the brain.

Thus, when deprived of this social connection, children are unable to develop optimally.

CONSEQUENCES OF ZERO PARENTING

So, what would happen if children were physically provided for but lacked human connection? Although this type of research would be unethical to do in a laboratory context, sometimes researchers are able to study this phenomenon as it occurs in the real world. A set of studies following children growing up in orphanages provides insight into the importance of human social and emotional connection.

In October 1966, Nicolae Ceauşescu, Romania's head of state, took an extreme action to counter declining birth rates: He enacted Decree 770, which banned abortion. Following the decree, it became challenging to find contraception tools, and, by 1977, people were being taxed for being childless. Birth rates rose significantly in the late 1960s. Children born during this time period were popularly referred to as *decreţei*, or decree. As a consequence of this policy, many parents were unable to take care of their children, so a number of these children wound up in state-run orphanages. These orphanages varied significantly in quality, and many, if not all, of these orphanages were unable to provide a supportive, loving environment that the human brain expects. There was minimal social interaction, the children rarely received one-on-one attention, and they had no primary caregiver on whom to rely.

Starting around the year 2000, researchers started gathering data on 136 kids growing up in these orphanages in Romania.[5] They conducted a randomized clinical trial, the most rigorous method of research possible, to examine the causal effects of practically zero parenting on children's outcomes. After several months of baseline assessment, half the children were randomly assigned to high-quality

69

foster care, and the other half remained in institutionalized care. The researchers gathered information on the children's social behavior, their emotional expressions, their intelligence level, their brain activity, and the size and shape of their brains. The children were assessed at 30, 42, and 54 months. In addition, data were collected at 8, 12 and 16 years of age. (The children are still being followed!)

Results from this study were definitive, revealing that institutionalized care was associated with profound deficits in a range of domains, including cognitive processes, such as intelligence, but also in social-emotional behaviors (e.g., attachment, peer relations). In addition, there were significant effects on brain activity and structure and increased incidences of psychological disorders. On the other hand, the children who were placed in high-quality homes did better and sometimes were indistinguishable from their peers who were never in institutional care.

Data from this body of work have also demonstrated what is called a *dose–response relationship*, such that the longer children remained in institutional care, the more severe and long-term the deficits they experienced were. Children who were placed in foster homes before 6 months fared the best, and children who were placed after 2 years of age fared the worst. This study provided some of the most definitive data on the importance of having close relationships with adults for children's development. It also highlighted the importance of timing on interventions.

In another study, researchers implemented a social-emotional intervention at some of the highest quality orphanages in St. Petersburg, Russia.[6] These orphanages had medical care, sanitation, and stimulation in the form of toys. Furthermore, they were free of physical or sexual abuse. At the same time, however, caregivers and children had minimal social and emotional interactions. The researchers implemented an intervention that trained personnel and encouraged caregivers to interact and behave in developmentally appropriate, warm, caring, and sensitive ways. For one of the sites, they also made structural changes to the caregiving arrangements, making it possible for the children to have a consistent caregiver. The study found that the children who received an intervention improved in social, emotional, and cognitive development. Overall, this intervention provides support for these essential ideas within developmental psychology: (a) adults can be trained to act in ways that are consistent with a loving and nurturing caregiver; (b) structure is necessary and consistency in caregivers is vital; and, as we would expect, (c) love matters.

WHAT IS LOVE?

But what is "love"? Is it a feeling? A thought? How do you know when you are experiencing love? Is it an action or a state of being? While psychologists are very good at understanding the benefits of love, characterizing what it may look like in all its forms, whether occurring in parent–child relationships, among friends, or in the context of romantic relationships, is a more complex enterprise. We are less eloquent when it comes to explicitly stating what love is. Especially among those of us growing up in a Western context, we frequently think of love as a *feeling*—a combination of intense fondness, positive emotions, and a strongly felt desire to be close. But feelings are not something we can always control. Not only that, but by their nature, feelings are impermanent: They come and they go. The danger in conceptualizing love as a feeling is that if we are stressed and tired, and we aren't feeling particularly loving, we may draw conclusions that may be erroneous about our ability to love our children effectively.

Consider, for example, Lauren. She is a stay-at-home mother with three kids under age 5. "I am constantly being touched, pawed on. The kids are always climbing on me. There is always someone who needs something," she says. "I can't even go to the bathroom in peace. Sometimes I resent my children." At the same time, however, just because Lauren has moments when she resents her children, it does not mean that she is still not kind and loving.

For us, one working definition that we use in the context of this book is to think of love as an *action* rather than a *feeling*. As Erich Fromm stated so eloquently, love "is a decision, it is a judgment, it is a promise. If love were only a feeling, there would be no basis for the promise to love each other forever. A feeling comes and it may go."[7] We asked one of our parents to think about love as an action and tell us what they thought it means. Franz, a new (and very articulate!) father of a baby girl, told us,

> It is an act directed towards someone or something that we see an alliance. The act of love, then, is the soul's cry, "I recognize you, and I want you to thrive in the world! I will act to support you, to hold you up, to give to you, sacrifice for you, so that you can be the best version of yourself possible."

In essence, it is in our actions that we "raise" our children.

The idea that love is better characterized as an action is consistent with traditions, such as Confucianism, which emphasizes actions and duty. A core concept, *ren*, places the emphasis on action in a relationship rather than on feelings of love. As a teenager, striding a culture that was profuse in its overt verbal expression of love (i.e., American culture), I (Stacey) remember clearly that my mother, a refugee from Vietnam, never said, "I love you" to me—even to this day. Even when, showing deep concern, she asked me about my first relationship, what she focused on was behavior: "How does he treat you?" and never, "Does he love you?" Despite the lack of verbal expressions of love, I, even as a child, never doubted my mother's love. It was evident in the way she asked, "con đã ăn chưa?" ("My child, have you eaten yet?"). Love was explicit in how my mother would wake up in the middle of the night to massage her children's feet when they ached.

It was evident in the way she stayed in her children's bedroom, telling them stories, waiting until they fall asleep before leaving. As trite as it may be, actions spoke louder than words. This is especially true in the context of love.

In contrast, my (Jessie's) father, who is the child of Italian immigrants, said, "I love you" most days. At the same time, my father would also give his children their daily back rubs. Expressions like this were free flowing, as was physical affection, which was dispersed to anyone who entered our home (even those who didn't want them). So, although feelings and expressions are nice, what has the most impact is the behavior, the daily interactions that characterize the relationship, and the context in which they must be interpreted.

While parental love and romantic love differ in multiple ways, one significant factor may be that parental love requires you to give unconditionally and does not necessarily demand anything in return. If you are with an adult partner and they are not contributing enough to the relationship or they are not giving you what you need emotionally or otherwise, you can leave. This is not the case with our children. Even if we could, few of us would want to. Thus, children demand and require that you love them but don't always return this favor. How many parents have felt the sting of a child who bluntly states, "Go away, Daddy, I want Mommy!" As the adult in the relationship, we cannot storm off in anger, and we can never make demands that our child must change—or else we will leave them! Can you imagine how shocked and appalled neighbors or friends would be if you were caught threatening your child to leave if they did not profess their affection for you? Being a parent and loving your child are perhaps some of the most emotionally challenging experiences in our lives because it requires us to be open, generous, and always compassionate.

Being resilient in the face of your child's rejection can be one of the most difficult experiences to endure as a parent. Children can be cruel in the way they reject their parents, and this comes up more during certain developmental stages than others. As in the previous example, toddlers and young children reject their parents in obvious ways (e.g., through preferring the other parent or saying things like, "I don't like the way Daddy sings") because they haven't yet acquired the social-cognitive skills to be able to understand that this could hurt another person's feelings. So, it's not that they are purposely trying to hurt their parent's feelings, it's just that they don't yet have the cognitive capacity to be able to put themselves in another person's shoes to understand what it would feel like to be the target of a comment like that. Teenagers, on the other hand, also engage in these types of behaviors, but, unlike toddlers, they have acquired the social-cognitive skills to know that it hurts. They may slam their door in their parents' faces and tell their parents they know nothing about what it's like to be a human being because they're so cold-hearted. Or they may sit through a meal in total silence, stonewalling them. This flavor of rejection can be particularly challenging for parents to weather because it requires a strong internal compass to guide your response—How do you not react with anger when your teen tries to provoke you in this way? And yet, reacting in this way is guaranteed to lead down the wrong path—and the faith that your teen will come back to you when they need you.

It may not be popular to say, but sometimes when your child has kept you up all night, your clothes are stained by the food they refuse to eat, and they are currently screaming at the top of their lungs while jumping on your favorite couch, it can be difficult to love your children. But if we think of love as an act, as a faculty that we are cultivating, as something that we must practice again and again, we can create some room for mistakes and resolve to do better. In the later chapters in this book, we seek to demystify love. By deconstructing and conceiving of love as an action, we hope to be able to highlight specific strategies that parents can use to reduce stress and uplift their children. If we think of love as a strategy that we can engage in, then it doesn't matter if we may not be feeling particularly "in love" with our child at any given moment; it just matters whether we can muster up the ability to act in loving ways. The expression of love, care, and sensitive responding looks very different, as we discuss throughout this book. We refer our readers to later chapters for concrete strategies and behaviors that allow parents to express love in ways that have profound impacts. For this chapter, we focus on describing the power of love. At this point, it is enough to say that loving someone means bearing witness to their lives, being present in their lived experiences, and responding contingently and sensitively.

THE POWER OF LOVE

No matter how much we deconstruct the idea of love, there will always be a mysterious magic to love partly because of just how powerful it is for humans. When we have social support or access to support and care through other individuals and groups, we see a host of benefits. As *The New York Times* noted in 2020,

> The most significant determinant of resilience—noted in nearly every review or study of resilience in the last 50 years—is the quality of our close personal relationships, especially with parents and primary caregivers. Early attachments to parents play a crucial, lifelong role in human adaptation.[8]

Not only are our relationships important, but relationships with parents and caregivers specifically have a crucial impact on the rest of our lives.

Study after study has shown that we have reduced risk of mental health problems and reduced risk of disease when we have strong relationships with others.[9-11] Many of these studies followed participants over a long period, sometimes even across multiple generations, to see the effects of social support and social connection (essentially love) over time. It's true that many other factors, including, say, health behaviors, can influence things like disease or mental illness, but in these studies, researchers can often parcel out the effects of these factors.

Some public health studies have also looked at trends over time within specific communities. For example, Alameda County, California, public health studies looked at residents' social ties and health over a 9-year period. They found that those with strong social ties were significantly less likely to die from heart disease, stroke, or cancer.[12,13] If that's not enough, there's biological evidence for the power of social support, too. In one study, researchers looked at the telomere length of adults who did or did not have a supportive spouse.[14] *Telomeres* are protein–nucleotide sequences that cap the ends of our chromosomes; they promote chromosome stability. Shorter telomere length is associated with chronic disease and increased overall risk of mortality; it is considered a marker of aging.[15] What the researchers found was that, among married couples, a supportive marital relationship was protective and associated with longer telomere lengths. Interestingly, when this support was absent, other sources of social support (e.g., friends) did not confer the same benefit. The benefits of social support have also extended to neurological responses and physiological stress response hormones in the body.[12]

In essence, then, human connection and close supportive relationships are crucial for optimal outcomes. This is particularly true for children. One of the principal pioneers in developmental science, Urie Bronfenbrenner, boiled down his decades of research into one belief statement: "Every child needs at least one adult who is irrationally crazy about him or her."[16] That's it. While we can provide endless opportunities for our children at home or in school, whether that is empowerment through community service or constructive use of time, such as theater or religious activities that would benefit our children, none of this is as powerful as having that one person who cares deeply about you.

LOVE AS A RESILIENCE FACTOR

While magical, love is almost common. And love drives resilience, which is also ubiquitous. Researcher Emmy Werner looked at a series of large, longitudinal studies around the world that were assessing early childhood factors that contribute to resilience. From a study in Minnesota tracking 200 low-income kids from birth to age 25 to a study in Australia tracking more than 5,000 kids from just after birth to age 21 to a study in Germany tracking them from 3 months to 8 years asking, "What makes children strong?" the answers were remarkably similar. Those kids who had strong, early supportive care had greater competence, which led them to a more resilient life. This doesn't mean these kids (who are now adults) have a perfect life free of negativity and stressors. Rather, it means these individuals were not as affected by negative events and had *less* risk than their peers who did not have the same early care and love.[17] Other studies have suggested that nurturing parenting can even be protective across generations, influencing an individual's parenting for their own family.[18]

Ann Masten, a professor of child development who teaches at the University of Minnesota, emphasized that while this resilience might seem like a kind of magic, it really comes about through everyday actions—like when a parent embraces their child or when a caregiver smiles warmly to show affection. The process of these ordinary interactions bringing resilience to children is what she dubbed "ordinary magic."[19] Love and our supportive presence are vital gifts that we provide for children. It is at its very essence the armor, sword, and shield that allow children to face the real and imaginary dragons they will encounter in their lives.

Eliana, 7

We (Stacey and colleagues) have seen this protective ordinary magic in our own research. The ordinary practice of being consistently responsive to your child can have an almost magical effect on working memory. We gathered data from 342 youths from rural, upstate New York, along with their families, and looked at a measure of chronic physiological stress. These markers can be found through blood pressure readings, urine samples, and body mass index measures. Mothers were observed in how responsive they were to their kids (and later, as they became teens through the duration of the study). Maternal responsiveness was also assessed through kids' direct reports. These kids also came in to perform memory tests. Data were collected over the span of 8 years. We had already guessed we would find a connection between biological stress and our memory test. What was exciting, though, was that those with more responsiveness from their mothers were less affected. In other words, maternal responsiveness buffered the impact of stress on memory functioning! A mother's love can quite literally protect their kids' brains from the harm of stress.[20]

A growing body of work has been able to replicate the finding that maternal love can act as a powerful buffer against stressors. Maternal warmth has been shown to buffer the effects of low early-life socioeconomic status on biological markers of health. In one study looking at people who had grown up in socioeconomically disadvantaged environments, the researchers found that upward mobility did not buffer the effects of early-life adversity on metabolic health, but the presence of a nurturing mother was indeed protective.[21] Even when a mother is suffering from depression, if she can engage in responsive behaviors, the effects of her depression are mitigated. In one study, mothers with depressive symptoms who nonetheless were more responsive and who engaged using more responsive touch during face-to-face interactions with their infants had babies with less DNA methylation of genes involved in the stress response compared to the infants of mothers with depressive symptoms but who were less responsive.[22]

Importantly, primate models have also demonstrated that parent–child relations can also influence how our genes shape who we are. At the National Institutes of Health Animal Center located in the Maryland countryside, scientists looked at gene–environment interactions in a colony of rhesus monkeys. About 20% of the monkeys in the colony were often anxious and fearful in new situations or, when separated from their relatives, showed a longer biological stress response compared with others. It turns out that there was a specific gene associated with more maladaptive behaviors and greater reactivity to stress when these monkeys experienced social separation.

However, that gene only had that fear association for those monkeys that did not develop secure attachments with their mothers early in life. Monkeys that did develop secure attachments did not have problems with that particular gene. Despite the genetic predisposition, if the monkeys had a solid, warm relationship to rely on, they could learn how to cope with stress effectively.[23]

WHAT CHILDREN LEARN WHEN THEY ARE LOVED

Once again, love can be conceptualized as a commitment to another person and as a series of acts we carry out over time for another person. On very concrete levels, when we love someone, we provide deliberate and overt support in terms of concrete instrumental aid, such as food and a place to sleep. Any parent who has struggled to help their child to sleep through the night knows full well this is no easy task. In addition to these concrete interactions, when we love someone, we place our attention on them and we act as active witnesses of their lives. This can mean celebrating an achievement together or even simply following the gaze of our infant to a toy they are interested in. As the child develops, physical needs shift to providing behavioral guidance or to teaching children. Viewed through an emotional lens, in the context of adversity, helping our children to cope, providing skills for problem solving, and even just listening and validating their emotions play powerful roles. All of these factors help children to be autonomous—to exert control over their emotions and to act on the world.

While we have argued that "love" is a verb and should not be conceptualized as an emotion, it is undoubtedly the case that the *feeling* of being loved is indeed a felt emotion. In other words, by acting in loving ways, we evoke and nurture in our children a feeling of being loved—of "mattering."[24] *Mattering* is essentially the belief that one is an important focus of another person's attention and that one is valued. It lays the foundation for the individual to value and take care of themselves and then later to expect that respect from others. Franz, the father of the baby girl mentioned earlier, relayed this heartbreaking story to me (Stacey):

> I was an excellent athlete, smart, amazing musician, and good looking, or at least I think so. On the surface, I had excellent self-esteem, but there was a part of me that never valued myself, and it influenced the decisions I made. For example, I left healthy relationships and sought toxic ones. Why didn't I have faith in myself? I trace it back to very specific aspects of my upbringing where my parents made decisions, said things, and behaved in ways that invalidated my experience and hence, in some ways, made meaningless my existence.

Note that Franz would never state he wasn't loved, but there were concrete behaviors, actions, that his parents engaged in that undermined his sense of "mattering."

By taking our children's perspectives, contingently responding to their presence and behaviors, validating their lived emotions (even if we don't necessarily agree with them), parents are conveying the message to their children that the child is an active agent in the world. Children learn that they have power to influence people around them and to change their environments. Consider how children love to build and knock down a tower of blocks—such joy they must feel to be able to create and destroy. When we, as parents, applaud the destruction, stop to help our children build another tower, and, together, knock it down again, we amplify this joy! On a basic fundamental level, children who are loved know that others care about them and that they can act on the world, and the world will respond empathetically. That is the gift that you can give to your child.

Peter Fonagy, a well-known psychologist and psychoanalyst at University College London, wrote about a concept known as *epistemic trust*, which describes a basic trust in the world around you and its ability to convey information to you that is trustworthy. Fonagy argued that a child develops epistemic trust when their caregivers have communicated with them in a way that speaks to the child's way of experiencing the world (e.g., making eye contact with the child, taking turns speaking with them, using an appropriate tone of voice), which enable the child to hear the message delivered by the caregiver as one intended for them and to store it in memory.[25] Fonagy argued that children who have epistemic trust grow into adults who have the sense that the messages they receive from the world are trustworthy. Furthermore, children who do not have the benefit of learning epistemic trust early in life appear to be less able to learn from experience later in life, which is one of the benefits of epistemic trust (it allows you to suspend disbelief so that you can learn new things).[25]

Through love, when parents not only care for children's needs but also are sources of comfort as well as active and engaged witnesses to their life, children develop a sense of purpose and meaning. In discussing the mechanisms for how social ties lead to better physical and mental health, Peggy Thoits at Indiana University wrote that "knowing who we are to others provides *purpose and meaning* [emphasis added] in life, which in turn guards against anxiety and existential despair."[26] The feeling of being loved signals that one is accepted and included, providing a sense of security that one's needs will be met. It acts as emotional sustenance that allows children to engage with the world effectively and with courage.

FACTORS AFFECTING OUR ABILITY TO LOVE

All of us are capable of loving, and that you are reading this book is a testament to your desire to love and to love better. But just like children are not born as blank slates, our ability to love is influenced by a variety of factors. Being aware of these factors and how they may impinge on our ability to love our children in ways that we would want is important, so we need to know our triggers and areas where we need growth. Only by knowing our limitations can we begin to address them.

Stress

One of the most important factors is stress. As we discuss extensively in this book, under stress, our brain short circuits, making it difficult to provide the patient, sensitive, nurturing care that our children need. Besides stress, many factors outside of our control also matter. Perhaps your child was born premature and had to spend extra time in the neonatal intensive care unit. When this happens, we can't hug and kiss them as much as we'd like; we aren't able to smile back at their smiles. Alternatively, it could be that you have another child who is ill and requires more attention. Leslie, a young mother of two, shared with us that she grew up with a brother who had multiple mental disorders. She was born when his symptoms started showing up. Because her parents were so caught up in visiting doctors, worrying about his symptoms, and managing every crisis, through no fault of their own, they weren't able to give her as much attention as a child. On an intellectual level, Leslie knows that her parents love her. But because they were unable to provide her with attention and time, she, on some primal level, didn't feel like she was loved.

Family History

If our own parents had trouble expressing love toward us, this can influence how we are able to express our love, too. For example, parents who show a great deal of aggression tend to have kids with social, behavioral, and health difficulties, and this cycle tends to continue as these children grow up and become parents.[15] However, breaking this cycle is possible; this is a common reason why people seek therapy—because they want to understand the impact of their experiences in childhood to avoid replicating them with their own children. Revisiting the events of the past with this intention, either alone or with the help of a trusted partner (e.g., a friend, therapist, romantic partner, support group), can be an effective means of preventing the past from negatively affecting our future relationships with children and partners.

As a parent, I (Stacey) often struggle with keeping my temper intact, yelling often at my children and saying things I often regret. I told myself I would never be like my father. Yet, here I am. My father was absent at his best. At his worst, he was emotionally and physically abusive. I was terrified of him as a child. I remember, however, one incident that completely changed how I saw my father. When he was learning to write English, he would leave scraps of papers around the house. They would have phrases such as, "I am lost. Can you give me directions?" or "How much does that cost?" "Where is the bathroom?" One day, I found a note that said, "My mother died when I was 3." The message written in neat handwriting on this scrap of paper stuck with me for years, and I spent as much time in therapy talking about my father's life as I did my own. But the pain in his note hit me the hardest when my first child was 3. I imagined my clingy, needy, 3-year-old losing her mother, and for the first time, I understood his insecurities, his fears that often manifest in unhealthy ways.

One of our (Jessie and colleagues) studies involved examining the parenting behavior and romantic relationship quality among a group of women who had experienced high levels of rejection and neglect from their parents as children. These women were pregnant at the time of their enrollment in the study. We interviewed them about their childhood experiences with their parents, assessing the degree to which they indicated they had been rejected by either parent. We also assessed the degree to which they were able to mentalize, or thoughtfully reflect on, their experiences with their parents as children.

We reasoned that being able to engage in this process might enable them to revisit their past, to reflect on how they might have been feeling as a child (e.g., upset, rejected, misunderstood, neglected), what they might have needed but not have gotten from their parents (such as acceptance, attention, love), and how this might have affected them over the long term. Being able to engage in this process might also enable them to mentalize for their parents, helping them understand what might have been going on that could have caused their parents to behave in this way (e.g., "My father was really overwhelmed because he had to work two jobs to support our family").

What we found is that mothers who had higher experiences of childhood rejection by their parents but who also showed average or greater levels of reflective functioning were more responsive with their infants at 5 months postpartum and had greater romantic relationship satisfaction at 17 months postpartum.[27] In a very real way, these findings demonstrated that by reflecting on our past experiences of hurt, we can gain clarity on them so that we prevent them from negatively impacting our parenting and couple relationships.

As a poignant example of this process, we invite you to witness this process within a Native American Indian father who resides in Kansas. He recounted how he worked hard to overcome his own experiences of being fathered, which he attributes to causes of intergenerational trauma and racism:

> I had a great dad. Don't get me wrong, I love him, but I had a hard upbringing because of the bad choices he made. The saying "children don't question the mistakes parents make, they suffer from them" captures the reality I faced every day as a child. My father struggled with drugs and alcohol, which eventually led to more and more problems not only for him but for my brother and myself as well.
>
> One night, I remember my dad came home, he was intoxicated, and he began to beat my brother and me for no apparent reason. After it was all said and done, I remember him leaving.

> Kyal and I were about 10 years old, and we were crying, holding each other, and I can remember thinking and asking God the question "Why? . . . Why did we have to go through this life? What did we do so wrong?" We were broken! It was then that I made a deal to my 10-year-old self: "When I become a father, I will never, never treat my children this way. I will never make them feel the feelings I feel, and they will never feel unwanted or unloved."
>
> Fast-forward 7 years later, I was a senior in high school, and my high school sweetheart and I were expecting our first-born child, our daughter, Lael. We spent a week in the hospital prior to her birth and nearly 2 weeks after her birth because of pneumonia and other complications. The first time I held and looked at my daughter, there was this energy that I had never felt before. I felt it go through my whole body, and during that exact time, a memory of my promise came to mind, and tears of happiness rolled down my face. As I held my daughter, my promises of a better life filled my mind, and I knew I was holding my whole world.[28]

Understanding and empathy are only the beginning of breaking the intergenerational transmission of trauma, but they are necessary. The process of actively reflecting on our own parenting and how our childhood experiences shape these parenting styles acts in the service of being able to write a new chapter for our children. We also need a resolve to do so, compassion for ourselves, and a commitment that our child will not suffer in the same way—all a solid recipe for change.

Limited Time

Like everything in life, actions take time. Lara, a single mom, works three part-time jobs but cannot afford a car. On some days, she doesn't get to see her kids except for when she gets up before her early shift or late at night just before bed. Lara is devoting a tremendous amount of energy and effort into raising her children by working so hard to support them, but she feels tremendously guilty about being unable to spend more time with them. She watches as other parents sign up to volunteer in their kids' school classrooms, bring baked goods for school events, and stay up late working on homework. These events don't pass her by unnoticed, but she simply can't make the time to give to them. Instead, she finds pockets of time to share stories and hugs with each child once a day,

Anastasia is a surgeon. She is up at 4 a.m. and is often in the operating room at 6 a.m. In addition to her clinical work, Anastasia is a research powerhouse, leading clinical trials and investigating new cancer drugs. Despite her accomplishments, she tells us that the most difficult thing for her to do is nothing:

> It is challenging for me to do nothing with my daughter. I used to schedule "time" for her: lunch dates, activities, like visiting a museum, to do together. But at the same time, I would "fill" up those in-between moments—like driving her to school. Instead of chatting with her, I took conference calls or just filled those times with my thoughts, planning for the next day, deciding what journal to submit that paper to. It wasn't until one day, when my daughter said to me, "I don't mind if you work on Labor Day. I want the babysitter to come"—in that moment, I felt my heart crack. I was flooded with mixed emotions—sadness but also a little bit of anger. It was like she didn't appreciate all the things I give her. When I asked my daughter why, she responded, "The babysitter *watches* me." At that moment, a memory flashed through my mind, of me coming home, and my daughter playing videogames, and our babysitter, just sitting there, watching her play and cheering her on.

Anastasia's story illustrates that, for children, attention is literally of the essence of love. To bear witness to someone's life can be an act of love.

A lack of time is a common challenge for many families. Fundamentally, however, it is important to remember that while time is necessary for you to love well, it is not the case that more time equals more love. Creating small moments of intense connection can mitigate some of the challenges of lack of time. Twenty minutes of engaging in play with your child can go a long way. Small signals, such as a hug before you leave, a note left in a lunch box, a story or conversation before bedtime, done consistently and regularly, can build up to powerful expressions of love.

In the modern era, parents invest tremendously in their children, and this investment includes extracurricular activities, ranging from sports to music to Russian math and Chinese language. But a common mistake parents make is thinking that these activities can substitute for quality interactions they have with their children. In reality, it may be the empty spaces spent together with no plans or activities that allow for spontaneous moments of connection—the times when you are lying on the floor with your child and giggling together, or the time when you spill something on the floor and clean it up together and make a funny game out of it. Or it may be the long, boring car drive during which you have a conversation about what would happen if there were no gravity on Earth ("Can you imagine?"). You have to find a way to create these moments with your child if they don't naturally occur. At the end of the day, the most powerful investment is time.

TOO MUCH OF A GOOD THING?

It is evident that love can serve an essential protective role in a number of ways, shielding us from the impact of stress and creating a context in which we can develop and thrive. But is there such a thing as too much of a good thing? Can we love too much? Well, let's reframe the question ever so slightly because we probably can't actually love too much, but there may be such a thing as focusing too much on our children, or devoting too much attention to our children, or engaging in parenting practices that are overly permissive. So, let's begin again with a new question: Can we provide our children with too much attention?

Research tells us that is likely the case. In a study combining the findings from more than 11,000 research articles on parenting styles and child bullying, researchers found that kids who had overprotective parents were at higher risk of becoming bullies, especially if they were victims of bullying already.[29] This finding has been replicated by researchers looking at adopted kids. By looking at adopted children, they can somewhat rule out the effects of genetics and focus on parenting behaviors that children are exposed to. These researchers looked at 382 adoptive families and assessed the children at 9 months, 18 months, and 27 months of age. They found support for the idea that it is possible to for parents' ostensibly well-intentioned behaviors to go too far. Parents who were overinvolved and too sensitive to children's behaviors had children with more temper tantrums and higher levels of acting out.[30]

Importantly, the negative consequences of overprotection can also extend to parents. Researchers published a study on parents and empathy in 2016 when they brought in 247 parent and adolescent pairs to take blood samples and complete surveys on empathy, well-being, self-esteem, and emotion regulation ability.[31] Unsurprisingly, more empathic parents—those who are able to better understand their kids' emotions and identify with them—had adolescents with better emotion regulation and less systemic inflammation in their blood. In other words, the adolescents could handle their emotions better and were also in better health. But what about the parents? That's what made this study particularly interesting. The study found that parents with higher empathy had better self-esteem and a greater sense of purpose than those with lower empathy scores, but they also had higher systemic inflammation in their blood. These data suggest that empathy and being sensitive to our own children can come at a health cost, suggesting that, as children grow up, it is important for parents to place some boundaries on their emotional roles. Although it is important for parents to support our children through challenges, it is just as important that we don't internalize or take their challenges on as our own. For children, learning how to confront challenges independently is an important skill, especially in terms of building up an arsenal in defense of anxiety.

So, one of the important tasks of parenting is learning how to feel alongside your child while not allowing this feeling to overwhelm you and also gradually transferring greater and greater responsibility to your child as they develop. Despite all of their good intentions, parents who continue to take on too much responsibility for their children's psychological well-being, despite their children aging, may be setting their children up for anxiety. We talk more about this in our discussion of empathy in Chapter 6.

CONCLUSION

In contemporary times, the cynic in us might raise our eyebrows at the idea of love being transformative. But the evidence is abundant: Love is like a powerful river that can shape landscapes. At the same time, it is not magical. Like most important things it takes time, and it takes great care and attention. Throughout the next chapters, we discuss how love may manifest and how it shapes children's lives.

Before we end this chapter, we would like to tell our audience the story about a little girl, "S." S was born to refugee immigrant parents. With two toddlers, S's mother was forced to flee a war-torn country. She was shot at, captured, and held prisoner. At a refugee camp, S's mother had to dig through trash to find food and bathe in swimming holes filled with human excrement. S grew up living in a one-bedroom apartment with her parents and four siblings. Her father suffered from depression and posttraumatic stress syndrome, and he was absent at best and abusive at worst. The neighborhood that S grew up in had one of the highest murder rates in the state. S should have become another statistic. But she had one thing going for her: Her mother loved her unconditionally. She made S feel enough. S grew up, went off to college, and eventually received a PhD from an Ivy League institution. Her own mother never even finished high school. Despite her adverse upbringing, S is living a "happily ever after." This is a true story, and we know this, because S—Stacey—is one of the authors of this book. Love is important to resilience. There are many more stories like this out there. Maybe yours is one of them.

TL, DR

- Love is powerful and lays the cornerstone for resilience.
- Conceptualizing love as a series of actions rather than as a feeling can be useful for parents. We can acknowledge that, as parents, we sometimes feel stress, resentful, and even irritable, but we can still behave in loving ways toward our children.
- Our family history, time, and stress levels can all affect our ability to parent effectively.
- Empathizing with our children is important, but we also need to avoid letting their challenges overwhelm us.

CHAPTER 4

PARENTING BEFORE BIRTH

Age reckoning refers to how culture and countries determine how old you are. "What?!" you may be exclaiming. "Don't we all count the years similarly?" Well, no. In certain cultures, for example, China, Korea, Japan, and Vietnam, the "beginning" occurs before birth. Historically, at birth, babies from these cultures are already considered 1 year old rather than zero, as they would be in most Western countries. While this practice is changing for multiple reasons (getting in line with standard international practice, the positive effect of being 1 year younger), for parents from these cultures, the general belief is that a baby's age starts from its time in the mother's womb.

Even though this way of counting highlights the importance of the prenatal period, parents from all cultures understand that even before the child is born, parental behavior matters. During the prenatal period, infants can hear, they are exposed to their mom's hormones, which pass through the placenta, and they experience certain flavors and absorb certain nutrients. Evidence suggests that all of these experiences can impact the developing baby both immediately after birth and even on into adulthood. Prenatal experiences are thought to affect mental and physical health, giving rise to resilience or increasing susceptibility to disease or developmental issues.

Regardless of if they want to listen to it all, mothers get advice from their doctors, from their own mothers, and even from strangers on the street. They get suggestions from people who don't have kids and won't don't want them. The advice can range from annoying but harmless ("No, no, you can't have a sip of wine") to outright nonsensical. When I (Jessie) got pregnant with my third child, I was told that now was the time to get serious about my family and stop working. Yet, I (Stacey) was once told to avoid horror movies because, if I didn't, the baby might look like the monster! This advice begins during pregnancy (or when a person begins trying to get pregnant) and extends onward.

All parents are invested in their children. Most of us will change our behavior, even if it is simply a matter of degree. Mothers will change what and how much they eat; they may limit alcohol, exercise differently, pick up new health habits (take prenatal vitamins), and drop bad ones (quit smoking). We change our habits and behaviors because, on some level, we know that they can impact our unborn children. Interestingly, the decision to change our habits may be driven not from our own top-down rational thinking but from the physiological changes that occur from being pregnant. I (Stacey), for example, was planning to limit, but certainly not cut off, all caffeine (which, for me, is truly the nectar of the gods). But while pregnant with my first child, I had a significant and severe distaste for the smell of coffee. I found it disgusting and, at 12 weeks, went off coffee cold turkey. I didn't miss it and, moreover, didn't suffer any withdrawal symptoms when I quit. No one knows exactly why we develop certain aversions other than that it appears to correlate with the pregnancy hormone, human chorionic gonadotropin (HCG). Even the obvious assumption that it may have developed to help us avoid dangerous foods that may harm the fetus is not clearly supported.

I (Jessie) was still nursing my second child (Charlie) when I got pregnant with my third. The way I figured out I was pregnant was that both Charlie and I started vomiting (Charlie almost immediately each time after he finished nursing). The coincidence was too uncanny to go unnoticed: The HCG hormone can really do wonders on a woman's (and, in some cases, a nursing baby's) body!

Changing our behavior during pregnancy is recognizing and acknowledging that parenting starts at conception, echoing the scientific literature on fetal programming. *Fetal programming*, or how experiences during the prenatal period shape the newborn baby, is a growing area of research that has immense implications for parenting, specifically the kind that occurs even before the child is born. Fetal programming emphasizes the idea that babies' brains and bodies are undergoing rapid cell differentiation during the embryonic and fetal stage. The *embryonic stage* refers roughly to the middle of the first trimester (3–9 weeks), when the major organ structures are forming (and when many mothers may have no idea that they are pregnant!). The *fetal stage* refers to the period following the embryonic stage when the fetus is expanding, growing, and developing.

The rapid growth and changes of the growing baby make them particularly sensitive to a variety of "stimuli" and "insults" both internally—within the mom's body—and externally—in the outside environment. *Stimuli*, in this case, can refer to a wide range of factors from nutrition to noise, whereas *insults* are stimuli that have a detrimental impact. A stimulus or insult during this period of critical development can, in turn, permanently alter the functioning of tissues and organ systems that can later affect health and disease. Indeed, prenatal influences have been documented in a wide range of areas from disease[1] to personality.[2]

The idea that fetal programming can affect health and well-being in adulthood is often discussed in the literature as the *developmental origins of health and disease* (DoHaD) hypothesis This hypothesis, also known as "Barker's hypothesis," emerged about 35 years ago, when researchers noticed that low birthweight was associated with higher rates of adult death from heart disease. Other observations, such as a link between regions of the country and certain types of adult deaths and infant mortality rates, led to the insight that individual differences or variation early in life, particularly during gestation, can program the structure and functions of the brain and body. This programming has important implications for physical health and psychological well-being. To put it simply, our experiences in the womb and early on in life affect how well we function in our adult lives.

Before we go into specific examples of how prenatal experiences can shape children and their children's health, well-being, and even personality, we provide a crash course on how a baby develops in utero. Understanding the time course of fetal development, or *what* develops and *when*, will shed insight into when and why certain types of stimuli and insults may matter most.

Here's a story that some of us who have gone to graduate school to study children have heard. An experimenter was interested in trying to understand whether babies cry in utero. To do this, he had to try and make a baby cry. His method to torture these poor and, as yet, unborn babies was to create a deafening and unpleasant noise right next to the mommy's tummy, where the ultrasound showed the baby's ear resides. He recruited new mothers who were just finishing up their first trimester, did his experiment, saw no signs of crying after blasting the loud noise, and concluded that babies don't cry in utero. The problem with his conclusion? Babies at 13–14 weeks can't hear! The auditory system doesn't start to develop until around 18 weeks, so it was likely that when he was blasting his noise, the babies heard absolutely nothing. For parents, that means we can wait a little before playing Mozart to our babies. More generally, it underscores the importance of timing.

WHAT BABIES LEARN BEFORE BIRTH

Protecting your unborn baby is a key part of being a parent, but nurturing the baby's growth is also another. Even babies in utero are active learners. Growth and development, after all, is not something that just happens but is shaped and molded by outside influences. Just as your muscles change and grow stronger if you work out with them, or you become more sensitive and knowledgeable to the variations of coffee if you spend a lot of time trying different types, the brain is also very much shaped by sensory experiences. In this section, we describe some fascinating studies demonstrating what babies are capable of learning in utero. We focus on auditory experiences, what mothers eat, and how mothers teach the newborn baby about what to expect regarding the outside world.

The Prenatal Sound of Parenting

In utero, some of the most critical stimuli, or sensory experiences, are the voice of the mother and the sounds of her heartbeat. It is a lovely thought that just by existing, mothers are not only providing a nurturing environment that holds all the necessary nutrients for physical development but that her heartbeat and her voice contain stimulation for significant brain growth. Indeed, prenatal exposure to the mother's voice provides the brain with the necessary stimulation to understand and produce speech later.[3] Relatedly, the lack of auditory stimulation, or auditory deprivation, can adversely affect brain development leading to despecialization in the auditory area of the brain.[4]

Thus, even before they are born, babies are already learning from their mother's speech. After all, birds learn the calls of their own kind while still in the egg![5] At least among male finches, exposure to songs improves the speed by which they learn to sing, which, in turn,

Eliana, 7

Sing! Your baby can hear you!

helps them to win adult mates![6] To illustrate this learning capability in baby humans, some researchers have examined how voices and languages outside the womb can influence the baby's vocalizations. As a reminder, around 6 months gestational age, the baby is capable of hearing voices and sounds, even though they're muffled, from outside the womb. Fascinatingly enough, there is evidence that postbirth, babies' cries reflect the languages that they were exposed to during the prenatal period. Researchers studied the cries of French and German newborns and found rises and falls in their cries that mimicked their native language.[7]

In another study, pregnant women were asked to recite one of two different rhymes between Weeks 33 and 37. At 37 weeks, when hearing the rhyme, the baby's heart rate slows down, suggesting that they somehow recognize this rhyme because a deceleration in heart rate often means increased attention.[8] More evidence that infants can hear comes from a study that examined how the brains of newborn infants respond to the sound of their mother's voice or the sound of a stranger.[9] Using electrophysiology, researchers exposed newborns to their mother's voice or a stranger's voice. They found a left-brain pattern (the left brain is intimately involved in language processing) of sustained activation for the mother's voice but not the stranger's. The researchers interpreted this finding as evidence for the preferential role of the mother's voice in language acquisition.

Not all sounds and noises are equal to the developing fetus, though. The fetal brain is particularly enriched by the voice of the mother and the rhythmic sounds of the heartbeat. The environment created by the womb is the environment in which the developing fetus is designed to thrive. However, not all fetuses have the privilege to develop until maturity within the maternal womb. For instance, neonates who are born prematurely must spend the remainder of their weeks of "gestation" in neonatal intensive care units (NICUs), which hardly resemble wombs. In one study, researchers looked at the outcomes of these preterm infants. Past research has already argued that the auditory environment of these NICU medical units, with their alarms, beeping, fans, and otherwise toxic, unpredictable, and loud noises is far from ideal. But the researchers wanted to see whether exposure to maternal sounds, including the mom's voice and heart, could counteract the deleterious aspects of this environment.[4]

They looked at 40 infants born between 25 and 32 weeks' gestation. The premature infants were randomly assigned to receive auditory enrichment in the form of audio recordings of the mother's voice and heartbeat or to just receive care as usual (in the case the noise they heard was what is typical in an intensive care unit). The results suggested that the groups that were otherwise medically and demographically similar at the outset of the study differed in the size of their auditory cortex by the end of the study. Specifically, using cranial ultrasonography measurements, the researchers found that the babies who had about a month of exposure to their mother's sounds had a larger auditory cortex at 1 month of age compared with the control newborns who received routine care (e.g., exposure to the everyday setting of the NICU). In other words, it's not just sounds but the mother's voice that matters, but even inserting the mother's voice into the sterile environment of the NICU helps to improve the brain development of these infants.

Prenatal Music Lessons?

While auditory stimulation like a mother's voice is important, limited evidence suggests that any auditory enrichment like exposure to classical music matters. In 1993, psychologist Frances Rauscher published a study with college kids in *Nature*, a well-known scientific journal, showing that college kids who listen to Mozart before doing several spatial reasoning tasks performed better on one specific task.[10] This task was not a measure of general intelligence but perhaps of spatial intelligence. Specifically, the kids were better able to guess what a paper folded several times over and then cut would look like when unfolded. Keep in mind that the sample was small (36 students participated), an improvement was only seen for this one task, and the effects lasted for about 10 minutes. This study, when reported in the media and dubbed the "Mozart effect," took on a life of its own and captured the imagination of everyone, but particularly parents (ever hear of Baby Mozart?). Even though the data never addressed whether listening to classical music would help babies, after hearing about the research, Georgia's then governor decided to distribute free classical music to every baby born in that state. Since then, an industry of classical, mostly Mozart, CDs have popped up.

As Jennifer, a mother of two stated, "It seemed like an easy way to try and give our children a leg up." She added, "I think every parent wants to do everything possible for their children, and, for me, walking around with headphones on my belly was a small price to pay if it would help my children's intelligence." It is appealing to think that simply listening to Mozart would improve our unborn children's intelligence. On the surface, there seems to be some sense to it right? Mozart, after all, was genius, and it seems exposure to the complexity of his music might help improve our own intelligence. The neurophysiological basis, the researchers argued, was that the cortical firings that arise from listening to complex music like Mozart were similar to those that arise from spatial–temporal reasoning tasks. But, like most things, it was too good to be true.

More research followed, and researchers conducted several *meta-analyses*, which involve pooling data from all the studies available and analyzing them simultaneously. The first, a meta-analysis of 16 different studies,[11] found that listening to Mozart did lead to improved cognitive performance, but the effect was tiny (an increase of 1.4 IQ points), a finding that was consistent with another meta-analysis that concluded the effect was not real.[12]

But, perhaps just as important, further studies have shown that Mozart is not special. Other kinds of music, including Schubert, are just as good, as is even listening to a passage from a Stephen King novel.[13] In a 2006 study involving 8,000 children, researchers found that pop music was just as effective as Mozart![14] The conclusion? It seems that all you need to be better at this cognitive task is exposure to some sound that will make you more alert! Although none of these studies specifically focused on babies in utero, they did tell us something: that music and sound can stimulate the brain, especially if the listener enjoys it. For parents, then, talking and singing to your unborn baby is one way in which you "play" with and "stimulate" your baby's brain growth!

Maternal Nutrition

In addition to exposing the baby to auditory stimuli, there are other ways in which the developing fetus can be influenced by prenatal maternal behavior. One of the most well-studied examples of fetal programming focuses on maternal nutrition. Kathryn, a first-time mother told us,

> I was looking forward to eating all my favorite food, and worrying less about how much I was eating. After all, I was eating for two! But my doctor informed me that the baby is getting nutrients from my blood, so what I eat and how much I eat, the baby is doing the same. This became even more salient after I was diagnosed with gestational diabetes. I cried after the diagnosis! In the end, though, it was a blessing in disguise. Knowing what I eat will influence the baby was an excellent motivation for me to eat healthier—motivation that I would normally never have.

Maternal nutrition affects the developing baby in fascinating ways. *Malnutrition*, or undernutrition, in a sense acts like an environmental insult similar to prenatal exposure to alcohol, and the effects depend on timing. The Dutch famine of 1944–1945 took place in German-occupied Netherlands and is known as *Hongerwinter* (hunger winter). At one point, adult rations were reduced to 580 calories. Keep in mind that the recommended daily calorie intake is 2,000 calories a day for women and 2,500 for men. Some 4.5 million people were affected, and it is estimated that 18,000 deaths were attributed to the famine. Even for those who survived the famine, the health repercussions were clear.[15] Audrey Hepburn, the famous actress and fashion icon, was living in the Netherlands during this time and developed acute anemia and respiratory problems as a result of malnutrition.[16]

But the Dutch famine did much more than affect the people living at the time. It left a long-lasting legacy on generations that followed. In 1949, the Dutch Famine Cohort Study was started and led by the Academic Medical Center in Amsterdam. Records of babies born in November of 1943 and February of 1957 were retrieved from the archives, and the individuals were tracked down. These individuals were then invited back almost 50 years later to participate in a study examining how experiences of the famine in utero would affect their health outcomes. Some of the first results emerged in the late 1990s, and they were astounding. Exposure to the famine in utero was associated with impaired glucose tolerance and obesity. Other research has demonstrated that exposure to famine during gestation was associated with a higher risk of type 2 diabetes.[17] Moreover, in a study looking at men who were exposed to the famine in utero, researchers found that exposure in the first trimester was associated with a 12% increase in mortality.[18] Socioeconomic or health characteristics did not explain this finding as adults.

The effects of fetal malnutrition appear to depend on timing. Individuals who were exposed to impoverished energy environmentally in late gestation (i.e., they were conceived before the famine) had an increased risk for insulin resistance and impaired glucose tolerance as adults, whereas those exposed early in development (i.e., they were conceived during the famine) had increased risk for coronary heart disease and high serum cholesterol as adults.

Notably, there is increasing evidence that the effects may also extend beyond the realm of physical health to psychological functioning. Evidence suggests that for babies who were conceived at the height of the famine and thus experienced severe malnutrition in the first and second trimesters, there was an increased risk of developing schizophrenia as adults. These findings have been replicated in a sample of participants from China. The researchers looked at those born during a massive famine in China that occurred in the Wuhu region of Anhui. Consistent with the Dutch sample, children who were born during the famine years had an increased risk of developing schizophrenia.[19]

As researchers delve into this naturalistic experiment of sorts to determine mechanisms, they are narrowing down epigenetic effects.

In examining DNA methylation, patterns of individuals who were exposed to the famine in utero and siblings who served as a comparison control group, they found that *methylation*, or the silencing of specific genes, may explain relations between famine exposure and metabolic health.[20] Prenatal exposure to the famine was associated with the silencing of *PIM3*, a gene involved in energy metabolism. Silencing of this gene seems to partially explain the relations between prenatal famine exposure and body mass index (BMI). Some evidence also suggests that these epigenetics marks are passed on to the next generation. The offspring of the women who were exposed to the famine has been found to have higher infant obesity and poorer health later in life.[21]

While nutrition and malnutrition can be types of "stressors," they are physical ones, and it is intuitive to think that what and how much mothers eat can have health consequences on their offspring. The takeaway for you is that if you can help it, make sure you get adequate nutrition throughout your pregnancy. This means ensure that you get sufficient protein, caloric content, and fruits and vegetables. Don't skimp because you're worried about gaining baby weight.

Getting Ready for Life Outside the Womb

At the same time, however, nutrition is different from environmental insults in that it cannot simply be seen as an "insult" that always has adverse effects. Rather, it is more appropriate to think of nutrition as a process of *plasticity*: What mothers eat can influence, shape, and mold the form and function of the developing baby's body. One of the most critical ideas coming out from the literature on maternal nutrition is that it can program the metabolic infrastructure, if you will, of the unborn baby. Specifically, researchers have argued that experiences in utero inform and shape "predictive adaptive responses."[22] In other words, the baby, as they develop in utero, is trying to predict what the outside environment is like with the goal of trying to grow and develop in such a way that would make them a good fit for the outside environment. One way to think about this is to imagine that you are about to go on a journey to a foreign planet. What do you bring? What skill set will you need? You would want to find out as much about this environment as possible so that you can be best prepared to survive on that planet.

Maternal nutrition provides clues the fetus uses to try to figure out how best to develop. To illustrate, if mothers do not have access to adequate nutrition, that will shape the baby's body to be thrifty and hold onto whatever calories are available. However, if plenty of energy is available, it may not be as important to be so thrifty. What are the possible consequences? If it is the case that the environment outside matches the baby's experience in the womb, then there is a better chance of survival. However, if there is a mismatch between the prediction and the outcome, then problems are more likely to emerge. In the case of nutrition, malnutrition may lead to what researchers called a *thrifty phenotype*, meaning that the body tries to keep energy and store as many calories as possible. However, if the environment outside of the womb is abundant and full of high-caloric food that is easy to obtain (think McDonald's on every corner), this approach may lead to problems, such as obesity.

Taste Preference

It is not only the amount but the type of foods that mothers eat that also seem to shape and inform how the baby develops. While in the womb, the baby drinks or gulps down several ounces of amniotic fluid. Taste pores develop around Week 16, and the baby's first taste is likely salty amniotic fluid. This fluid that surrounds, protects, and nourishes the baby is influenced by what the mother eats. Even adults can tell whether mothers had recently ingested garlic by sniffing their amniotic fluid.[23] And, yup, even this early on, the fetus is likely to prefer sweets! Thus, what mothers eat influences what the baby will be exposed to and, in turn, can shape their preferences.

In one study, researchers had some mothers drink carrot juice (and water) during the last trimester of their pregnancy, and they had a control group of mothers stick to water.[24] At around 5 to 6 months of age, the researchers gave the infants cereal with carrot juice and observed their facial expressions. The babies who had been exposed to carrot juice early in their development ate more of the cereal and seemed to enjoy it more than the babies whose mother just drank water. This kind of finding has also been extended to strong flavors, such as garlic. Peter Hepper at the University of Belfast gave mothers a cookbook with plenty of garlic recipes and asked them to eat three to four meals a week containing fresh garlic for the last month of their pregnancy. At age 8 or 9 years, the children who were exposed to all that garlic (yum!) ate more garlicky potatoes than the control group!

But it's not just innocuous taste preference that can be shaped by a mother's diet. In a fascinating study with rats that were fed a *junk food diet*—a diet with foods that are high in fat, sugar, or salt but nutrient poor—researchers found that the diet could alter brain pathways and receptors associated with pleasure and reward.[25] The idea is that junk food is delicious. The way the brain's reward system works is this: The consumption of junk food leads to an increased concentration of opioids, which leads to that pleasurable feeling you get when you consume a delicious slice of chocolate cake! Results from this study found that the offspring of the rats that were put on a junk food diet during pregnancy and lactation were smaller. This might seem surprising—after all, shouldn't eating more fat and sugar lead to bigger babies? Not necessarily. It's not just about calories but the type of nutrients being offered by those calories. Protein is important for growth, and the junk food diet tends to lack protein and key nutrients, including magnesium and calcium. But just as important, the offspring of the rats that were fed junk food experienced functional consequences on the reward pathway in the brain, leading to increased levels of desensitization. In other words, these rat pups would need more and want more junk food to obtain the same level of pleasure than rat pups whose mothers ate a healthier diet. This finding highlights primary idea of this chapter: that parenting begins before birth because prenatal experiences can shape the baby in fascinating and critical ways. The exposure to a maternal junk food diet was powerful enough to not only affect the size of the rat pup but also its drive for junk food.

Maternal "Impressions"

The idea that intense psychological experience in mothers can some how leave a mark on the baby is not new—and not just stories circulated at baby showers. Belief in maternal *impressions*, or psychological experiences as capable of causing physical anomalies in the offspring, was pervasive even in ancient Greek culture. The Greek physician Galen thought, for example, that a pregnant woman need only to look at an image or statue of someone, and her child might bear similar characteristics. This could, of course, then be used to one's advantage; many mothers would spend a significant amount of time gazing at beautiful statues with the hope that their children might grow up looking like Adonis.

The medical literature is also full of stories with depictions of how traumatic events during pregnancy shape the physical form of the baby. In a paper written in the 1800s, the author detailed the story of how a woman, about 5 months pregnant, became extremely shocked and filled with revulsion on seeing her husband kill a goat.[26] The intestines of the goat left a significant impression in her mind, and she could not stop thinking about it. When the baby was born, a large, bulbous tumor was found at the back of the baby's neck.

When she saw the tumor, the mother exclaimed, "Oh, the intestines of that goat!"

While the notion of maternal impressions has been mostly discredited, modern science suggests that there might be some truth in it. In prior chapters, we highlighted the critical role of stress in affecting biology and behavior, so you likely are not surprised to see the concept of stress here again. Although DoHaD theories originally focused on nutrition and food intake, a growing body of work has now shown that maternal emotions during pregnancy can also affect the developing newborn.

Similarly, the evidence is mounting that maternal prenatal stress can predict more behavioral problems and biological dysregulation in the offspring.[27] Essentially, mothers who are highly stressed during pregnancy tend to have children who are emotionally reactive and who show higher levels of negative emotions, such as sadness, frustration, and fear.[28] To illustrate, with my (Stacey's) first baby, I was working my first real job at a major university in a department that was not supportive of new mothers. I was under a lot of stress trying to meet tenure guidelines by writing grants and papers, and by mentoring students. Simultaneously, I had a senior faculty member who was, to put it simply, a bully. I was also stressed about all the things that new mothers are stressed about. Is the baby kicking? Can I eat just one slice of deli meat? Does this dish have wine in it? Does it matter? Even before my child was born, I could feel her crying at loud noises, and, to this day, Eliana is a contrarian. She is sensitive, moody, and reactive, and she is likely to get upset at the littlest thing. (Recently, she was upset because she could not get her blanket to lay "straight" and "flat" while she was using it! [Insert face-palm!].) Interestingly, research suggests that although firstborn children are, on average, high achievers and leaders, they also are most fearful in new situations and more vulnerable to stress.[29] Does it have to do with their parents' stress levels? We think so!

PARENTS' SUBJECTIVE EXPERIENCES OF STRESS DURING PREGNANCY

Remember in Chapter 1, we discussed how stress could mean many things, including subjective self-reports, the occurrence of stressful events (stressors), or the physiological bodily response. The research literature on prenatal maternal stress has reflected these differences with studies examining a mother's subjective reports of stress, her exposure to stressful events, and the role of cortisol. Results, however, are all over the place. Sometimes stress is associated with negative outcomes, sometimes there's no association, and sometimes prenatal maternal stress is even predictive of positive outcomes. In the next sections, we synthesize some of these findings.

Mom's Own Feelings

When I (Stacey) was pregnant with my firstborn, I was in a tough position at work. In a high-pressure job with unsupportive colleagues and living in a city with no family, I spent most of my pregnancy exhausted and tired. I also spent the first few months after giving birth crying and counting the minutes until my husband came home from work. On the outside, you couldn't really say I had a concrete reason for being stressed. I had a decent job and my husband was very supportive. But I felt the lack of support at work, and I worried about the future. I also found it surprisingly lonely and challenging to stay inside a small apartment alone with a screaming infant for hours on end.

To understand the role of stress during pregnancy, we really need to have data that take into account stress after pregnancy. In one study, for example, mothers reported on their levels of depression and anxiety in the third trimester and also after birth.[30] Having these data points both pre- and postnatally is crucial because those data points allow researchers to look at the unique effects of prenatal stress in particular. After these children were born, the babies were brought back into the lab at age 4 months. This is when the researchers started to have some fun.

They were interested in each infant's levels of emotional reactivity or how emotionally intense the baby was when presented with novel objects and experiences. We know that how people react to new situations is a marker of potential vulnerability later in life. To elicit the infant's emotional reactions, the researchers used a range of tasks, including presenting different tastes from sugar water to lemon juice, having a cotton swab (dipped in diluted alcohol) placed in the infant's nostril, and popping a balloon behind the infant's head. Most babies will get upset, but there is variability: Some babies cry longer and louder.

What the researchers found was that maternal distress during the prenatal but not the postnatal period was associated with more negative reactivity in the 4-month-olds. This study was limited because the sample size was small, but what is notable was that instead of using the mother's reports of children's emotions and behaviors, they had an outsider observe and rate the baby's behavior. This is important because it could be possible that moms who are more stressed are simply more likely to perceive their baby as more emotionally reactive.

Other work has found that maternal stress during pregnancy affects other outcomes, including more sleep problems at ages 18 and 30 months.[31] In another study, researchers followed more than 7,000 women.[32] They looked at measures of anxiety and depression multiple times over the course of pregnancy and during the postnatal period. When the child was 4 years old, they also had parents report on their children's behavioral and emotional problems. What they found was that maternal prenatal anxiety in late pregnancy and postnatal depression contributed independently to children's outcomes. Specifically, the more anxious a mother is during pregnancy and the more depressed she is following the child's birth, the poorer the child's emotional outcomes later in life. These data suggest the importance of timing and type of stress (e.g., depression vs. anxiety) as well as the specific child outcomes. Despite these compelling data, parenting still continues after birth, and research suggests that as the child grows up, maternal psychological distress was only modestly associated with child outcomes.[33]

One of the problems with these studies is that the relation between prenatal maternal stress and children's outcomes are confounded with genetics. It is unclear, for example, whether and how much of a mother's contribution is her genetic makeup or her stress and anxiety during pregnancy. In a unique study that offered some assurances for the idea that it may be a mother's emotions during pregnancy rather than her genetic makeup, in general, that matter, researchers took advantage of families that used in vitro fertilization.[34] Some pregnant women in that study were genetically related to their children and also carried their baby. Others, through the process of in vitro fertilization, were not genetically related to their mothers, but these mothers carried the baby in their womb.

The researchers looked at both depression and anxiety during pregnancy. Their results suggested that prenatal stress was related to birthweight and antisocial behavior in both groups of moms. However, prenatal stress was only associated with attention-deficit/hyperactivity disorder (ADHD) in genetically related mother–offspring pairs. These data suggest that maternal stress during pregnancy may be more important for some outcomes rather than others. Some researchers have argued that a straight genetic story is unlikely because the effects of maternal stress and anxiety on babies have been found when stress and anxiety were reported when the mother was pregnant but were not reported not postnatally.[34–36] They argued that if genes were what was driving the relationship, you would expect to see the relationship between maternal stress and infant outcomes during both periods. Regardless, however, the effects of stress are not uniform. Families with more resources may be able to mitigate its impact, and individuals with more social support may be able to better buffer the effects of stress on their children.

Stressful Life Events

Rather than look at subjective experiences of stress, others have examined exposure to stressful events. The data that looked at exposure to a stressful event as a proxy for the subjective experience of stress, such as self-reported anxiety or depression, were much more mixed. In one study,[37] for example, researchers looked at 164,753 infants who were born to active-duty military families. They compared babies who were in utero on September 11, 2001, when the United States experienced a series of terrorist attacks, with babies born in the same period the previous year (2000) and the year after (2002). This study found no group differences with regard to congenital disabilities, preterm birth, or growth deficiencies.

Others, however, have found that these large-scale disasters do seem to matter. In 1986, Olof Palme, the prime minister of Sweden, was killed by a single gunshot. His assassination was a terrible loss and was a significantly painful experience for many Swedes. Then in 1994, the *MS Estonia*, a cruise ferry, sank in the Baltic Sea while en route to Stockholm. It is considered one of the worst maritime disasters of the 20th century and second deadliest only to the *RMS Titanic* during peacetime. Analysis of birthweight data among the Swedes suggests that the incidence of very low birthweight rose significantly following the months of the Palme murder and the sinking of the *MS Estonia*.[38]

As we discussed in Chapter 1, the impact of any stressor is not uniform. There is much individual variability with regard to how the same stressor may affect different people. The impact of September 11 on babies in utero likely depended on how their mothers responded to the event and did not just depend on the event itself. Indeed, in one study of pregnant women who were directly exposed to the World Trade Center collapse, mothers who developed posttraumatic stress disorder (PTSD) in response to 9/11 had abnormally lower morning and evening cortisol levels.[39] They were also more likely to rate their infants as more distressed when encountering loud noises, new foods, or unfamiliar people compared with mothers who did not experience PTSD. At the same time, the events of 9/11 also led to increased incidences of discrimination, harassment, and violence among individuals from Arab descent. In analyzing birth certificate data, researchers found that for women who gave birth in the 6 months following September 11, the risk of poor birth outcomes was much higher for Arabic-named women than for other groups.[40]

Physiological Response

One important proposed mechanism for how maternal stress can affect the newborn is our old friend, cortisol. As a reminder, cortisol is the end product of the hypothalamic–pituitary–adrenal axis (HPA), one of the body's main stress response systems. Cortisol naturally increases dramatically over the course of gestation.[41] Fascinatingly, elevated cortisol levels can trigger preterm birth. Maternal cortisol can pass through the placenta, and cortisol can pass through the blood–brain barrier. Because cortisol targets receptors that are present throughout the nervous system, it is thought that this can, in turn, lead to a range of behavioral changes in the offspring.[42] Higher levels of cortisol in moms during pregnancy is associated with greater infant negativity, even when controlling for maternal postnatal psychological state.[43] Amniotic cortisol levels during the second trimester of pregnancy is associated with lower birthweight and temperament at age 3 months.[44]

Another unique and ingenious study design used the consumption of licorice during pregnancy to tease apart prenatal stress and genetic effects. Licorice has a compound, glycyrrhizin, which inhibits a placental enzyme that is responsible for breaking down maternal cortisol. By breaking down cortisol, this enzyme can greatly reduce the amount of cortisol the fetus is exposed to. What this means is that pregnant women who eat a lot of licorice may be exposing the baby to higher levels of cortisol. Interestingly, a series of studies have found that greater licorice consumption does lead to higher levels of HPA reactivity in children[44] and an increased risk of externalizing behaviors, such as acting out[45] plus greater risk for ADHD-related problems![46]

The Timing of the Matter

When we talk about development, we must consider timing. Consistent with the idea that timing matters, researchers looked at mothers who experienced the 1994 earthquake in Northridge, California, in 1994.[22] The earthquake was a magnitude 6.7 and killed 57 individuals and injured more than 8,500. Property damage was estimated to be $13 to $50 billion, making it one of the costliest natural disasters in the United States. Mothers who were invited to participate in the study were either pregnant or within 6 weeks of delivery. In the study, mothers were also asked to rate how upsetting the earthquake was. The earthquake was rated as more stressful if it occurred in the first trimester and less if it occurred during the third trimester. The timing of the earthquake was also related to gestational age at birth; stress experienced early in pregnancy was associated with shorter gestation. The researchers concluded that women become less sensitive to stress later in pregnancy.

Although that study was small (only 40 women participated), it is consistent with some prior research suggesting that, as pregnancy advances, to protect the fetus, women become less physiologically reactive to stressors. When researchers[47] had women under mild stressors, such as performing challenging tasks like tracing an image from a mirror or doing serial subtraction, pregnant women appeared to have reduced blood pressure changes compared with their prior nonpregnant selves. The maternal body is sophisticated and perhaps protects the unborn baby by producing levels of placental enzyme that offers partial protection from cortisol and rises as the pregnancy progresses.[43]

What About Dads?

Do fathers contribute more than just their genes? Compared with mothers, the research with fathers is still in its infancy. Still, a growing body of work suggests that even though the dad is not the one to carry the baby physically, his experiences can influence the unborn baby.

One study was able to obtain detailed information on the mortality rates, socioeconomic information, and family structure of children of former prisoners of war (POWs), veterans of the U.S. Civil War (1861–1865).[48] What they found was that the sons of Union Army soldiers who were imprisoned when the camp conditions were at their worst were less likely to survive than the sons of those who were imprisoned when camp conditions were better. Interestingly, there were no effects on daughters. Importantly, however, maternal nutrition in utero was an important protective buffer. The effect of the father's POW status was absent when maternal nutrition was adequate. This suggests a one–two punch and lays out the importance of considering multiple factors when we think about stress. In this case, mothers' nutrition can potentially prevent or reverse the effects of the father's stress. In that study, socioeconomic effects, family structure, and maternal effects did not appear to explain the findings, suggesting that an epigenetic mechanism might be driving the effects.

Around the turn of the century, researchers from England and Sweden looked at data from families that spanned multiple decades (the Avon Longitudinal Study of Parents and Children). They found that smoking before age 11 in men was associated with greater BMI for their sons at age 9. Interestingly, the same effect was not found for daughters. Other studies have shown that alcoholic fathers can have children with fetal alcohol spectrum disorder (FASD), even if the mother did not drink before or during pregnancy. Up to 75% of children with FASD had dads who drank heavily. In addition, parental prepregnancy BMI is associated with the BMI and waist circumference of the offspring during adulthood.[49] The problem with this type of work, though, is that we do not know whether the pattern of associations are driven by common shared environments or genetic predispositions shared by parent and child.

This is where animal studies can tell us a lot. By being able to randomly assign rats to different types of diets and being able to control their environments, researchers are able to look at whether paternal behavior can have programming effects on their offspring. These studies in rats generally show that a high-fat diet in fathers can change both the newborn's weight and adult growth trajectories with effects on glucose and insulin tolerance, fertility, and excess fat. These effects appear to last for two generations. While the exact mechanisms are unknown, researchers have hypothesized that diet can affect sperm quality. At the same time, once again, the beauty of development is that few things are set in stone. When fathers were placed into an exercise intervention, the offspring displayed normalization of their metabolic health.[50] Thus, exercise can indeed counteract the effects of an unhealthy diet for you and your unborn children. In general, dads, here is a great excuse to take care of yourself!

CONCLUSION

As we were starting to write this book, an image—not quite a meme but perhaps more of an infographic—started appearing on the internet. In the image, there is a fetus, and you can see the outline of the fetus's uterus. The fetus is shown inside the body of a woman. Notably, what the graphic was meant to convey is that, at some point in time, part of who you were (the part contributed by your mother) was located inside of her, and that she as a fetus was located inside your grandmother. The implication is that your grandmother's experience might have had an effect on you. Indeed, in humans at 20 weeks, a female fetus has a fully developed reproductive system. She has in her all the eggs that she will ever make: nearly 6 million to 7 million eggs.

Consistent with the thesis of our book, genes and the environment constantly interact. Both the developing baby and her eggs do not exist in a vacuum but within the environment of a living, breathing person. Thus, at birth, there have already been months of "environmental" impact because the womb is an open system in which a wide variety of elements from hormones to drugs to noise are passing through. So, even before birth, "parenting" is happening. Singing to the unborn baby may lead to stimulation of neurons and connections that lay the foundation for later language development.

Moreover, eating a healthy and nutritious diet may protect your child from adverse outcomes later in life. Because the brain is rapidly developing at this time, the effects of the environment, both physical and social, may have outsized effects. Most research has only focused on how prenatal experiences can program and affect the first generation offspring, but emerging evidence suggests that this programming phenomenon may continue across a number of generations.[51]

Before we wrap up this chapter, we want to revisit some ideas of stress that we discussed earlier and discuss throughout this book, namely, stress does not simply equal "bad." How stress affects you and your unborn baby depends on timing and dosage. To illustrate, studies have found that some psychological distress during pregnancy can be beneficial for children. As we discussed in prior chapters, the world, for better or worse, can be a stressful place. And being emotional and reactive can help you deal with said stress. Sometimes, *not* being stressed can be problematic.

Evidence that suggests some moderate levels of stress can be good for development has been reported in the scientific literature. Maternal psychological distress during pregnancy was associated with higher scores on the Bayley Scales of Infant Development! (The Bayley Scales is a commonly used comprehensive tool to test the development of very young children.) Higher levels of prenatal distress were associated with more advanced motor and mental development![52] It is plausible, maybe, that moms who are more anxious and stressed may be parenting in such a way that leads to faster maturation, so the researchers looked at brain activity during the second week of life when it is unlikely that parenting behaviors would matter at this point. They found that prenatal maternal stress was associated with faster brain maturation.[53] It is important to note that these mothers were somewhat low risk. They didn't smoke, had no birth complications, were relatively mature with an average age of 32 years, were well educated, and were married. In other words, it is likely that these women had the resources to deal with stress and that their levels of stress might be, on average, relatively lower than for other populations.

In addition to psychological reports of distress, maternal cortisol after 31 weeks of gestation has also been associated with faster physical[54] and mental development.[42] Timing does seem to matter because cortisol levels early[42] and late[55] in pregnancy are associated with worse outcomes. In Chapter 1, we discussed the *U*-shape roll of stress on performance, whereby moderate levels of stress are motivating and can ready the body to respond effectively to challenges. In essence, it is likely that the developing brain and body require moderate levels of stress to learn how to react and regulate emotional and behavioral responses.

The prenatal period is critical, yes. But brain and body development do not just end when the child is born. If that were the case, then we could give up all the annoying things like finding a house that must be located in the right school district; deciding whether eating mac 'n cheese every single day is really all that bad; and paying for music lessons and swim lessons and. . . . You get the picture! Like the body, the brain continues to grow in size, volume, and in the connections that it makes during the early childhood years. In the next chapter, we look specifically at the newborn baby.

TL, DR

- Babies can learn in utero, including developing taste preference and recognizing the sounds of their parents' voices.
- Some research suggests the experiences that grandparents went through can affect their child's outcomes.
- Mom's experiences of stress do matter, but, at the same time, the data are mixed, and it is likely that moderate amounts of stress may even be beneficial for the baby. So, in other words, it's okay to be a little bit stressed!

CHAPTER 5

LAYING THE FOUNDATION: THE EARLY YEARS

Newborn babies are born equipped with surprising capabilities. After already learning so much in the limited environment of the uterus, imagine what babies are capable of now in the outside world! Mothers may use their voices and expose their infants in the womb to music, sounds, and other auditory stimuli. The world of possibilities and the range of interactions explode almost beyond comprehension postbirth.

Throughout this book, we elaborate on a range of parental behaviors with a focus on ones we think are pertinent to both psychological and biological adaptation. But the type of parenting behavior that matters most depends on developmental age. Consider, for example, the importance of savoring positive experiences with your child through memory sharing to help them shore up their competencies to deal with stress later on (we talk more about this topic in Chapter 8). This advice doesn't quite fit, though, when you are staring into the eyes of a newborn. Yes, there is intelligence there, but language may not be the most effective way to communicate emotions to your newborn. It may be more helpful to communicate nonverbally (for instance, through your facial expressions and your tone of voice) to your child.

The period of early life (the first 3 years or so) is unique in that experiences during this time exert an inordinate effect on later development. This is true of physical characteristics and psychological ones. For example, the trajectory of growth in body mass index (BMI) gains from 2 to 11 years of age is strongly predictive of cardiovascular health in adulthood—more so than BMI at any other age.[1] And, with regard to attachment, behavioral problems, and peer relations, children adopted out of orphanages and placed into loving homes earlier tend to fare just as well as children who were raised in loving homes from birth.[2] The notion that timing matters is encapsulated under the idea of *critical* or *sensitive periods*, which refer to time windows in which certain events must occur for the organism to develop most optimally.

In a critical window, if the appropriate input is unavailable, the window closes, and it is much more difficult, if not impossible, for that skill or trait to be developed. A classic example of a critical period is *imprinting* in which a young animal is exposed to an object and develops a strong preference for that object. Zoologist Konrad Lorenz demonstrated a critical window of 13 to 16 hours after hatching when imprinting occurs in geese. Lucky for us, in humans, the window for forming relations and attachments is lifelong! However, some functions, such as binocular vision, are thought to develop between 3 and 8 months. If one eye is injured or covered during this critical window, binocular vision may not develop normally.

Sensitive windows, although similar to critical windows, are less strict. They are windows during which the brain is particularly sensitive to input. Language is an example. Children excel at learning language and can learn quickly and easily. Language learning is not impossible for adults but is much more challenging.

Early development is also a time of immense plasticity. *Brain plasticity* refers to the idea that brain structure and the neuronal connections are not set in stone but change and adapt through exposure to a variety of different experiences. In other words, the brain is malleable. Despite this malleability, the brain does need stimulation from the outside environment. *Experience-expectant development* refers to neurobiological development that is driven by experiences that are common to or universal among our species. So, the brain expects certain inputs whether those inputs are a ground on which to practice crawling and walking or a sensitive, warm caregiver who will meet its emotional needs. When there is a violation of expectation— when these factors are not present early life—a host of problems can ensue.

Newborn babies are unique simply because of their immaturity. While capable in many ways (e.g., training mothers to jump out of bed in the middle of the night to feed them), babies are also quite dependent. But they are not quite capable of regulating their emotions or distress. They cannot feed themselves when hungry, and some, including ours, are incapable of putting themselves to sleep. Humans are what biologists call an *altricial species*, or a species with young who cannot move, often lack hair, and cannot obtain their own food. The word "altricial" is from the Latin root *alere*, which translates to "nurse, rear, and nourish." Contrast this state with other animals, or *precocial species*, that are mature and mobile at birth or pretty soon after. A baby horse, or foal, can stand within 30 minutes and walk as fast as its parents within hours. And then there are the *superprecocial species* like baby sharks, for example, that are raring to go even before they are born, gobbling up their siblings in utero!

The altriciality or dependency of human babies makes them particularly susceptible to the influences of their caregivers. And one of the main advantages of immaturity may be the plasticity we referred to earlier. Brain plasticity is important because it allows flexibility in development. To illustrate, humans live in a wide range of culture and contexts. We have, for example, roughly 6,500 languages. These languages differ in multiple ways, including the use of different sounds and how the sounds are used together to make words; and of course, languages also differ significantly in their grammatical structures.

The brain doesn't really know exactly which language will be most important, so it prepares. The infant's brain is capable of hearing all *phonemes*—or distinct units of sound—such as the difference between *p* and *d* in every single language! At the end of the first year, however, infants lose this ability and become specialists in their own language. This process has often been described as "brain pruning." Just as pruning a plant can direct the growth of plants into a specific form, control its size and shape, and improve fruit quality, the type of information that our babies are exposed to shapes the brain to function best in the context in which the baby is born. It doesn't make sense for the brain to waste its resources in knowing sounds that are not used in its current environment.

Knowing all of this probably doesn't help the anxiety associated with being the source of life and love for a newborn. Franz, the father of a baby girl, tells us,

> I was in a constant state of anxiety over how fragile she seemed. More than anything, I wanted her to just grow a little bit—and holding her head up, and start eating solids, et cetera—so that I felt like we were over that hump! I did gain confidence as a parent and a sense of peace with every passing day that she survived. Yet, it was an underestimation of how hard parenting a 1-year-old is—the constant need for attention which hinders you, the parent, from really focusing on anything meaningful in your own world.

As Franz's comments illustrate for us, parenting a newborn is hard! Newborns make incredible demands on our time and patience, leaving parents with little time for much else. But this is also an ideal period for laying down a strong foundation that will support their growth for the rest of their lives.

So how best do you parent a newborn? We argue that parents must serve a regulatory function with regard to the newborn infant's basic physiological needs and a facilitative function with regard to social-emotional development. When we say "regulatory function," we are referring to control. The newborn baby requires us to help it regulate its physiology, and we, as parents, can do this in a variety of ways. The most basic form of parenting sensitivity may be responding to infants' most basic human needs, such as food, warmth, and shelter. Parents must hold infants in ways that support the head and neck and make their body feel protected. Parents who feed their infant when the infant shows signs of hunger are helping to regulate their infant's physiology just as parents who help soothe their infant to sleep by rocking them and entering a dark, warm environment help to regulate their circadian rhythm. In this way, parents' ability to train infants' basic physiology begins before parents are needed to interpret infants' emotions or cognitions.

Parents also must serve a facilitative function with regard to social-emotional development. Human beings are incredibly social creatures, and, at birth, the baby is equipped with competencies that help build social connections. An obvious example is how a baby's cry can activate an area of the brain linked to urgent, immediate, do-or-die actions.[3] Moreover, hormones during pregnancy have rewired the mother's brain to make her more susceptible to the baby's influence and to receive intense emotional pleasure from the rug rat.[4]

Even the way a baby looks is designed to capture our attention. Think puppies, kitties, and, yes, the human baby. They all kind of look alike. Babies are cute with wide eyes and a big head; this characteristic of "cuteness" is universal in mammals. This cuteness activates reward, emotion, and attention pathways in the brain.[5] Babies are also designed to have a preference for looking at human faces.[6] In other words, they are primed for social connection. Nature has done a lot of work to make sure that the baby is ready to form social-emotional connections. A parent's job is to foster those social connections.

Cute!   Eliona,
7

WHAT DO BABIES NEED?

Like all of us, newborns need adequate sleep and sufficient food. Sleep for newborns is primary; it's what they do 80% of the time! In addition, nutrition is vitally important—whether breastmilk or formula. In this book, we do not elaborate on nutrition and sleep because hundreds if not thousands of parenting books, blogs, and Instagram posts center on these factors. Instead, we focus on factors that are vitally important for children's psychological health and well-being—variables that are just as critical as sleep and nutrition for resilience and well-being but are rarely discussed. They are sensory stimulation, synchrony, and stability.

Sensory Stimulation

Touch is the first sense to develop in the infant: The fetus responds to touch around the lips at 8 weeks gestational age, and by 14 weeks, all of the body, except the back of the head, responds to touch. Touch is powerful. It can be used to soothe, and it can be used to hurt. Touch can be used practically for support, such as when we hold our child's hand so that they can walk. It can be used to stimulate, such as when we tickle our baby to make them laugh.

Some of the most controversial studies and disturbing stories that underscore the importance of touch and comfort come from the work of psychologist Harry Harlow. Harlow was born in 1905 and attended Stanford University. He was interested in the study of emotion—and not just any emotion but arguably the most powerful emotion of all: love. In trying to understand the love between infants and their mothers, Harlow designed a series of studies to look at whether sustenance (food) or physical comfort (namely, touch) was the driver of the infant–mother bond. He created puppetlike mothers for infant monkeys. One "mother" had a bottle from which the infant could receive milk; however, she was made of wire. The other "mother" did not provide sustenance but was made from comforting cloth. The monkeys vastly preferred the cloth mother over the wire mother even though the wire mother was the one providing food. They would only go to the wire monkey as needed for nursing and then right back to the cloth mother the rest of the time.

Monkeys raised by these two mothers were more likely to explore and interact with objects when a fake cloth mother was present. When new objects were introduced, they would be hesitant and run to the cloth mother for support before exploring the new objects. Monkeys with only a wire mother present when a new object was introduced would exhibit disturbing behaviors, curling up in a ball in the corner of the room and screaming. Further studies have demonstrated that touch in Rhesus monkeys affects the immune system.[7] Early contact and grooming were associated with the ability to produce an antibody response after receiving a vaccine. These studies, highly problematic, and, as mothers, painful for us to recount and teach, nevertheless showed the importance of comforting touch for the infant.

In other studies using rat models, researchers have demonstrated that a particular pattern of touch, namely, licking, is pivotal for physical growth. Saul Schanberg, a neuroscientist and physician at Duke University, where he also was a professor of pharmacology and cancer biology, was studying growth in rat pups when he and his students realized that when the pups were separated from their mother, they would not grow no matter how much they were fed. The experiment was looking like it might fail. But, at the same time, it intrigued the researchers and forced them to ask a different question: What was it about the mother's presence that was helping to grow these rat pups? Nursing? Pheromones? He and his students and collaborators spent hours observing mother rats interacting with their pups and realized that it was touch, specifically, vigorous licking, that facilitated the rat pups' flourishing. Once they realized that it was licking, they spent many more hours trying to figure out what type of licking. They used wet paint brushes to vary speed and pressure, finding that moderate pressure and rapid rate similar to what the mother rats were doing worked! Being stroked by a paint brush in this way revitalized the rat pups and allowed them to grow. Further research in their lab demonstrated that other types of stimulation, including vestibular (the rat pups were rocked back and forth in their incubator) or kinesthetic (the limbs were moved passively by an experimenter) were useless. It was the licking that was key.[8]

Serendipitously, at a conference, Schanberg met a researcher, Tiffany Field, who was studying the effects of touch in preterm human babies. Field's research on touch in infants was failing. She had thought that touch, such as caressing premature babies, would help them to grow. However, in sharing her data with Schanberg, she realized that perhaps the caresses were too soft and more like annoying tickles compared to the deep and stimulating touch that the rat pups received. She went back to her lab and started a study massaging the premature babies gently, but firmly, stroking their arms and legs. Astonishingly, she found that premature babies who received a massage three times a day for 15 minutes each time gained weight 47% faster than the group of babies who did not receive this massage.[9] The massaged babies did not eat any more than the controls but showed signs that their nervous systems were maturing more rapidly, demonstrating more responsiveness to a face and rattle. And just as important, the massaged babies left the hospital, on average, 6 days earlier than the babies who didn't received massage.

The benefits seemed to have long-lasting effects. One year later, the massaged infants performed better on tests of cognitive and motor functioning compared with their peers who did not receive the massage. Results from Field's work have continued to be impressive. Findings have revealed that massaging lowers stress hormones in infants of depressed mothers and also benefits infants exposed to cocaine, HIV, and other medical conditions. Hospitals now routinely massage premature infants and engage in *kangaroo care* in which most of the baby's body is allowed close skin-to-skin contact with the mother or other caretaker. Kangaroo care stabilizes breathing and heart rate, and it is most beneficial right after birth.[10]

This research is astounding, but, at the same time, many of us as parents either consciously or unconsciously know exactly what to do. When our child falls and cries, we immediately pick them up and rub their back. We give kisses on boo-boos, and while we humans don't tend to go around licking our babies, this stroking behavior can be seen in how we pat our babies to sleep, scratch their backs, and rub their arms and legs. Even as adults, we reach out to hold hands, we hug one another, and we get professional massages. Touch is a powerful way to sooth our bodies and relax our minds. It is important to understand why we (Stacey and Jessie) think touch is as important as sleep and milk for babies. Oftentimes, parents tell us, "I check to make sure she is fed, that her diaper is dry, and that she is not too cold or too hot. If all of this is fine, I try not to pick her up." However, we realize that, for infants, being held and feeling the warmth of a human is important; it doesn't make sense to say, "Don't pick her up. You'll spoil her." We are here to tell you that in the first few months of life, you cannot spoil your baby; your baby needs your touch.

Touch can be characterized in a variety of ways. It can be used instrumentally (e.g., simply moving the baby's hand from their mouth), to express affection, or to stimulate the infant.[11] Affection is characterized as holding and caressing the baby, often to comfort the child. Stimulating touch is designed to rouse the infant. It is firm and active and can be used to encourage social attention, such as when a mom helps the baby to clap their hands together. It is part of a larger communication system between a caregiver and child. For infants, one important expression of love is touch. Touch, whether to physically support, express affection to, or stimulate the baby, is important for building a social-emotional relationship as well as for physiological functioning. In addition to touch that occurs in everyday interactions, infants can benefit from deliberate soft touches and massages.

Mothers who are breastfeeding have the advantage of being able to be both a source of comfort and of food, unlike other family members like the father, sibling, or grandparent. Many parents we have talked to regularly tell us, "Oh, yes, I am also bottle feeding so that my partner has a chance to feed the baby." We know that the opportunity to feed the baby is important; however, the opportunity to cuddle, comfort, and hold the baby is just as, if not more, vital. By allowing multiple people to play this important role in the lives of our children, we parents are providing our babies with many sources of love and connection, which is a priceless gift. Babies don't always like this because they quickly develop a preference for one parent over the other, yet being consistent—for example, "Daddy puts you to bed"—helps the child to learn that other people can also meet their needs. We discuss coparenting further in Chapter 10.

Synchrony

One of the simplest yet most profound ideas about what it means to be human is that human beings are social creatures. Even the most introverted of us would wither away if we were deprived of all social interaction. With infants and children, this is even more salient. The role of parents and caregivers is more than just meeting our child's physical needs; we also to meet the social-emotional ones. While physical touch is a concrete way in which we express our care and nurturance, another just as important one lies in our emotional expressions and behavioral interactions. The "dance" that occurs during the interactions between the primary caregiver and child is referred to as *synchrony*.[12]

When we interact with one another and our children, we are actively responding in verbal and nonverbal ways that are often contingent on the behavior of the others. For example, if someone looks a certain direction and points, we turn our head accordingly. If the baby picks up a toy, a mother may respond by labeling the toy. In addition to behaviors, there is an emotional element to synchrony: If someone smiles at us, we smile back. If a baby starts laughing and clapping their hands, they are often looking to their mom to laugh and clap back. If she doesn't respond, the child will often get confused or distressed.

In our everyday lives, we often get a sense of whether our interactions with others are synchronous or not. Consider when you are hanging out with a close friend: There's a lot of back and forth, a sharing of emotions. You might feel that they know your thoughts even before you verbalize them. The conversation flows, and you get energized. In contrast, consider when you are talking to someone, and they interrupt you (and you are not used to the interruption). You don't understand their perspective, and they respond in some ways that you find jarring. That's an example of perhaps feeling out of sync with someone; their rhythms and ways of relating to you are out of step with yours, which can translate into a feeling of being misunderstood or unseen. Another illustration of feeling out of sync is when people from different cultural backgrounds interact for the first time—say, the New Yorker and the Californian. The stereotypical New Yorker is rough around the edges, says what's on their mind, and is edgy, whereas the stereotypical Californian is warm, syrupy, and lighthearted. When the two first meet, they will seem out of sync, a real mismatch in terms of their way of speaking, standing, gesturing, and intonations.

Synchrony between parents and infants looks slightly different over the course of the first year. Early on, synchrony looks more like imitation or the mirroring/matching of infants' emotions. After this is the development of mutual gaze and attention. Then, synchrony morphs into something that looks more like explicit turn-taking.

Affective Mirroring

When you look in the mirror, you see a reflection of yourself that matches your own movements. *Affect mirroring* is when that reflection is someone else who is matching your emotions, especially positive emotions. It's when two people are so in tune with each other's emotions at that moment that they start to mirror each other's movements, sometimes without being aware of it. When someone smiles at us, and we smile back, it increases positives feeling for both. In essence, this mirroring is a sign of affirmation.

In parent–child relationships, affective mirroring is often an empathetic response from the caregiver. The parent or caregiver is responding to the child's expression of their emotions, and the caregiver is picking up on that emotion and reciprocating it. Who doesn't laugh when they see a baby laughing? This kicks off a reciprocating process by which the parent and child keep reinforcing each other's emotions and movements. The baby responds with a continued, and possibly bigger, smile. The mom keeps smiling back, and the spiral of positive emotions continue. In one of the studies we conducted, we asked mothers of 2-year-old children to try to make their children laugh. We told them to do whatever they would normally do to make their children start laughing. What we saw was mothers engage in this elegant back-and-forth, affective volleyball game during which they started out with a small, playful gesture toward their child. The child then reciprocated, usually with a slightly larger facial or vocal expression. Then, the mother would take it up a notch higher to which the child would then respond, and so on, until both child and mother were laughing.[13]

Affective mirroring can lead to social benefits for children. For example, in a study with forty-one 2- and 3-month-old infants, researchers observed mothers interact with their infants at two different time points. They ranked moms on how long their attention was on their children, how emotionally sensitive they were to their children, and how often they displayed social responsiveness. They also looked at how often infants smiled and made vocalizations as responses. The researchers found that moms who ranked higher in affective mirroring had children who showed more positive behavior and attention toward them and who had a stronger expectation for social feedback.[14] This mirroring may help children to not only understand that they have an impact on others but also help them get a strong sense of how others might react and, through this process, be able to build empathy and social trust.[15]

Shared Attention

Another important aspect of synchrony is mutual gaze, or *shared attention*. Consider, for example, that humans are able to use our eyes or fingers to direct attention. It might come as a surprise to you that infants do not understand pointing until the end of the first year. Rather than looking at where you are pointing, they will look at your finger! Fun fact: Wild chimpanzees do not point and do not seem to understand pointing gestures. But dogs and captive chimpanzees do seem to understand the idea of pointing, suggesting that there is something about being around humans that leads to this ability.

In addition to pointing, our eyes can also illuminate what is going on in our head. For example, if someone is looking very intently at a painting, we can infer that they are thinking about the painting. Interestingly, infants don't even begin to follow another's gaze until age 9 to 12 months. However, when they start to do so, we parents can use our infants' pointing and gaze direction to follow children's lead. As we carry our babies around with us, having them in front so that we can see where they are looking is beneficial because it allows us to capitalize on this interest to label or explain their objects of attention. When we are playing and talking with our children, making eye contact with them, and making sure that they are sharing attention with us, we are facilitating connection and cognition (including language abilities)!

Mind-Mindedness

The last aspect of parenting that is important for synchronous interaction between parent and child is something researchers have called reflective functioning or mind-mindedness (see Chapter 6 for more on this topic). *Reflective functioning* is the tendency of some parents to actively consider and label their children's psychological internal states.

For example, a baby cries, and her mother might respond by saying, "Oh no. You must be sad because you miss your sister." Parents who do this tend to have children with higher levels of emotion understanding[16] and better capability at understanding and predicting the behaviors and intentions of others.[17]

Reflective functioning is illustrative of how we conceptualize our babies. If we think about their thoughts and their feelings, we think of them as humans with intentions and an inner world. An important aspect of reflective functioning, however, is a sense of curiosity and comfort with ambiguity. In reality, we can't ever truly know what is going around in babe's head, but being curious about it and being sensitive to what they are expressing through their cries and behaviors are critical for appropriate reflective functioning. Relatedly, understanding how children develop and what they are capable of helps immensely in being able to "read" our children's thoughts. For example, sometimes we hear parents say, "She's trying to manipulate me with her cries. I feel like, if I respond, I would just be spoiling her." But the reality is that it is impossible for an 8-month-old to ever be manipulative. When an infant cries, they are expressing a real need. Responding contingently and sensitively is not spoiling your baby but laying the foundation for healthy attachment.

The disruption of synchrony—this intricate emotional and behavioral dance—can be seen in a fascinating paradigm called the *still-face paradigm*. In these types of experiments, after a few minutes of normal face-to-face interaction between a parent and the infant (usually around 6 to 9 months or so), the parent is then instructed to hold a "still face." That is, they are asked to simply look at the infant but not respond verbally or nonverbally to the infant's changing facial expressions. They are told essentially to freeze.[18,19] When confronted with this behavior, infants will first try to interact, moving their hands and making faces, but after a while, they will start to look away and cry. The data suggest that infants expect parents to smile, coo, and interact with them, and that breaking this synchronous interaction is a stressor.

Another example that we sometimes see is intrusive parenting, which, in some ways, is the opposite of not responding to the child at all. *Intrusive parenting* describes an interaction style whereby the adult insists on maintaining a higher level of interaction and stimulating the child when the infant is tired. The infant may look away, start to cry, and become increasingly distressed. The paired nature of parent–child interaction is an intricate balance, a coordinated ballet that requires parents to respond contingently and sensitively to the child. Being finely attuned to the infant's signals, interpreting them accurately, and responding promptly and appropriately are fundamental for helping children to regulate their physiology and for social-emotional development.

Stability

When we try to understand environmental impacts on children's development, researchers in the past have often focused on harshness. *Harshness*, in this case, can mean insufficient resources, including poverty or neglect; it also can refer to threatening situations, such as child abuse. More recently, however, another dimension of environmental experiences has been shown to exert unique effects: stability and consistency. *Stability*, or a lack thereof, can describe everyday interactions with a primary caregiver, changes in marital status, and residential changes. It can also be used to describe the extent to which the home environment is calm and organized or is chaotic and characterized by noise, crowding, and disorganization.[20]

Stability is important throughout children's development, but it's important to lay the groundwork early in a child's life. Stability is vital because it is key for predictability. Children like to know what they can expect from their environments, and children who know they can expect a consistent response from their parent(s) are able to better learn how to adapt to their environments. Predictability helps children to understand cause and consequence, which is important for developing *self-efficacy*—the idea that one can shape and influence other people and one's surroundings.

The ability to manage one's emotions and behaviors also requires predictability of events and situations; so does planning for the future. In this section, we look at predictability in parenting behavior, mood, and the presence of daily routines in children's lives as well as how these factors may influence children's outcomes.

PREDICTABILITY IN PARENTAL BEHAVIOR

Infants and young children benefit from parental responses that are predictable and sensitive to their behavior. This can happen at the level of daily interactions, such as when the infant smiles and the parent routinely smiles back in return, as opposed to the parent who sometimes smiles, sometimes frowns, or just ignores the infant. Predictability can also occur when infants learn, for example, that the noise machine always precedes sleep. When children do not know what type of response they will get from their parent ("Will my parent be friendly to me when I reach for them?" "Will my parent comfort me when I'm scared?" "Is my parent quiet or loud?"), the unpredictability is a source of stress. Consider, for example, having a boss at work that you just don't know to please. Sometimes you make a joke that goes over well, and sometimes a similar joke offends them. In some ways, it would be better if you knew that they *always* hate it when you joke around. If they were consistent, then you would learn how to behave in front of them. But if they were inconsistent, you can't adapt; you just never know what to do in any given situation. This lack of consistency can make one feel like you have little control, and the lack of control is a significant source of stress.

When parental behaviors are erratic or unpredictable, children's outcomes tend to be more negative. Unpredictability of maternal behaviors when children are 1 year of age was shown to be associated with worse cognitive outcomes in children.[21] In that study, the researchers videotaped mothers interacting with their 12-month-old infants for 10 minutes. They looked in close detail at how the mothers talked to the child, the nature of the physical contact (holding, touching) initiated by the mother, and how she played with the toys with her infants. From these observations, researchers were able to quantify how predictable her behavior was. Did she tend to look the infant in the eye first before showing the baby a toy? Did she tend to smile before soothing the baby? When the children were 2 years old, they were bought back into the lab, and the children's memory, problem solving, and language skills were tested. At age 6, the children were bought back, and their memory was tested. The predictability of the mother's behavior predicted cognitive abilities both at age 2 and at age 6½. This effect was true even after the researchers consider overall maternal warmth and sensitivity.

Predictability in maternal behavior during infancy is also associated with a lower likelihood of an infant's having a secure attachment with the mother at 12 months of age. Unpredictability has also been shown to lead to cortisol dysregulation in infants[22] and worst self-control in children.[23] What these studies suggests is that being warm, nice, and responsive is important, but that is not enough. We also have to be predictable. The relationship between infant and primary caregiver is also affected by unpredictability in maternal behavior.[24]

As children grow older, their behavior is also affected by parental predictability. Consistency in disciplining has been investigated experimentally, and results suggest that parents who were inconsistent by both reprimanding and providing positive attention had the highest rates of toddler misbehavior and negative emotion.[25] Another experimental study found that children's hitting behavior was least frequent when met with consistent disapproval.[26] These data suggest that when parents are inconsistent or variable in their disciplining behavior, children have an increased likelihood of acting out.

Another way to think about parental predictability is whether children can expect adults to be reliable. In one experiment, researchers wanted to see how long children could wait for a prize.[27] Before the wait task, they were told that an experimenter would come back with nice art materials. For one group of children, the experimenter came back as expected. For another group, the children were told that the experimenter had made a mistake, and no art supplies were available. After being told this, the children were asked to participate in the infamous marshmallow task. In this task, children are presented with a marshmallow and told that they can eat it right now, or, if they can wait until the experimenter returns, they will get two marshmallows. What the researchers found was that children who were, in essence, mislead were less willing to wait. If parents are unreliable in their disciplining, it would be much more difficult for children to learn from their mistakes and be willing to engage in appropriate behaviors.

PREDICTABILITY IN MOOD

In addition to variability in behavior, variability in caregiver mood influences early development. One study examined the association between maternal mood predictability during the prenatal period and child negative affectivity over time. Greater unpredictability in maternal mood was associated with a higher level of child negative affectivity at 12 months, 24 months, and 7 years of age.[28] Another perspective on parental mood and its consistency is evident in research on caregiver mental illness. To illustrate, borderline personality disorder (BPD) is characterized by an unstable sense of identity, volatility in relationships, and mood dysregulation.[29] Unsurprisingly, BPD strongly influences parenting. Mothers who have BPD score higher on levels of intrusiveness and insensitivity to infants[30] who, in turn, manifest levels of disorganized attachment comparable to that found among maltreated children.[31]

Parenting behaviors and mood can be characterized along the dimensions of instability and unpredictability. Increases in unpredictability tend to disrupt parent–child bonds and lead to higher levels of disruptive behavior in children. Beyond the specifics of parenting behaviors, how families organize their lives is also linked to developmental outcomes.

PREDICTABILITY IN ROUTINES

Another way to think about stability is regular routines (e.g., mealtimes and bedtimes). Routines provide children with a sense of constancy in their environments, which gives them a sense of control and mastery. From routines, they learn to anticipate what's coming next. Young children are like sponges who build associations between different events in their environments. They like to make these connections; it's what learning is all about. Routines enable them to learn that a precedes b and that c leads to d. They learn that people's behavior can be predicted and is lawful—and that they can have some impact on their environments.

Research suggests that routines lead to positive developmental outcomes. Family routines benefit children by providing organization and predictability but also by establishing young children's daily biological rhythm, which, in turn, lay the foundation for higher cognitive and social-emotional learning. Sleep, for example, is necessary for physical health and growth as well as psychological well-being. Family routines help children to fall asleep faster and to sleep enough. Family routines also are linked to less nighttime awakenings.[32] On the other hand, lack of sleep routines in early childhood is also associated with higher levels of BMI.[33,34] This research suggests that family routines, perhaps by offering stability, are necessary for behavioral development and physical health.

Transitioning from one activity to the next is notoriously difficult for young children. In particular, transitioning from a favored activity (e.g., play, watching a video) to a less preferred activity (e.g., having a diaper changed, going to bed) is particularly disliked. Transitions are even more difficult for children who have special needs (such as children on the autism spectrum and children with anxiety disorders). Parents can help children manage the distress associated with these events by providing warnings before transitions (e.g., by giving a 5-minute warning, then a 4-minute, then a 3-minute, then a 2-minute, then a 1-minute warning) and by offering a fun event following the less-preferred activity (e.g., "When we wake up in the morning, we will read your favorite book!"). Beginning the activity with a preview of what will happen afterward can also help as can having a clock or schedule visible for children to see. Even when children can't tell time, having a clock visible is helpful because it provides a tangible signal that time changes, and one activity moves to the next. As children age, you will need to do less of this previewing with them because they will internalize the skills you have taught them and develop better self-regulation skills.

METAPARENTING

Before we wrap up this chapter, we'd like to state that the newborn period is also an important time to engage in something we call "metaparenting." Just as children are not born as blank slates, we, as parents, bring our own histories, moods, and personality into our parenting style. As Susan, a mother of three, said, "My mother was controlling. I told myself I would never become her. Yet, here I am with a monitor on my child's wrist, so I know exactly where she is and when." While being controlling isn't ideal, being able to reflect on one's own parenting is critical for being able to parent mindfully. Whenever we reflect on our own parenting, whether it's on the way we discipline our children or the way we play with them, we are engaging in metaparenting. The prefix "meta" refers to the notion of reflecting on an idea or process itself. So, *metaparenting* involves reflecting or thinking about our own parenting. Understanding our own parenting styles and their origins and causes helps us to understand both our strengths and weaknesses as parents, and helps lay the foundation for fostering change, if necessary.

In the context of metaparenting, there are four main processes that parents can engage in: anticipating, assessing, problem solving, and reflecting.[35] As you can guess, *anticipating* the effects of our parenting behaviors comes before an event has occurred ("How will my child react if we have to get up early for tomorrow's flight?"). So much of parenting is about planning—planning for children's futures but also planning and anticipating how the day will go, the routines that will be played out. As much as we would like to "go with the flow," this rarely goes well when you have young children. By anticipating what your child may need and how they may react as well as what *you* may need to be an effective parent, you can be prepared for any challenges.

The second possible direction is *assessing*. Assessing our parenting style always depends on a specific event; you can't evaluate yourself if you're not picturing some specific example. In the process of assessing, we focus on exploring why we, as a parent, behaved a certain way and also why a child may react the way they did to our parenting style. This can be challenging and can play out in obvious ways, such as when a parent loses their temper and they simply know it was because they didn't get enough sleep or they are currently very stressed out planning for the holidays. Sometimes, however, assessing can illuminate our behaviors in surprising ways.

I (Stacey) remember once being a test subject for my students to practice on in my developmental psychology lab. I was also asked to fill out a questionnaire that assessed the way I handled my child's negative emotional outbursts. Although my students learned a lot about the interview process, I learned about my parenting style. I knew what the questionnaire was assessing, but as I was filling it out, I realized, shockingly, that even though I *knew* intellectually that I should acknowledge my children's emotions and give them space to express themselves, I wasn't doing that in practice. In practice, I would get irritated when my daughter couldn't control her emotions. It also dawned on me that, for a host of reasons, my parents did not tolerate bursts of negative emotions in their children. As a child, I was always taught to keep my emotions—both positive and negative ones—under control. Through this process of reflecting, I became more conscious of how certain types of parenting behaviors get passed on to the next generation. Importantly, being more aware of it, I am now better able to change my behavior.

The third skill of metaparenting is *problem solving*. This one is actually a little more complex and often involves another person, such as your child (if they are old enough), to be engaged in the process. Generally, the steps in solving any problem, parenting-related or otherwise, involve recognizing the problem, identifying the source of the problem, coming up with possible solutions, anticipating possible outcomes, testing solutions, and evaluating how those tests went. For example, you might see that your child is throwing a tantrum every time they go to the doctor's office. You might notice that you haven't been framing the trip in a positive way each time, so you start to think about ways you could communicate better to change their view of the trip, thus hopefully changing their behavior. Given that it's a process, problem solving in metaparenting isn't necessarily tied to any one specific interaction with your child. However, problem solving could involve trying to figure out why you end up feeling frustrated or angry when your child reacts by yelling when you set limits with them. Does this make you feel like they are challenging your authority? Or like they don't respect you? Does it make you feel ineffective? How can you deal with these feelings? Does your child's yelling have to mean that you are ineffective? Is there a different way to interpret this yelling, such as that your child feels safe sharing their anger with you, trusting that you can hold the limit and absorb their anger?

The fourth type of metaparenting is *reflecting*. This one is similar to assessing: You're thinking about behavior or outcomes from interactions but the reflecting is broader and could be longer term. For example, you might reflect on how the family is getting along over time. Reflecting can even happen before the birth of your child! You might reflect on how your parents raised you and what type of parent you might be or wish to be. You might reflect on your own emotions and worries. By reflecting on our thoughts and emotions, we have the potential to see how our thoughts and emotions affect our behaviors. Maybe our guilt about working too much is leading us to buy a lot of toys for our kids. Maybe experiences from our own childhood (e.g., our own experiences with getting hurt) are making us obsessed with baby-proofing every corner of the house. In other words, engaging in metaparenting behaviors shows us what types of parents we are and can prompt us to think about ourselves and these interactions with our kids, thus opening the possibility for change, if necessary.[7]

If multiple adults are engaging in the care of your child, however, we encourage everyone to discuss and share their parenting philosophies. Through this discussion, you'll get a sense of where your philosophies overlap and where there may be tension and conflict.

Relatedly, whoever becomes involved in your child's care, whether a nanny or a preschool teacher, it is worth investigating and reflecting on the way that they "parent" your child. Do you share the same philosophy regarding how a child should or should not be disciplined? Why? How important is it to nurture children's cognitive versus emotional development? What are the goals that they have for your child? Making all these notions explicit can help reduce conflict later on and foster a mutual understanding.

CONCLUSION

The first couple of years of life form a unique period full of rapid change and development. The infant is an open system whose biology and psychology are heavily influenced by the world around them. Fundamentally, for most infants, the "world," in some ways, is very small, encompassing mostly the primary caregivers. At the same time, given the plasticity of the brain, primary caregivers can exert an inordinate influence.

In this chapter, we discussed how basic parent–child interactions can exert profound effects on children's outcomes later in life. We focused specifically on stimulation, synchrony, and stability, and we argued for the importance of touch—using touch and emotion to stimulate your child in a responsive and contingent manner. We believe these parenting strategies are particularly important during the early infant years and are just as integral to children's health development as are sleep and nutrition. At the same time, positive parenting is dynamic; it should change and adapt to each child's growing needs. In the next couple of chapters, we focus on parental behaviors during toddlerhood and the early preschool years that continue to foster children's social and emotional development.

TL, DR

- The brains of newborns are plastic, malleable, and affected by the type of inputs they are exposed to.
- For newborns, touch is a powerful way to support, stimulate, and sooth.
- Mirroring the baby's emotions, following their gaze, and taking the time to reflect on what the baby may be thinking, feeling, and experiencing are important strategies that help foster positive development.
- The newborn stage is also a time when fostering a stable and predictable environment is crucial. Stability and predictability can mean being consistently available to meet the baby's emotional and physical needs as well as having regular family routines.
- This period of development is also an important time to reflect on our parenting philosophies and dive into the philosophies of other adults who are engaged in the care of our children.

CHAPTER 6

IN THE MIND'S EYE: MENTALIZING AND EMPATHY

In some ways, infants are easier than toddlers. While they are unable to express their needs as well as a toddler, it is often the case that their needs are simpler to decipher. We can cycle through their needs almost like a checklist: Are they hungry? Cold? Is their diaper wet? Toddlers are much more difficult. Their feelings are big, their needs more complex, and yet they don't fully have the capacity to understand and express their thoughts and feelings. If toddlers themselves don't know what they want and need, how are we, as parents, supposed to meet their needs?

Older children can be even more challenging. They are now aware that we do not know everything about their lives, they can hide their emotions, they don't always tell us the truth, and they may not share their personal experiences. To be good parents, we, in many ways, have to be mind readers and to teach our children to understand their own minds. It has taken scientists a long time to prove it, but we now have a lot of solid evidence to suggest that the nuts and bolts of being able to care for someone breaks down into two essential components. The first is cognitive in nature—we have to be able to mentalize (understand what another person is thinking or feeling[1,2])—and the second is emotional—we have to experience empathy (feeling alongside our child's feelings).[3-6] These two skill sets may just be the core psychological skills that are needed for parents to behave toward children in a way that promotes healthy development. In this chapter, we unpack these concepts and illustrate how and why they are so important to children's development.

Let's start with this example from Jessie:

> My 8-year-old son, Charlie, came home from school the other day and was in a really bad mood. He was irritable and kept picking at his siblings. He was breaking all the family rules and no amount of gentle reminders was working to help correct his behavior. My instinct was to give him a consequence, which is what I did at first. But then, when I did, he started crying and told me that one of the members of the "doggy club" (a club he helped to start at school that's very important to him) had kicked him out of the club because he had defended another member of the club from some teasing. He started crying and told me that this is the worst thing that could have happened to him because he loves that doggy club so much.

This example illustrates the importance of mentalizing and empathy. Charlie's feelings when he arrived home from school were not obvious to me (Jessie)—at least not his true feelings. What was apparent to me was that he was irritated, but this was only the feeling that was clear. That irritation was on the surface. That could be seen. However, what was really going on underneath the surface for Charlie (and this is important because it is where the meaningful action was) had to do with something about which I had no knowledge. As his mother, I might have been able to mentalize and recognize that this behavior was outside the norm for him (he doesn't usually pester his siblings—at least not to this extent), and I could have wondered whether he might have been feeling upset about something.

Being in this state of curiosity about Charlie's thoughts and feelings, wondering what might be motivating or causing his behavior—

this is *the* crucial ingredient of mentalizing, which is sometimes also referred to as reflective functioning within the world of parenting and attachment research.[2] This insight or awareness into what might be happening with Charlie (what is causing his upset) is also likely to be important in helping parents feel empathy for their children. In my (Jessie's) case, understanding what was going on within Charlie— that he felt hurt and angered by the teasing boy's actions—inspired a great deal of empathy within me and softened my reaction to Charlie. Had I not had an explanation for his misbehavior other than what was immediately apparent through his actions, I would have been left to make up a more simplistic, limited explanation for his behavior that would not have allowed me to fully resonate with Charlie's emotions. This feeling of being moved with Charlie, of feeling his pain alongside him, well, that is the crux of empathy in the parenting role.

It turns out that mentalizing is one of the strongest predictors of *sensitive parenting behavior*, that is, parenting behavior that is responsive to your child's underlying emotional needs.[7] In turn, sensitive parenting behavior is a strong predictor of attachment security,[7] one of the best indicators of developmental health. *Attachment security* is the state that results when children experience a sense of confidence and certainty that the primary people in their lives who care for them, usually their parents, will be there for them when they need them.[8] This sense of safety and security in these important adults early in life generalizes to other relationships throughout children's lives. So, children who can trust that the important adults in their lives are going to be there for them also come to trust that their closest friends and ultimately their romantic partners (when they are adults) will be trustworthy.[9] They also develop a strong sense of self-worth and confidence, the kind of inner strength that results from feeling that they deserve to have been cared for and protected.[10] Given the vast number of characteristics that security relates to later in development, security in one's primary relationships may very well be the most important predictor of psychological resilience going forward.

Empathy, too, has been linked to parenting behavior that is more responsive to children's emotional needs[11] and to attachment security in children.[12] When parents are empathic, they feel their child's distress or pain along with their child. Feeling with the child allows the child to sense that another person shares their emotional experience (for the child to feel that they are not alone). In addition to being empathetic to children's emotional states, it is important for parents to be empathetic to children's physical states and competencies. Long before I (Stacey) had children, I used to say to my friends that I do not want my life to revolve around my children. Parents shouldn't be so child-centered. When I have kids, I told them, I'm going to continue living my life. This was, of course, the foolishness of youth. When I had children, I realized that even though I didn't need to eat regularly and that I was a night owl, it was ridiculous to expect my children to be like me.

It wasn't until a massive meltdown, complete with head banging on the cement floor by my toddler, that I realized how silly it was to expect children to conform to adult expectations. To be a good parent, I (Stacey) needed to think and feel like a child. In addition to their physical needs, it is important to understand what children are capable of at each developmental stage, I remember clearly when my younger sister said to my boyfriend, "You have a big, ugly, red bump on your face." I was mortified, but to a 3-year-old, the comment was merely an observation. My sister was unaware of social norms (that you do not mention someone's zit!), and she certainly wasn't aware that the comment may be perceived as insulting or hurtful. Mentalizing and empathy go hand in hand; being aware of why a child is behaving a certain way and having a good understanding of what they are developmentally capable of help us to be more emotionally understanding. In the next section, we dive deeper into the subcomponents of each of these skills.

THE CENTRAL COMPONENTS OF PARENTAL MENTALIZING

Mentalizing can be broken down into several different subcomponents. It is the capacity to reflect on mental states (thoughts, feelings, intentions, desires) and to understand that mental states can impact behavior in the self and others.[13] For our purposes, we are most interested in mentalizing as it pertains to parents' understanding of mental states in themselves (referred to as "self-focused mentalizing") and to their children (referred to as "child-focused mentalizing").[14] Parents are mentalizing when they are able to look at a child's behavior, typically a behavior that, at first glance, is a bit mysterious or confusing, and tease out a mental state that might be motivating or causing that behavior. For instance, a parent may wonder if a child hit them because the child was feeling overstimulated or was in need of connection, and was trying to get the parent's attention. A state of curiosity, and a desire to tease out the child's feeling that might be motivating the behavior are essential to the art of mentalizing.

We are mentalizing when we can acknowledge that we can never be 100% certain what another person is thinking or feeling because that other person's mind is not our own. In the research literature, this is referred to as acknowledging the *opacity of mental states*, the property that mental states in another person are ultimately unknowable because it simply is impossible to be completely certain of the contents of another person's mind (as much as we would like to have this certainty). We can make informed inferences regarding what is going on with our child, but we cannot, with certainty, know. Furthermore, people can intentionally mask or disguise what they express or share in terms of their emotions. Young children are not very skilled at hiding their emotions (many parents wish their kids were a bit more skilled at masking their emotions), but, as kids age, they get better and better at hiding how they are feeling from the world.[15-18] This can create benefits for the outside world, including for parents (for instance, it's a bit of a relief when children stop telling their grandparents that they didn't like their birthday present), and can also create some challenges (such as not knowing what your child is thinking and feeling at every juncture). This opacity of mental states may increase the importance of parental mentalizing. Parents may need to exert that mental effort if they want to have a prayer of figuring out what is going on in their children's minds when their children are better and better at not showing how they are feeling.

Given that it is never possible to truly know what another person is thinking or feeling, it may be the ability to stay engaged in the process of mentalizing—to tolerate the ambiguity and the not knowing—that may be the most important aspect of mentalizing. Conveying to your child that you continue to be interested in what they are thinking and feeling and in getting to know their inner life better is one way of getting this message across. Parents are also mentalizing when they demonstrate the knowledge that a child may not be capable of thinking or feeling certain things because of developmental constraints on thinking or feeling processes. For instance, when a parent expresses the awareness that children are unable to fully separate their own feelings from those of other people, which is a developmentally acquired skill, or when a parent senses that a child only understands a few basic emotions but does not yet understand certain other emotions (e.g., embarrassment or guilt), parents are mentalizing.

Furthermore, mentalizing can take the form of parents being able to make explicit links between mental states and behaviors in their children or themselves, such as when they ascertain that their child felt angry and reacted to that anger by leaving the room abruptly and disengaging from their friends for the rest of the evening. Parents can also make these connections with respect to themselves and their own mental states and behavior. For instance, a parent may realize that they were feeling really anxious about their child's safety, and that made the parent overreact by becoming rigid or controlling when their child asked if they could go play with a friend.

THE CENTRAL COMPONENTS OF PARENTAL EMPATHY

Empathy, or feeling with your child's emotions, often necessitates knowing what your child is feeling before you can feel alongside your child. Sometimes it's obvious what your child is feeling such as when the cause of a child's upset is quite clear (e.g., your child falls down and gets hurt). But, many times, as in the earlier case of Charlie, it isn't so obvious what our children are feeling, and we have to dig a little deeper before we can get to the place of empathizing with our children.

Most definitions of empathy hold that it involves three core components: (a) *affective empathy*, which is feeling a sense of emotional connection with another person's emotions; (b) *cognitive empathy*, or understanding another's emotions and having the ability to take their perspective; and (c) *empathic concern*, or a concern for another person's well-being.[3,4,19,20] Empathy often is closely linked with parental mentalizing because having insight into a child's mental states is important for empathy.

Importantly, for empathy to truly be empathy, the feelings have to stay focused on the other person. For example, if a child was emotionally hurt at school and a parent responded by getting wrapped up in their own emotional experience (e.g., their anxiety or fear about the hurt, or their guilt about having allowed their child to get hurt, or their frustration regarding the school environment or their child's choice of friends), they are drawing attention away from their child's experience and not engaging in empathic responding. In other words, a defining feature of empathy is that the feelings must stay focused on the child and cannot morph into feelings focused on the self. This distinction can be tricky because, in both cases (true empathy and self-focused distress), the emotional expression can be one of distress. However, in one case, the attention stays focused on the child, and in the other, the focus turns toward another person.

THE BENEFITS AND COSTS OF PARENTAL MENTALIZING AND EMPATHY

The benefits of parental mentalizing and empathy for children are clear. Decades of research now support the conclusion that children parented by people who score high on measures of mentalizing or empathy (or better yet, both of these) are more likely to have better psychological adjustment as measured by attachment security, prosocial behavior, and the ability to regulate negative emotion.[21–24] The findings of some studies suggest that the links between these parenting qualities and the outcomes in the children may be explained by the differences in the parenting behaviors they exhibit. Specifically, parents who are higher in mentalizing and empathy are more sensitive in their behavioral responses to children's needs.[12,25] They demonstrate behavior that is more attuned to their children's emotional and developmental needs and is less hostile, critical, rejecting, or harsh.

It is worth mentioning that although these parenting skills have clear benefits for the child, there may also be a cost for the parent. Being high in mentalizing or empathy can exact a toll on the parent. Many parents may be able to relate to this on an experiential level. Caring for your child, spending time wondering what might be happening inside of them, feeling their pain alongside of them—all of this can be quite taxing on the parent. These effects have been documented within the research literature. For instance, one study found that parents higher in a self-reported trait like empathy had higher systemic inflammation.[26] Importantly, the parents also derived psychological benefits: They reported greater purpose in life and higher self-esteem, and unsurprisingly, their children had lower inflammation and better emotion regulation.[26] However, that the high-empathy parents exhibited a health cost (and the children, a health benefit) is unsurprising because it's meaningful but hard work to care for another person.

Another study, conducted in our (Jessie and colleagues') laboratory, used a different method to test for a measure of being in tune with one another. We examined mothers' and children's linguistic synchrony by measuring the degree to which mothers' and children's language use paralleled one another; we used a metric referred to as "language style matching." After measuring the degree of linguistic synchrony, we exposed the child to a stressor while the mother watched. We then tested whether the degree of language style matching was associated with mothers' and children's physiological stress response to a laboratory stress task. We predicted that children from in-sync pairs would show lower stress reactions, whereas their mothers would show greater stress reactions. Such a result would suggest that this linguistic synchrony was suggestive of a dynamic in which the mother was absorbing some of the stress of the child. We found that mothers who were more linguistically in sync with their children, which may be suggestive of a dynamic similar to empathic behavior, showed a higher heart rate when they watched their school-aged children complete a stressful task.[27] However, the children of these in-sync pairs showed lower levels of the stress hormone, cortisol, following a stressor.[27] We interpreted these findings to suggest that the "cost" of being in sync with one's child may be physiological engagement in the child's stress exposure (i.e., the mothers had more physiological stress); however, the benefit is that the children showed lower levels of stress physiology.

These research studies validate what many parents know: Parenting in an engaged way is effortful and often quite stressful. It's hard to stay engaged, and it hurts to feel your child's pain. However, the data also reveal that it's worth it. Parents who are higher in empathy report having a greater sense of purpose in their lives.

In addition, we (Jessie and colleagues) conducted a study in which mothers were asked to report on their feelings throughout the day. Results suggest that ratios of positive emotion such as joy and excitement were more intense when mothers were with their toddlers than when they were away from them.[28] They also report more variability in their emotional experience. Thus, being with your child can be associated with more varied and sometimes more challenging pattern of emotional experiences. Being with our own children is rarely ever a neutral experience but an experience that is often highly charged, full of color and intensity. No wonder all parents remember evenings when they are exhausted to the bone, even after a day of "doing nothing, but hanging out with the kids." Notably, parents who are more empathetic, more sensitive, are more susceptible to the roller-coaster.

If you add being an empathic and mentally attuned parent into the mix, parenting can come to exact a significant personal emotional cost. However, the trade-off may mean that you gain a greater sense of meaning and purpose in life and a better sense of connection with your child. Furthermore, the benefits for your child are clear: Children parented in this way are more likely to experience a range of benefits, including being more likely to have secure attachment and better emotion regulation.

PARENTAL MENTALIZING AND EMPATHY ACROSS DEVELOPMENT

The tasks of parenting change as your child ages and so do the requirements of parental mentalizing and empathy. When children are infants, the aspect of mentalizing that involves identifying what a child is thinking or feeling is made more difficult by the fact that a child has limited skills to express themselves. So mentalizing requires paying attention to overt and not so overt cues. Infants are able to let us know through their crying, protests, and smiles what makes them happy and sad. Thus, mentalizing here involves listening and paying attention to how they express themselves. But they also communicate in other ways: They rub their eyes when tired, their back arches when they are mad, and they look at things that interest them. Mentalizing here means engaging in *joint attention*, that is, looking at where they are looking, gaining an understanding of their rhythms (e.g., the period from 6 p.m. to 8 p.m. is peak fussiness), and even counting and inspecting their dirty diapers (e.g., "Hurray! Eliana did a poop every day for a week. She's getting enough to eat!").

By the time children are age 3 or 4, they have the capacity to broadly describe their emotions but only using two or three labels, such as "happy," "angry," or "sad."[29] This limitation in expressive capacity makes it difficult for a parent to engage in conversation with a young child regarding their thoughts or feelings because the child cannot articulate what mental states occupy their mind. However, at this age, mentalizing is made simpler because young children are less skilled (relative to older children) at disguising or hiding their emotions.[15–18] When a toddler is mad or sad or afraid, you probably know it. Young children do not have the desire to hide their emotional expression from the external world, and this makes identifying children's emotions a far more straightforward task. But while toddlers can express their emotions, they often do not have the words or cognitive capacity to explain why they feel the way they do. If the child is angry, the child may be screaming and pounding the floor with their fists while crying but also be unable to clearly articulate the reason why. At this stage, helping to them to label their emotions and helping them to figure out the reasons underlying their emotions helps children learn to mentalize for themselves—in other words, it fosters children's abilities to understand the interconnections between mind and behavior.

Furthermore, in communicating that emotions make sense and obey certain laws or principles, this conveys a sense of control to children, assisting them in developing skills to regulate their emotions.

However, as children age, their ability to hide, mask, or even alter their emotional expressions grows significantly.[17,18] Although, in many ways, parents may be grateful for this growth in emotion regulation capacities in their children—because most parents would prefer that their teenagers not have all-out, on-the-floor, fist-pounding tantrums during their high school years—this does make it more difficult for parents to be aware of how their children are feeling. Teenagers, for example, are highly skilled at being able to mask their true feelings from people they don't want to know about their feelings. It is not uncommon for parents to find out about their teen's breakup with a boyfriend several weeks after the entire high school class found out through Snapchat. In times like this, the teen is able to keep their emotional experience under wraps so that feelings of personal vulnerability, anger, or sadness remain hidden from the parents.

Thus, the challenges in mentalizing during adolescence involve using contextual information and knowledge of your child's unique personality and experiences to guide your predictions of how your child is feeling or what your child is thinking at any given time. These changes are complemented by relational changes that are also occurring during this phase. During middle childhood, parents and children transition from a caregiving relationship to a stage that researchers have referred to as a *supervision partnership*,[30,31] which means that parents and children share the responsibility for managing the child's supervision. Children increasingly turn away from their parents and toward their peers for social support.[32,33] As a result, parents get less and less intel from their children regarding their children's interests, wants, and desires, which also makes it more difficult for parents to understand their children's mental states.

Parental empathy also changes as children age. Empathizing with young children may sometimes be simple in that the source of their discomfort is fairly obvious: Infants experience hunger, fatigue, hurt, fear, and crankiness. However, it may, at times, be more difficult to empathize with infants because their emotions cannot be named or recognized or because some of their internal states do not evoke deep empathy—in other words, they may be perceived by adults as superficial or physical in nature (that is hunger, tiredness). Furthermore, if a parent has tried to satisfy a child's need and is unable to do so, they may have difficulty maintaining empathy for that child for a long period.

As children develop, their needs and feelings become more complex. No longer is your child upset because their diaper is soiled; suddenly, you have a third-grader who is sad because someone at school teased them. Next, you have a junior high school student who feels embarrassed because no one asked them to dance. Then, before you know it, you have a high schooler who is upset because they do not feel they are living up to their potential. These are just examples, but they illustrate the ways in which children's emotional reactions and cognitive capacities become increasingly more complex as they grow into new social worlds.

So, although parents of young children may have difficulty empathizing with certain states of an infant because the states are difficult to name or are somewhat superficial, parents of older children may struggle to empathize with their child's states if they do not understand what their child is going through. Parents also may struggle to empathize if their own defensive emotional reaction to the child's emotion blocks their empathy. Furthermore, because children's emotions increase in complexity as the years proceed, it may become more difficult to accurately appraise children's emotions as they age. For instance, it is not uncommon for school-age and older children to experience multiple emotions (some of which may be conflicting) simultaneously or for older children to experience emotions that are difficult to articulate or pertain to bigger picture issues (e.g., loneliness, angst about their future, or feeling they can't live up to others). These feelings may be harder for some parents to empathize with, especially if parents feel like they had things harder as a child than their child does.

THE HOW-TOS OF MENTALIZING AND EMPATHY

Parents often ask for tips on and tricks for engaging in the practice of mentalizing for their child and be empathic toward them. Parenting is such a dynamic, fast-paced process, something that occurs amid a flurry of other activities. For instance, parenting occurs in the spaces between making lunches, returning emails, and driving kids to different activities. It's not like parents are just sitting around with nothing else to do but calmly reflect on their children's behavior. If parents had all of the resources in the world in terms of attention, time, patience, and emotional robustness, mentalizing and empathy would be easy. However, it's rarely that simple. For instance, we know from the research literature that as parents' emotional arousal increases, their capacity to mentalize decreases.[34] If mentalizing and empathy are related—for example, if understanding why a child is upset is necessary for a parent to empathize with a child's distress—then parents' emotional arousal may limit the ability of a parent to empathize with a child.

This has led us (Jessie and colleague)[35] to introduce the OPENing Up framework as a way of thinking about mentalizing and empathy. Like most therapeutic practices, it is best to engage in and practice these strategies in moments when we have time and energy rather than wait for an acute stressful situation. In this framework, the O refers to the importance of parents reflecting on their "own emotions" as a first of four steps in this process. Parents must first be aware of how they are feeling and what is transpiring inside of themselves. They must ask themselves, What is happening inside of me that could be affecting me, my parenting, or my child at any given moment? Parents can pause

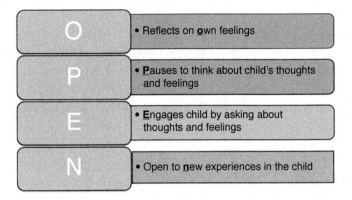

and ask themselves these questions when they notice that their child is distressed or when they notice themselves experiencing some stress. Engaging in mindfulness practices in which you stop to check in and notice your feeling without judgment can help keep you aware of your mental state and help keep it from spilling over and affecting your child. An abundance of research evidence suggests that children are acutely aware of and affected by their parents' emotions,[36-38] so finding ways to tune into the vibes you are sending out into the universe is an important part of being a tuned-in parent. This strategy is even more salient when you have had a challenging upbringing that might influence how you parent.

I (Stacey), for example, had a father who was hot-tempered and extremely critical of any behavior he perceived as laziness. He would often yell at his kids when he saw them just lounging around. I hate to admit it, but, somehow, I internalized my father's ideas about laziness. It would really irritate me when Eliana would get up first thing in the morning and open the iPad, even though we had a rule that she could have some cartoons if she got up early, brushed her teeth, and got dressed. I would get irrationally annoyed and harass her about all the other things she could be doing: getting her lunch ready, organizing her school materials, and so on. The ironic thing is that the first thing I do when I get up is open my phone and read the news. This is one example. How my father parented me continues to affect me in many and somewhat frightening ways I am not even aware of. This story illustrates the importance of reflecting on what triggers us. Reflecting is the first step toward parenting mindfully in ways that we consciously want to—not in ways that we may have been programmed to.

The second step in this process is "pausing to reflect" on your child's thoughts and feelings. You can engage in this process whenever your child is showing a behavior that is perplexing or unusual. Enter into a wondering stance in which you become curious about what your child might be thinking or feeling that could be leading them to behave in that way. Try to think of many different explanations for any given behavior, remembering that feelings and thoughts are often layered, so it's possible that many different explanations are true at the same time. Also remember that some feelings can be big and scary to experience and express, especially for members of certain groups. For example, boys often are often socialized to express assertive emotions, such as anger, whereas girls are socialized to express "softer" negative emotions, such as sadness or fear,[39–41] so it might be particularly hard for some children to give voice to these feelings. Thus, you may need to look carefully for their telltale signs. Sometimes imagining that your child is not your child (but instead your friend's child, for instance) can be helpful, especially if you yourself are feeling overwhelmed in the situation because it can be hard to mentalize for our own children in times of stress.

The third step in this OPENing Up process, *E,* is "engaging your child." You can test your mentalizing hunches by asking your child how they are feeling or whether they are feeling the way you think they might be feeling. Here, we recommend you use open-ended questions with a tone that conveys true interest and curiosity. It is best to ask these questions when you have time to sit and talk to your child (i.e., not when you are rushing busily from thing to thing). You don't want your child to feel like you are just checking a box by asking them how they are feeling; rather, you want your child to feel that you are truly interested in their thoughts and feelings and that you have the time to do a deep dive with them into their internal worlds. You can start off the conversation with a statement or question that sets the right tone for conveying interest, such as, "I want to know how you're really doing." Next, you can ask specific questions regarding how your child is feeling or what they are thinking. Usually giving children options for several feelings they might be feeling (e.g., "How angry are you?" "How sad are you?" "How afraid are you?") gives children permission to feel multiple feelings simultaneously and sends a message that it is expected and normative to feel negative emotions in the first place. What a powerful message this conveys to your child.

You can follow the OPENing UP framework even if your child is preverbal, knowing that your child may be unable to respond with words. Some parents, for example, will naturally mimic their children's emotions, expressing emotions in an exaggerated manner. In essence, by embodying your child's emotion, you are able better able to understand their psychological states but also signal that you feel what the child feels. New research shows that the way in which you convey your curiosity about children's mental states through your body language can affect their own ability to understand their mental states. This has been referred to as *embodied mentalizing*.[42,43] Through facial expressions and tone express, you can express concern to an infant who may not understand language. Or, imagine that you notice that an infant is orienting their body toward an object (e.g., they are facing a toy and then begin lifting up and leaning toward that toy). You can

embody mentalizing by showing, through your body language, that you understand that your child is interested in that toy. You may wish to also move your body so that you are facing that toy and even get down close to the ground so that you are at eye level to it. Children understand nonverbal emotional cues long before they understand words. Indeed, at 6 to 7 months, children will look to a trusted caregiver to figure out how to respond. If a child falls and is not hurt, if they see an adult say, "Oh my, what a fantastic fall! Look at you, so brave," they are much less likely to cry than if an adult expresses undue fear and concern.

The fourth step in this part of the process is being open to "new experiences in the child." It is easy to assume that we know our children based on our past experiences with them, but we must remember that our children are ever-evolving creatures who can surprise us in all kinds of ways. Our kids can surprise us in the extent to which their interests and proclivities and feelings can change from day to day. Our job is to roll with it, to be open to the child we have in front of us each day, and to communicate that we want to get to know that version of our child every day.

Once we've got a handle on what our child is feeling, then we have to move into an empathic state. The two tricks here are both feeling empathy for our child and then expressing empathy for our child. Children are astute perceivers of falsehoods, so they know better than anyone if someone's faking a feeling. Therefore, our initial advice here is to never fake feeling empathy for your child if you don't actually feel concern for them. Often, the empathy you need will come right to you once you identify what your child is feeling and why. You may easily be able to understand why your child is feeling a certain way and be able to resonate with this feeling.

However, when children respond to their feelings in ways that are destructive or antisocial, certain barriers can sometimes prevent our normal feelings of empathy. For instance, imagine Tom, a child whose feelings were hurt because his brother, Miles, excluded him from his play when a more attractive playmate appeared. Tom reacted to feeling hurt by pushing Miles. While you may have loads of empathy for Tom's feelings of rejection, it may be difficult to access this empathy perhaps because you feel anger toward Tom for pushing Miles or because you feel concern for Miles. So, how can you go about accessing your empathy for Tom? You could approach this by first recognizing that your anger toward Tom is getting in the way of feeling empathy for him. You could express this frustration to Tom or acknowledge it to yourself. Pausing to recognize this anger and give it a place in your mind may allow it to ease so that you can then focus on the deeper root cause of Tom's outburst, which was his feeling rejected by his brother. If you can feel and express empathy for Tom's pain at being rejected, you can then move on and discuss alternate ways that he could have handled this pain that would have been more helpful than pushing Miles. But it is unlikely that Tom will be able to hear anything before he receives some empathy for his pain at being rejected, so this is the best place to start.

In terms of the how-to of expressing empathy, we recommend two key ingredients. The first is an acknowledgment of the feeling the child is likely experiencing (e.g., "You must be feeling so sad right now . . .") and the second is a statement in which the parent joins the child in the emotion, avowing that the parent is sorry that the child has to go through this (e.g., "and I'm so sorry you're suffering so much"). These two statements combined provide the child with a mirror of the emotional state (the acknowledgment) plus a sense that it matters and that someone else cares that they are experiencing that feeling (the joining). These statements must be uttered with some feeling so that they don't come across as empty words— children will know if the parent doesn't feel the empathy behind the words. Thus, if the parent doesn't feel with the child, the parent may wish to only reflect back the child's emotion and not offer a joining statement because a joining statement without a joining sentiment could feel hollow to the child. Recall the story of Charlie at the beginning of this chapter—when Charlie arrived home and acted out. I (Jessie) was unaware exactly why he was behaving in this manner. So, I initiated the interaction with him by acknowledging his emotional state: "It seems like you might be feeling hurt or angry, and I can completely understand that. I'm really sorry for it—feeling upset is really hard."

At this stage, we suggest that the parent be tentative in the language they use here, which grants the child autonomy in terms of owning their mental states. It gives space for the child to say, "Actually, you are wrong." The parent reflects back the presumed mental state(s) and then joins the child in expressing empathy for the child's emotional pain:

Charlie, I can see how deeply that hurt you. It must have felt terribly unfair to you that he kicked you out of the doggy club for protecting a friend. I'm so sorry that happened to you. But I'm really proud of you for being so kind to the friend who was being teased. I wonder if you might want to share what happened today with your sisters.

Here, I (Jessie) am reflecting Charlie's emotion and then join in it. I praise Charlie for his behavior with the child at school and then suggest a counter-behavior that he could use with his siblings (directly expressing his vulnerable feelings to them rather than expressing irritation toward them).

CONCLUSION

Mentalizing and empathy are two psychological processes that are extremely important in helping parents enact sensitive responses to children's needs. They are key ingredients in responsive parenting, which helps to promote children's socioemotional well-being. In this chapter, we reviewed the science supporting the case for the importance of these two factors and simple tips for how to enact these factors in everyday parenting situations. Remember that it's nearly impossible to mentalize or be empathic when you are overwhelmed yourself, so, to use these skills, you need to clear out some mental space first. As always, taking care of your children means taking care of yourself first.

While this chapter focused on cognitive processes in us, as parents, our next couple of chapters focus on emotions in our children and how by being able to be empathetic and mentalize, we can better understand their emotional experiences. In doing so, we will increase our capacity for helping them to learn and control their emotions.

TL, DR

- One of the important skill sets parents need to have is to be able to "read" their children's thoughts and to empathize with their children's emotional experience.

- The process of understanding children's mindsets is challenging because (a) they don't always know exactly how they think or feel, (b) they may not be very good at conveying their big emotions and complex thoughts, and (c) they start to learn to hide their emotions and thoughts.

- The OPEN framework provides a process by which parents can begin to understand their children's experience: *O* equals reflect on one's own emotion and response; *P* equals pause in heightened moments of stress, take a moment to pause, and pay attention to both your and your child's emotions; *E* equals use open-ended questions to engage your child and help them to explore their own emotions; and *N* equals understand that most experiences are new experiences for your child that are free of encumbrances from the past and don't always let how your child has responded before shape your understanding of how they are responding now.

CHAPTER 7

TEMPERING THE TANTRUM: REGULATING CHILDREN'S NEGATIVE EMOTIONS

We have discussed extensively the role of stressful life events and how they can have enduring influences through biological and epigenetic pathways. At the same time, humans are complex creatures. Even negative life events do not affect us all the same way. Just as important as the actual events themselves is how we perceive them. Do we see these events as formidable obstacles that will derail our lives? Or are they exciting challenges and opportunities that we can cope with and learn from? Do we perceive that others are there to support us, to help guide us through? These perceptions lead to our emotional responses. And it is our emotional responses that trigger the cascade of bodily responses that, in turn, affect our health and well-being.

Just as stressful events lead to biological changes, perceptions of love and social support affect health and well-being through their influence on biological systems. To understand how this works, consider, for example, that when we are upset or stressed, our blood pressure and heart rate goes up. Chronic elevations can lead to cardiovascular disease. But the presence of supportive, nurturing others serves as a buffer against the negative impact of stressors on our bodies. In other words, when children are upset, their physiological reactivity is up, and their stress response is in full gear. When we help them deal with these emotions, we are putting a gentle brake on this system.

Perceptions of love and support lead to higher levels of the infamous "love" hormone called oxytocin.[1] Oxytocin plays various important roles in the body, but more recently, its role in buffering our stress response has been studied. When couples discussing a conflict were exposed to oxytocin (through the administration of a nasal spray), they had more positive communication and lower levels of cortisol.[2] Importantly, oxytocin level increases when we feel supported and cared for. It's often described as the love hormone (although it is much more) because of its importance in building bonds and social connection. By acknowledging children's emotions and being responsive their emotional needs, we are shaping their adaptive stress physiology.

Humans connect and provide social support to other adults and to strangers, but children in particular need this source of strength the most. Children experience emotions often and intensely. Any parent who has ridden their 2-year-old's emotional roller coaster knows this to be true. In terms of time course and intensity, children's emotions are a force! This sensitivity to their emotional lives can be a vulnerability because these emotional reactions can shape their health and their ability to learn and grow. At the same time, the emotional reactions offer a window of opportunity—they are lessons by which, with their parents' help, children can learn to manage and take advantage of the power of these emotions. With such frequently occurring "opportunities," parents have ample chances to teach children about what their emotions mean and how they can learn to manage them.

In this chapter, we unpack the importance of responding to children's distress, reviewing the scientific evidence on the topic, and offering concrete tips parents can use to deal with children's negative emotions. We take important issues confronting parents head-on, providing a reasonable, science-based approach to responding to children's distress—one that may actually help save your sanity as well as your kid's. First, we provide a basic overview of what research tells us about these strange things called emotion, and we describe the reasons why children's distress can be challenging for parents to handle, which we hope will provide you with a context for understanding the nature of children's distress. Then, we discuss the aspects of children's emotions that can be most vexing for parents. We conclude by offering potential solutions for parents dealing with children's negative emotions. We focus on negative emotions in this chapter, but in the next chapter, Chapter 8, we switch gears and discuss the role of positive emotions.

THE SCIENCE OF EMOTION

Children's brains and emotional centers are unlike those of adults. The part of the brain that sits right behind the forehead is the prefrontal cortex. This area of the brain controls emotions, is involved in planning and decision making, and plays a large role in guiding our interactions with others. Psychologists group all these higher order abilities, including self-control, under the larger category of *executive functioning*. One can think about this area of the brain as the CEO, or director, of the whole operation. The best word to describe the prefrontal cortex in children is *immature*. The most recent data from scientific research suggest that the prefrontal cortex is still developing long past the teenage years. Thus, while there is some variability based on children's temperament (see Chapter 9), as a whole, children are much more emotional than adults, and it is because of primarily one reason. The area of the brain responsible for controlling children's very strong feelings is not fully formed. Imagine if a large company were operating without a CEO, and you will have some sense of why children are the way they are.

Emotions are powerful, even transformative; they affect all aspects of our lives from our relationships to our health. They motivate us, drive us to succeed, and in many ways, can be thought of as a form of energy. Both positive (e.g., happiness, joy) and negative emotions (e.g., fear, anger) serve essential functions in our lives. Consider, for example, how fear of failure may drive a student to study, and pleasure from receiving attention from one's parents can motivate children to behave or act out. The guilt we feel from doing something wrong drives us to make amends. Embarrassment leads us to act in socially appropriate ways (at least in front of others)!

In addition, emotions are sources of information. They provide us with clues about our bodily states as well as our physical and social environments. It is critical to understand the information that our emotion offers and also the causes of these emotional experiences. Understanding these aspects of emotion allows us to capitalize on the power of emotion, to use the information our emotions provide us, and to diminish their negative effects.

It is important to understand the sources of emotion (in other words, where they come from) so that we know whether to trust them. When we feel fear walking down a dark alley, this fear may be telling us that walking down this alley is not a safe activity at night, a feeling we might want to listen to by deciding not to take that first step. But at other times the causes of our emotions are less obvious. Consider the following example. For me (Stacey), the emotion of being "hangry," which I experience as a mix of anger and irritation when hungry, is a genuine phenomenon. It is often a signal that it is time to have a snack. Before I realized this about myself, I would often lash out at my partner right before lunchtime, thinking that he was behaving in a way that was making me upset. In fact, the culprit was low blood sugar. Now, I carry around a granola bar. While this is a somewhat innocuous example, not understanding the sources of emotions can also exert more significant impacts, such as making us behave in ways that are biased or discriminatory.

Second, emotions are essential because, at the end of the day, how we respond to events that happen around us is often more important than the events themselves. If we see a stressful event as a challenge that we can overcome or a mistake as a lesson to be learned, we will bounce back much more quickly from that event. Because we can never truly control our world or other people, being able to control our emotional response is perhaps the most significant step toward happiness and well-being. A large body of research now suggests that the link between stressful events and health, such as cardiovascular disease, is not so much the result of the event itself but our response to the event.[3,4]

Interestingly, sometimes it is not so much that responding with negative emotions is always a bad thing but that the lack of responding can also be harmful. For example, in one of our (Stacey and colleagues') studies, we found that people who report both high and low levels of negative emotion in response to life stressors have the worst physical health.[5] In addition, in studies in which researchers bring people into their laboratories and have them watch emotional video clips, the people who show the greatest cardiovascular responses, including blood pressure and heart rate, are the ones who are told not to show their feelings.[6,7] We (Stacey and colleagues) have also found that being stoic and exerting high control can lead to higher levels of biological dysregulation.[8] We remind our reader of the Yerkes–Dodson law we discuss in Chapter 1: Just as a moderate level of arousal is beneficial for performance, moderate levels of emotions are better for health than too little or too much.

Being able to experience emotions, both positive and negative, is the core of what it means to be alive. As parents, we try hard to protect our children from negative emotions, such as disappointment or fear. But as the emotion researcher Susan David stated, "Only dead people don't feel." Inevitably, in life, despite our best efforts, our children will be disappointed, they will feel fear, and they will have tremendous loss and grief. While we can't and should not protect our children from these emotions, we can use certain strategies to help them manage these emotions so that they are a source of energy and provide opportunities to learn and to feel connected to others.

If emotions are a form of energy and a source of information, we can view the role of the parent as that of an emotional coach.[9,10] Our role as coaches is to teach children to be aware of their emotions, be curious about their origins, attempt to understand where they come from, and learn how to express and control them. Importantly, when we say "control," we don't just mean that children should learn when *not* to express their emotions or to suppress their emotions. Rather, they should also learn which emotions to express, when to express them, the benefits of expressing emotions, and how to express them in socially appropriate ways. Children should be encouraged to experience and express a wide range of negative and positive emotions given that ample research demonstrates this has a positive effect on health and well-being.[11] We want children to understand that they can learn to use their emotions to influence themselves as well as other people. We want our children to have rich emotional lives.

THE PARTS THAT STING: RESPONDING TO CHILDREN'S DISTRESS

We mentioned earlier that the CEO part of children's brains are not developed. Thus, it is vitally important that parents take on this role. In our discussions of parents, we have found that parents frequently fall into one of two categories: One group comprises those who take on this role with gusto to the point at which they are overcontrolling. This is the parent who calls a child's professor to demand that the professor regrade their child's exam [please don't do this]! The second group consists of parents who, for a host of reasons, hesitate

Responding to Child's Distress Sam 12

to make demands of their child. As one mother explains, "I don't want to discipline them. I want them to know that I love them unconditionally" And some, like my (Stacey's) husband, just state, "When I ask her to do something and she doesn't do it, I just simply don't know what to do!" Imagine being on a plane and the flight attendant comes and says, "There's no pilot"—or even worse, the emergency lights go on and the pilot doesn't seem to know what to do. We all need experts in our lives. We need people who are charge, who know what to do, and who know how to do it effectively. Children are no different. They need us to be their CEO.

Does it sometimes feel like children have endless numbers of complaints and an exhaustingly long list of feelings to express? And that they get upset over the most inane things? How in the world are parents to respond to children's displays of distress, especially when their distress spills out all over the place, erupts at inconvenient times, and often pertains to topics that it's extremely difficult to care about (coming from an adult's perspective)? Before diving into our recommendations, we thought we would first consult with some experts. So, we asked Sam, my (Jessie's) 11-year-old; Charlie, my (Jessie's) 8-year-old; and Eliana, my (Stacey's) 7-year old, to tell us what helps and harms when they experience negative emotions. Here, first, is the conversation with Sam:

> *Jessie:* Sam, what different negative emotions do you have?
>
> *Sam:* Yikes, I have a lot—um—when I'm angry or mad. When I'm stressed, overwhelmed—uh—sad.
>
> *Jessie:* What do parents do that are helpful or not so helpful when you are experiencing these emotions?
>
> *Sam:* It's really helpful when, like, I ask them for help, and they give me a hug, and they say, "It's gonna be okay" rather than—um—saying, "Ah, that's not a big deal" or "That's nothing" or something like that, and making it seem like—like it's not important to them. And, it's also more helpful when they say, "It's gonna be okay" rather than just say, "Well, of course you could do this, follow this as a solution" because I don't really want a solution. I want more empathy from my parents when I ask them for help.
>
> *Jessie:* How does that make you feel when they give you a suggestion, but you want empathy?
>
> *Sam:* It makes me feel upset and, like, it kinda makes me feel like they just wanna solve the problem and get it over with. And make it be done with rather than help me feel better slowly.

For Sam, the importance of acknowledging the emotional experience far outweighs the importance of problem solving. Charlie, however, makes the distinction between the types of emotions. "When I am mad," he says, "what helps me feel better is having some alone time, but when I am afraid, what stops me from being scared is being with Mommy."

Interestingly, when Stacey asked Eliana, "What can you do to make yourself feel better when you are upset?" Eliana replied with the following: "When I am mad, I can punch a pillow. Sometimes running can also help. I can also exercise with Pops." It's interesting to us, as parents who study emotions, the diversity of these responses and where they came from. Children's choice of strategies clearly come from *socialization practices*, or what their parents have taught them about how to deal with these emotions. Despite her focus on being physically active to release stress, Eliana, when asked, "What can adults do to help you?" responded simply: "Cuddling!"

The conclusions from these little experts are clear: Be there, be ready to listen, and err on the side of empathy rather than give advice. If you feel tempted to give advice, try this one trick first and ask this question: "Would it help you if I gave you some tips?" Or: "How would you feel about me giving you some suggestions?" If the answer is yes, then, by all means, lean in and give your child advice because they've given you permission to do so. However, if your child indicates they aren't in the mood to receive that kind of help, then you have your answer. What they really want is a different kind of support—the kind that looks like empathy (care, concern, and love). Moreover, of note, these anecdotes also highlight that there is no one strategy that will work for all negative emotions and for all children. Just as when adults are stressed the type of coping strategies that we may use—talking it out with a supportive friend, relying on our faith, spending some time on self-care, even using humor or retail therapy—depends on the situation at hand and the type of stress we may be experiencing. Sometimes the best and only strategy is to sit with our emotions, experience them, and have them pass through us, to tell ourselves, "This, too, shall pass." Just as there is a diversity in emotional experiences, we need to be aware of the diversity of ways in which we can help our children cope.

When it comes to meeting or not meeting children's emotional needs, the messages are loud, and everyone has an opinion: "Spare the rod, spoil the child." "If you don't meet your child's every need, your child will be insecure." "Let your child cry. It will teach them to self-soothe!" "Don't let your child cry it out. They will be less attached to you!" Messages such as these are extreme by nature, leaving reasonable parents with nowhere to go. Stranded and paralyzed in the middle, parents may have the subjective experience of "failing" at whatever approach they have selected as their gold standard. That's because these extremes aren't reasonable, and they aren't feasible unless you have (a) no heart or (b) no need to ever care for yourself or accomplish any task besides caring for your child. So, where's a reasonable parent to turn? We got ya.

THOSE DOGGONE KIDS AND THEIR FEELINGS

Why are kids' feelings so inconvenient? Well, there are many reasons for children's feelings, and none of them is random. Kids' expression of feelings doesn't have to do with your child being a bad kid, trying to manipulate you, or purposely timing their upset to have the greatest negative effect on you, although it might feel that way sometimes. We cannot underscore this point enough. If we, as parents, interpret our children's emotions as a form of manipulation or as intentional bad behavior, we are more likely to respond in harsher, more negative ways, which may worsen our kids' behavior. Kids' feelings make sense to them and exist for a reason. Here's what the science has to offer.

My Kid's Distress Spills Into Everything: Charlie and the Epic Alarm Clock Incident

When children get upset, it's extremely hard for them to recover. For instance, one morning, my (Jessie's) then 7-year-old was upset that his alarm clock didn't go off an hour earlier, mostly because this reduced the amount of time he would get to spend cuddling with me before getting ready for school. His crying, loud enough to shake the bed, woke my partner and me, jolting two unwilling, sleepy people into a day that was bound from the start to be rocky.

As a method of protest, Charlie refused to settle into cuddling with me because he wasn't going to get as much time as he wanted anyway, so why enjoy any of what was left (totally makes sense, right?). After I was able to help him calm down about the alarm clock, he then became very upset about the placement of his sister's arm on my body (by this point, she, too, was cuddling in bed because his crying woke her up early). His argument was that her arm crossed the imaginary line that cuts my body in half and therefore had intruded into "his half" of my body. That intrusion would limit his ability to maximize his cuddles—if he were to actually cuddle me, which he wouldn't because he didn't get enough time to cuddle this morning because of the doggone alarm clock timing.

Why does Charlie's distress seem free-floating, that is, at first focused on not having enough time to get his cuddles followed by his refusal to do cuddles in the first place and then his getting upset that his sister's arm placement was interfering with his cuddles? Kids' feelings are kind of like the "fly in the punch bowl": If there's one tiny fly in that punch bowl, the whole darn thing is ruined. It doesn't matter that the fly touched less than 1% of the punch in the punch bowl—it's the principle of the whole thing. And the principle is that one small bit of fly ruins a whole large batch of punch.

Kids' distress is catching and it's long lasting. Children's ability to cope with or manage this distress is immature relative to adults (remember the missing CEO?). This is, in part, because of their underdeveloped prefrontal cortices. Whereas it may take you or me 30 minutes to get over something that upset us, it may take children several hours. Children have far fewer tools to use to manage their emotion, and the effectiveness of the tools that they have depends heavily on luck (e.g., "Can my daughter find her favorite stuffed animal before she reaches total meltdown? Depends on how messy our home is!"). Furthermore, the tools that they do have are poorly developed, will collapse under too much stress, and ultimately may not work that well unless everything goes just so.

Similarly, children's insight into why they are feeling the way they are feeling is underdeveloped. This means that my (Jessie's) kid really may believe that it's his sister's arm that is the ultimate culprit in making him mad and not that the feelings are ones that are left over from the alarm clock incident. Not knowing *why* they feel the way they do makes managing their feelings that much harder. One dominant way in which adults manage feelings is by expressing them, but if children are unaware of why they feel the way they do, expressing them is, at best, imprecise—like trying to write neatly when holding a pencil with your fist. Children's grossly uncoordinated efforts to manage their emotions lead to spillover—distress that seems contagious as it jumps from one focal point to the next—and this spillover can also affect those around them, not just the children themselves. This quality of children's distress can be enraging for parents, but it makes perfect sense when we consider that children's skills for managing these intense feeling states are extremely rudimentary.

My Kid Gets Upset at the Worst Times (the Most Inconvenient or Imprudent Occasions)

"On the way out the door." "Right before bed." "When you are already 5 minutes late to school." "Right before the bride walks down the aisle." "On a holiday." "Just as you are boarding the airplane." Basically, whenever is be the very worst time for your kid to get upset is the exact time they get upset. This gets us every time. It's puzzling and it's infuriating, and yet it actually makes so much sense.

Children's main source of security—of emotional anchoring— are the people who care for them. When their parents are with them and are calm, all is right in the world. A child's caregivers are their environment, so how their caregivers are doing goes a long way for setting the stage for how a child is doing. When caregivers are stressed or harried or rushed, this sends a cue to children that something is awry—something's in the air, and it's ambient anxiety! This ambient anxiety sends a clear message to children: Pay attention, don't let your guard down, and stay alert because danger is on the horizon. It's kind of like a low-level buzzing in your ear at all times or the feeling that comes when multiple children are talking to you at the same time while you are trying to do complicated math. Similarly, for a child, having a parent be distracted (or not paying attention to the child) can also evoke low-level anxiety, leading the child to launch attempts to return the parent's attention to the child. Situations in which parents are behaving differently in these alarming sorts of ways—such as when parents are tired, distracted, stressed, or rushed— are a complete setup for system meltdown—for the worst temper tantrums and the most unreasonable demands. This *is* the time when children are bound to get upset or lose it because the time when you, as a parent, need them to get with the program, to behave, to not be noticed, is exactly the time when they become frightened and are most apt to lose control. And this, ladies and gentlemen, is exactly what makes parenting so incredibly challenging. It's that when you most need their cooperation, you're least likely to get it.

So, it's not an unhappy accident and it's not bad luck that your child becomes upset at the most inopportune moments. It's because these inopportune, stressful moments are not only that way for you, they are that way for them, too. This pressure puts too much stress on the system and is a surefire way of creating overload. The actual secret to this whole thing is that *you* have to be the CEO—a sort of prefrontal cortex that exists outside of their bodies. And at the times when your prefrontal cortex is already on max, you may not have the bandwidth to also manage their company. But their company needs more managing when your company is under duress. You can fix this with (a) a whole lot of empathy for yourself (these situations are *hard*!) and your kid (your stress makes them worry, and, in all honesty, they lost a competent CEO), and (b) lots of planning in advance because knowing when hard times are on the horizon can allow you to talk things through with your child so they know what's coming and to create systems that will help them get through times that are bound to be more harried or when routines are out of whack.

My Kid Gets Upset About the Silliest Things

One time my (Jessie's) oldest child got extremely upset about leap year—that there was such a thing. Our kids have also gotten upset that weekends aren't 3 days long. One of them became intensely distressed that his underwear didn't match his socks (because he wanted to tuck his underwear over his shirt—it was a phase). My (Stacey's) daughter cried because she couldn't stay home and go on a walk at the same time. While we agree that these are regrettable facts of the human condition, they are fairly silly things to get upset about—and so are about 99.99% of the things kids bemoan. These sources of upset are often unassailable facts of the universe ("Why is it getting dark so early?" "Why are eggs yellow when they are scramble-cooked instead of white?"), or they are minutiae that just don't seem to matter to an adult but are exceedingly important to children ("I want this door to open out rather than in!"). In thinking about why children get upset about these things, it's important to remember that children have a completely different frame of reference than we adults do. Children have different perspectives on life from so many different angles. From the perspective of perception, we know that children can hear different sounds than adults can and that they see different things than adults (both because their vision is better and because their eyes are typically 2 to 3 feet lower than adults' eyes). Their sense of time is different from that of adults—much slower, typically. Remember when the summer used to last for ages? In a sense, children are much more perceptually sensitive than adults. So, the things they notice are things that pass under adults' radar. While adults are focused on bigger picture concerns, kids notice the details.

Furthermore, what matters to them is completely different than what matters to adults. But, like adults, the things that matter to children are actually the things that children think about all of the time. I (Jessie) will never forget how, one morning before school, my daughter was extremely upset about the shape of the door handles in the car. I thought it was a bit silly at the time, but when I picked her up from school 8 hours later, I was bowled over by the fact that she was still thinking about those silly door handles. Instead of being more frustrated about this than at the beginning of the day, the experience gave me pause as I contemplated this: Since that morning, I had gone about my day thinking about at least 100 things that were different from the door handle, yet my daughter had been thinking about that door handle all day long and wishing that it was shaped differently so that her hand would feel different when it was rested on the handle. Even though I still thought it was a bit ridiculous that this mattered as much as it did to my daughter, it was incredibly clear that it did, in fact, matter that much.

Several weeks later, when I (Jessie) was talking to my daughter, I learned that when she was riding in the car, she wanted to use the door handle as a place to rest her hand (so she didn't have to hold her hand in the air or set it on her car seat, which was sticky from something she had spilled a few days ago). Of course, there are other solutions to this issue, such as cleaning the car seat, but this hadn't occurred to my daughter likely because she wasn't the one who cleans the car seats. This got me thinking a lot about how reality is subjective—we only know what we experience—and for my daughter, one of her greatest adversities that day pertained to that door handle. But there's no arguing with subjectivity. What matters to our kids is what matters to them. We may wonder why it matters or feel frustrated that it matters, but we can't argue with the fact that it does, indeed, matter.

REASONABLE RESPONSES FOR REASONABLE PARENTS

So, the question is, How do you best balance your sanity and your child's needs when they are upset? And how do you do so when their responses last a long time, occur at the worst times, and are inspired by things that seem unimportant to you? Here's what we recommend.

Acknowledge Children's Emotions

For children of all ages, the first step to acting as an emotion coach is to acknowledge children's emotions even when they aren't aware of them. Remember Sam's and Charlie's words? The most important thing you can do is be there and listen to them. Our way of describing what Sam and Charlie are referring to is acknowledging their feelings. This simple act of acknowledgment, which may be as effortless as saying, "I can see that this upset you" or "It seems like you're worried about something," can go a long way. If you don't actually know what your child is feeling but you can tell that they are feeling some kind of negative emotion, you can ask them about it ("Are you worried about something?" "Are you feeling sad?"). This strategy might work better for older children, too, who are likely to have more insight into their thoughts and feelings. If your child is unaware of what they are feeling, making a statement like this (or asking a question, as the case may be) can help increase your child's awareness of their emotional experience by drawing their attention to the change in their state.

If, on the other hand, your child is aware of the emotion, then acknowledging affirms that you are paying attention to them, that you think their feelings are important, and that you care about what they're feeling. By acknowledging your child's feelings, you are sending a powerful message to your child: Your feelings matter. This very act alone is a powerful way to diminish the negative emotion. This strategy works for children of any age (or for adults, for that matter!), but you may want to vary the words you use depending on their level of comprehension and their emotion vocabulary in particular.

When Eliana, my (Stacey's) daughter, was a toddler, she was what developmental psychologists would call a highly reactive and emotional child. She would get upset because she felt her cheeks were slightly puffier than she was used to in the morning or that the pea soup was a slightly different shade of green than normal. More often than not, it was not always clear why she was upset. Often, when Eliana was crying (which was often), my response was to ask (and often in an exasperated tone of voice), "Why are you so upset?" I frequently followed this question with, "It's not a big deal. There's no need to be upset." These statements are problematic in so many ways. (And it wasn't until I was a test participant in my own research study on emotions and parenting that I became fully aware of my errors.) First, children are not always aware of why they are upset. And the "why" can have a presumption of judgment. It asks first for an explanation, but not only that, it asks the *child* to explain. To have to explain your feelings when you are upset can actually make things worse. Unless this "why" comes from a genuine sense of curiosity and empathy, it can be perceived as a judgment.

Rather than asking why first, we encourage parents to provide validation. When parents validate children's emotions, they are not asking the child to explain but, instead, are affirming and responding to the child's needs. And as emotion coaches, it is the parents' role to be responsive and to scaffold children's experiences—not the child's role to justify their experience. Second, it is obvious that the events and experiences that trigger emotions (both positive and negative) in adults are different than in children, but this difference certainly doesn't make children's emotional reactions any less valid.

Eliana's response to my (Stacey's) questions was often to become more upset and ultimately to be less responsive to my attempt at understanding and consoling her. I soon realized that understanding the *why* should always come after acknowledging Eliana's emotions with both verbal—"You seem really upset, honey"—and nonverbal behavior (pulling her in close). Eliana responded immediately to this simple change in behavior. Often, simply acknowledging the emotion was enough for Eliana to calm down. Once calm, she was much more capable of responding to my question, "Do you want to tell Mommy why you are upset?" Phrased this way, the assumption is that (a) it's okay that Eliana is upset, and (b) it's up to her to share that with me. Importantly, it also emphasizes the idea that Mommy will still be loving and understanding, regardless of whether Eliana even knows why she is upset. Acknowledging children's negative emotion is often a fundamental first step to diminishing the negative hold it can have on children.

Sometimes children prefer to have more control over the extent to which others perceive their feelings, wishing to be the ones who inform others how they are feeling rather than being informed that people can see what they're feeling. This can happen when children are embarrassed about how they feel in general, when the situation or feeling itself causes more discomfort about the feelings, or when children have been criticized in the past for feeling a certain way and thus are hesitant to express feelings. In this case, it can be helpful for parents to phrase their acknowledgment more tentatively, such as in the form of a question—"Did that upset you?"—or a statement that implies a lack of complete certainty—"I'm wondering if that might have upset you." Phrasing the acknowledgment with more tentativeness gives your child the freedom to be able to agree or disagree with your statement. It allows for the possibility that the child might be experiencing a feeling but doesn't place pressure on the child to agree that they are experiencing that exact feeling. This type of statement is akin to giving the child permission to feel without telling the child that they must be feeling a certain way.

In my (Jessie's) clinical practice, I have found that even when children disagree with a certain type of acknowledging statement from me (Jessie: "I'm wondering if that made you feel a bit upset." Child: "It didn't"), sometimes just having made the statement in the past can increase the child's willingness to talk about feelings in the future. For instance, the next time a similar situation occurs in a child's life, if an acknowledging response has previously been made, the child may be more comfortable sharing these feelings. Thus, even when a child's response to an acknowledging statement is a repudiation of the feeling, your message may not be lost on the child. Hold out hope and wait to see how the child responds to this type of situation the next time it occurs.

Acknowledgment is a reminder to the child that you see their suffering and that you care. In other words, you are providing social support. This type of emotional support profoundly influences children's ability to adapt to stress and also influences their health.

Emanate Empathy

In Chapter 6, we discuss the importance of fostering empathy in ourselves. Empathy is vital for being able to respond sensitively to our children's displays of distress. We experience empathy when we feel with another person. Empathy is one of the most powerful forces in human relationships. In our species, which is so strongly driven toward human connection, we have a powerful need for understanding from others. We also want our experiences to be shared because it takes us out of the uncomfortable state of being alone with the feelings. If we had to sum up the essence of empathy, it would be to communicate a very simple message to the child: "I understand, and I'm sorry you're hurting." When working with parents, we often advise that before they say anything else to a child, they first provide empathy. Anything said following an empathic statement will be processed more deeply by the child.

Empathy can also be infused in all aspects of this emotion coaching process. For instance, when parents acknowledge the child's probable experience, they can offer a bit of empathy: "You must be upset about that. And I'm *so very sorry* that you are." In so doing, the parent not only draws the child's attention to the emotion but also lets the child know that they care about how the child is feeling—that the child is not alone with their hurt because the parent feels a little bit of that hurt, too. Another way in which we can show our empathy is to use our own experiences, to let them know we have gone through something similar. When Eliana was 7, she came home from school, very upset that her two best friends looked alike with their blond hair and blue eyes. Eliana has brown eyes and dark hair, so it was heart-breaking when she said to me (Stacey), "I wanted Pops to buy me this color ChapStick because A had the same ChapStick, and I wanted to be twins with her!" She went on to list the ways in which her two best friends were alike and to explain how sad she felt when they often declared themselves as twins. After acknowledging her emotions, I proceeded to share my own experiences of feeling left out. By sharing the experience, this feeling was normalized for Eliana but also conveyed to her that her mother understood. In doing this, we must be careful that we continue to center our children's experiences by bringing it back to their own feelings and giving them room to express the possibility that our experience is "not the same."

One obstacle to parents' expressing empathy is when parents do not like the way the child is expressing their feelings. This can happen when children behave aggressively when they are angry. In cases such as these, it is important to separate the child's emotion from the child's reaction to the emotion. Emotions *always* deserve understanding and empathy. Always. Emotions are real and valid as they are; they are a reflection of the child's perception of a situation, and whether the perception itself is accurate or not, the feelings are always real. If you are struggling with your child's reaction to their emotions, we encourage you to comment specifically on the emotion itself by expressing empathy and then speak to the child's reaction to the emotion. For instance, you may wish to say something like the following:

> I see that you are feeling angry, and I'm really sorry. It's awful to feel that way. [Pause for 10 seconds.] "When you're angry, it makes sense that you want to do something about it [here, you are empathizing with the desire to take an action of some kind], but next time, instead of hitting your sister, I want you to use your words to tell her and me why her behavior made you angry [here, you are providing a suggestion for a different kind of action].

Encourage Children to Express and Verbalize Their Emotions

Acknowledging statements and empathy can go a long way in helping children become aware of their feelings, and the next step in the emotion-coaching journey is to help children elaborate on the expression of their emotions. Typically, when we have emotions, simply saying the name of the emotion isn't enough for us to feel like we have fully expressed it. Adults often use many different words to give a full flavor to their emotional experience, invoking metaphors and sensory descriptors to bring into narrative an experience that lives in the senses ("It was just crushing—it knocked the wind out of me, just left me aching and empty"). Children are less apt to use lengthy narrative and metaphor to express their feelings, but they may be able to elaborate some on their feelings when parents can ask them questions that prompt this type of discussion.

For instance, if a child says that they were upset in response to something that happened at school, a parent could respond by saying, "What kind of upset was it? Was it the kind where you feel sad and lonely, or was it the kind where you want to get mad and yell?" Or they may be able to draw comparisons between different situations that have created this kind of feeling in them. This type of initial follow-up helps the child hone in more specifically on the nature of the feeling. Subsequent follow-ups can focus on helping the child get deeper into the feeling—for instance, by asking the child what about the incident bothered them the most or which part of it was the most painful. Inquiring about the *emotion's action tendency*, or what the emotion makes the child want to do, also heightens the child's processing of the emotional experience ("Did the feeling make you want to go out there and scream at [that other child]?"). Parents can also encourage children to think about their emotional experience in a more nuanced way by asking the child what else they were feeling at that time. Sometimes it helps to refer back to the original feeling the child expressed when helping the child refine their emotion expression. Doing so reminds the child of how they were feeling and also implicitly communicates that it's possible to feel more than one thing at the same time (e.g., "So you were angry about that. What else were you feeling?"). And it can also be valuable to give the child permission to feel things that might be harder to express by minimizing their strength (e.g., "Okay, so most of you was feeling angry. Was there any part of you that felt afraid?").

For some children, words and narrative are not the dominant or most accessible form of expression. The inability to articulate and express emotions is particularly true in younger children whose verbal skills are undeveloped or in children who are less oriented toward language as their main mode of expression. If you sense that this is the case for your child, it can help to ask your child to draw how they are feeling or to draw the situation that caused the feeling. Children could pick out a color that shows the feeling or choose a shape that best expresses the feeling. Or they might like to find a song or play or sing a song that shows the feeling they are having. Some children even like to act out the feeling, for example, by running away, cowering in the corner, or pretending to be an animal that best represents the feeling (e.g., a big angry bear, a trembling mouse).

In general, society discourages males from focusing on their emotion, and they are often encouraged to suppress certain emotions (like sadness and fear). It always saddens us to see a parent say to their little boy, "Don't cry! You need to be tough!" By not allowing our male children to experience and express a diversity of emotions, we risk emotionally stunted adults who have trouble connecting and empathizing. Parents may have to work harder to evoke awareness and open expression regarding these emotions within their male children. Using techniques other than talking (e.g., drawing) may also help to loosen things up with male children as well as acknowledging that it can be hard to talk about and share feelings.

Your child will let you know they are done expressing a feeling, either by straight up telling you or by becoming disinterested, getting distracted, finding something else to play with or talk about, and so on. It is best to follow their lead in terms of whether, when, and how long to spend focusing on an emotional experience because these techniques do not work if a child is resistant to them. You can always tell your child that you are willing to talk about this if they want to at any point, which will leave the door open for continued or deeper exploration of their feelings.

Know Which Coping Strategy to Use: Emotion-Focused Coping Versus Problem-Focused Coping

Broadly speaking, there are two ways to cope with distress. One is referred to as *emotion-focused coping*, which involves coping with the distress by focusing on the feelings. The other is *problem-focused coping*, which means coping with the distress by changing the situation that is creating the distress. Some situations call for emotion-focused, parent-assisted coping, whereas others call for problem-focused coping. You can ask yourself several questions to figure out which type of coping your child is asking for in a given situation. The first question is this: What type of help is my child looking for? Are they looking for help in the form of understanding/empathy/expression coaching? Or, is my child looking for help in the form of information or concrete behavioral change? Some of these distinctions are easy to spot. For instance, when my (Jessie's) daughter comes to me to tell me that she's upset because her sister is wearing her shirt, my daughter is not looking for empathy and understanding—there is a situation to be solved here! Conflicts and disputes often call for problem-focused coping. When a child says something like, "And I don't know what to do" after describing feeling upset, this is a sign that they are probably looking for some type of insight or ideas into how to solve a problem, which is often a call for problem-focused coping.

However, much of the time, children are actually looking for emotion-focused coping, which typically involves the provision of empathy, understanding, and expression coaching. Situations in which the child felt rejected, was disappointed by the outcome of something, or got hurt feelings are prime candidates for emotion-focused coping. Going back to the example of Eliana's being upset that she did not have blond hair and blue eyes like her two best friends. Clearly, the solution was not to dye Eliana's hair blond and buy her blue contacts. Rather, the situation called for acknowledging emotions to help Eliana to see her own beauty ("Mama made you to be different so that you can be unique! I also wanted you to look like me and Papa! I love your warm eyes and soft hair!"). It also called for a deep conversation about how friendships are not built on physical similarity ("Remember Mom's friend from college? She has black hair, brown skin like Mom, and also two daughters. She looks like Mom's twin, right? Well, she's Mom's frenemy! Mom's best friend is a tall, White, Russian lady with super-short hair!") and also lots of hugs and reassurance.

Sometimes after this emotion-focused coping happens, it can be helpful to move into problem-focused coping mode. For instance, in a circumstance in which a child has hurt feelings, it could help to ask the child if they want to talk to the child who hurt their feelings about the situation. But this problem-focused coping should not occur before the child has received the emotion-focused coping. If it does, this can send the negative message to the child that it's not okay for them to have these feelings or talk about these feelings; instead, the child should just solve the situation and move on. This is the opposite of the message you want to send to your child.

While there is much talk about talking about emotions, we believe that there is such a thing as doing it too much. *Rumination* is when one keeps thinking the same thoughts, and those thoughts are often sad or dark. All of us have been in that situation. Maybe we said something embarrassing in public, or we made a mistake that was easily preventable. Despite the event having come and gone, despite the fact that no one died, we didn't lose our jobs, and no major consequences are going to come from that event, we stay up all night, replaying the event in our head. At some point, endlessly analyzing a situation can become unproductive. At some point, we need to be able to say, "Okay. Let's go get ice cream."

Practice Forgiveness

Despite all of our best efforts, we still get what our kids need wrong a lot of the time. Welcome to the club: You are officially a parent now because all parents make mistakes with their kids. Don't worry if you reach for the wrong form of assistance for your child because your child will let you know if you do! And it's never too late to turn it around! If you start with problem-focused coping, and your child rejects all of your suggestions, then you know they were actually looking for emotion-focused coping. Sometimes children give a cue that they are looking for problem-focused coping when they actually are looking for emotion-focused coping (in this case, it was the cue that was misleading). A sign that it was a misleading cue is if the problem-focused coping you provide doesn't help. Or, perhaps, you misinterpreted their cues. No big deal. All you need to do is back it up and go to the emotion-focused coping. You can even apologize for starting where you did ("I'm sorry. I thought you wanted me to help you solve the situation, but I can see now that you actually wanted me to understand what happened").

The good news for all of us imperfect parents out there (aka all of us) is that loads of research out there shows that the mistakes we make in relationships offer us opportunities for repair and that it's the degree to which we repair these stumbles with our children that matters. In these situations, make sure to praise your child for telling you when what you were doing wasn't working. We want to be responsive to our kids and to be giving them what is actually going to help them. Sometimes kids worry about correcting their parents' efforts to help, so you want to clearly tell them that you appreciate knowing what works and doesn't work ("Thank you for telling me so clearly what you need. That really helps me know best how to help you").

Don't Take It Personally!

It is so easy to take children's feelings personally—to feel like they would feel better or be less angry or sad if we had done something differently—but the bottom line is that it just isn't true. Childhood is full of a messy mix of intense emotions, many of which are highly charged negative emotions. Childhood is not a carefree time of emotional levity; it is the time when we have the greatest uncertainty and face the most of intense of all experiences. And the lion's share of children's fluctuating emotions is not your fault, even when those emotions are related to things you have done or the way you have acted.

It's easy for a parent to get caught in the guilt–worry spin cycle of parenting in which they feel guilty or anxious regarding the way their child feels, and this guilt or anxiety then makes the situation worse by affecting the child's emotions or by changing the parent's behavior. But, in reality, this sense of responsibility is not deserved! Just think about the types of things that upset children—such as the shape of the door handles. This can't possibly be your fault, and taking this on is only going to hurt your sense of self-efficacy—and you don't deserve that kind of treatment from anyone, especially not yourself.

CONCLUSION

Negative emotions have a terrible reputation. Scientists often argue that it is the negative emotional responses to events in our lives that lead to mental and physical health problems rather than the events themselves. But we know now that this is a simplistic understanding of negative emotions. Negative emotions, like all emotions, are a useful and essential part of our everyday lives. It is neither possible nor advisable to protect our children from these emotions. Rather, by accepting our children's emotions and encouraging children to be aware of them, we are training them to understand and, hence, shape their emotional reactions.

Importantly, our behaviors and actions have consequences not just for children's current state of mind but for their developing stress response systems. Our behaviors have consequences on biological systems that play important roles in health and well-being. In this chapter, we focused on negative emotions. Positive emotional experiences also play profound roles in shaping children's lives! In the next chapter, we switch gears and discuss positive emotions, their importance, and what parents can do to cultivate and capitalize on children's positive emotional experiences.

TL, DR

- It's not simply stressful events that impact our health and well-being but also how we respond to these events that matter.
- Children have big emotions that they need help controlling.
- Children's brains are not fully mature; parents must act as the child's CEO. As CEO, we need to help children deal with their stress and be aware of the range of strategies that exist because every child is different—just as every stressor is not experienced the same.
- In helping deal with children's emotions, acknowledging and respecting their lived experiences comes first.

CHAPTER 8

CAPITALIZING ON CHILDREN'S POSITIVE EMOTIONS

"Tickle me! Tickle me, again!" the child squeals with joy. This simple activity is repeated across many households all over the world. It is a simple, yet profound task. In these types of games, parents are doing something crucial: They are generating positive emotions in their children. In the previous chapters, we extensively discuss the importance of downregulating or mitigating children's negative emotions. But downregulating stress and reducing negative affect are not enough. Being able to upregulate children's positive affect to create and accentuate moments of joys is just as vital.

For far too long, the field of psychology concentrated on understanding negative emotions, such as depression, sadness, anger, fear, and grief, and the field of parenting and parent–child relationships was no exception. Parenting researchers' primary area of focus was on understanding parents' responses to children's negative emotions. And although nobody would dare dispute that the way in which parents respond to children's distress as being a defining feature of the quality of the parent–child relationship, it is now widely acknowledged that it is also important to understand how parents and children (and people, in general) engage with one another in terms of positive emotionality.

Positive psychology is the discipline within the broader field of psychology that has brought into focus the importance of understanding positive emotionality as a central aspect of human experience. This discipline is based on the premise that thriving in life is more than simply the absence of mental illness and distress. In other words, leading a life full of satisfaction, meaning, and purpose is not at the opposite end of the same continuum on which lie mental disorders, hopelessness, and despair. As such, positive psychologists argue that it is important to specifically study the processes by which people achieve these higher order states rather than just study the absence of illness.

Positive psychologists weren't alone in the emphasis they placed on the importance of cultivating positive emotionality. Long before positive psychology was in vogue, attachment theorist John Bowlby argued that it was important for parents to delight in their children's positive emotion and to find joy in the day-to-day moments they experienced with their children.[1] But this point was overshadowed by other messages in Bowlby's writings. People instead focused on Bowlby's work showing the prominent role that parents and other attachment figures play in helping children regulate negative emotions, such as fear, anger, and sadness.[2] Now, however, Bowlby would be pleased to find that mutual positive engagement between the parent and child is widely acknowledged to be associated with superior physiological emotion regulation in children[3] and better regulation of negative emotion.[4] In this chapter, we briefly review what is theorized regarding positive emotions in general and then discuss how positive emotions operate within the parent–child relationship context. We end by discussing techniques for enhancing positive emotionality within the parent–child relationship.

BENEFITS OF POSITIVE EMOTIONS

One particularly influential theoretical perspective within the field of psychology that holds a great deal of explanatory power regarding the role of positive emotions is Barbara Fredrickson's[5-7] *broaden-and-build theory of positive emotions*. This perspective suggests that positive emotions have the effect of broadening the individual's thought processes, prompting them to consider a wider array of possibilities (in terms of thoughts and actions), which, in turn, has the effect of leading them down different paths. According to a theorist named Isen,[8] positive emotions afford the ability to "integrate diverse material" to do the kind of complex and difficult thinking that many tasks require.[9] By virtue of the ability to think more expansively—and be less hindered by "what-ifs" or self-doubt and instead be fortified with confidence and possibility—the individual is able to "build" the resources necessary to accomplish the goals they are setting out to accomplish. Positive emotionality provides fuel (expansive thinking, attention, and energy) that enables individuals to approach situations with a different perspective than they might otherwise have. For example, someone might feel particularly generative and creative after having received a promotion at work. Buoyed by the positive emotion they have as a result of this accolade, they may stay up late redecorating their bedroom; learn a new song on the guitar; and, somewhere in the evening hours, even rekindle a relationship with an old friend. Positive emotion is a force that has a certain type of energy that sparks ideas and brings people together in new and different ways.

Positive emotions have an opposite action tendency as negative emotions, which tend to narrow people's attention, make them concrete and limited in their focus, and render them shortsighted. If you think of a highly depressed or anxious person, someone who can only focus on what troubles them and has a difficult time envisioning different ways of approaching problems, this is the counterpoint to positive emotionality. And this makes good sense from an evolutionary perspective: If there's a threat in sight, it would behoove the individual to shut out extraneous stimuli and narrow attention on the threatening stimulus. This hyperfocus on negativity and threat enables fast and precise responses to potential threats and ensures that resources crucial to one's safety are protected.[7,10] The fast-acting, defensive/protective response is adaptive from an evolutionary perspective and is thought to provide survival for brief moments of danger. However, when this type of response is repeatedly triggered over prolonged periods, it can lead to a state of hypervigilance that is associated with poor health outcomes, including heart disease,[11] headache,[12] and immune system suppression.[13] Positive emotion experienced over the long term, on the other hand, is considered to be associated with action tendencies that promote health and survival.[5]

One amazing fact about positive emotions is that spending time experiencing positive emotions helps buffer people during times when they later experience negative emotions. Barbara Fredrickson and colleague[14] referred to this idea as the *undoing hypothesis* wherein positive emotions help to regulate or correct the impact of negative emotions. What they meant by regulate negative emotions was to reduce the physiological arousal associated with negative emotions. Put more concretely, this theory states that negative emotions turn on our body's stress response system, whereas positive emotions reduce or even turn off the stress response. This buffering effect of positive emotions helps to speed the body's recovery from the negative emotions and makes positive emotions worth pursuing.[15] It has also been shown that experiencing positive emotions in the aftermath of a traumatic event (e.g., the September 11th terrorist attacks) is associated with posttraumatic growth[16] that allows us to make meaning out of trauma and to learn and grow from these experiences.

STRATEGIES TO ELICIT POSITIVE EMOTIONS

To take advantage of positive emotions, you first need to have positive experiences. This goes without being said. At the same time, however, the type of activities children take joy in can be mundane and boring to an adult; thus, mentalizing and empathy (see Chapter 6) are crucial. It is important to understand from your children's perspective the things they find most enjoyable because this will help you share in their joy. What children value and desire are often not what adults would expect. Consider, for example, that I (Stacey) grew up with very few material resources. I do not remember a single vacation that my family went on together when I was growing up.

I felt like I really missed out. All my friends were backpacking across Europe, sunbathing in the Caribbean, and shopping in New York City. I had none of these experiences and none of these memories. As an adult, I am privileged enough to take vacations and to bring my children along. By the time my daughter was 5, she had gone to Hawaii twice, Europe three times, and Asia once. I asked her once, "What was your favorite vacation?" She replied, "Hawaii." I wasn't surprised. But when I asked her, "What about Hawaii did you like so much?" her answer was simple: "I really liked the pool." I thought to myself, "It costs like $2 to use the city's pool. Instead, I spent hundreds of dollars to trek to the other side of the world to give my child this experience." It dawned on me that while I don't remember any big family vacations, I do have wonderfully fond memories of going fishing, of baking with my mom, and having "sleepovers" during which my siblings and I would run into my mother's room and jump into bed with her. She would then tell us the most terrifying ghost stories. We would cling to her in fright and love every minute of it.

When children are young, it does not take much to make them happy. Playing pretend, building a fort, and collecting rocks are favorite activities. But parents can find such activities dull and boring. I (Jessie) find putting together model planes and Lego sets trying, but I love to sing and dance and engage in any kind of play that involves utter silliness. For me (Stacey), engaging in "play" with my children is a challenging task. I find playing with my kids utterly boring. Going through the rigamarole of using dolls to enact out mundane everyday events is excruciating. At the same time, there are things that

I love to do that I don't do as much as I would like as an adult. I love to paint, and painting rocks is an activity that my children and I enjoy together. I love building things, and so we find crafts to make together. And, of course, I love eating, so baking is very gratifying for my kids and me. So, the strategy, here, is to bring about contexts that evoke joy in both parent and child. This might require a little creativity and it might require us to slow down and think about what brought us joy as a child, but, in the end, it will allow you to create rewarding play experiences for you and your children.

As you cultivate positivity, consider also the type of positive emotion. Although joy and happiness from birthday parties and movie nights are wonderful, these are not the only positive emotions. We often neglect or ignore a range of positive emotions, including emotional states, such as curiosity, contentedness, generosity, gratitude, and purpose. For example, investigating the night sky, reading books to children about their topics of interest—whether dinosaurs, planets, or bugs—cultivate interest and curiosity. When we share in this sense of discovery, we are nurturing profound positive emotions.

Contentedness is an emotion that is often overlooked in favor of the flashier feelings of joy and excitement. But unlike joy and excitement, too much of which can be exhausting, contentedness is not tiring. Just as important, events that lead to contentment—snuggling in bed, enjoying a warm bowl of soup, sipping milk tea—are mundane and can occur daily. They also require little planning, resources, or energy (and, for a tired parent, this reason alone might make it the best positive emotion to elicit!). We can amplify and prolong these moments by savoring them (more on this later).

Gratitude is another strategy that elicits feelings of positive emotion. A large body of research suggests that *gratitude*, reflecting on and expressing appreciation, can boost our mental health.[17] Gratitude can be a spontaneous emotion that occurs when someone does something nice to us, but it can also be a feeling that we cultivate. Asking children to reflect on things that they are grateful for or modeling gratitude for them can nurture this skill. Gratitude can also lead to higher levels of prosocial behavior,[18] which leads to our next strategy for cultivating positivity.

Create opportunities for children to give, whether that means donating food or helping out their grandmother. When children can be of service to someone, when we provide them with this opportunity, we lay the foundations for a meaningful life. Children love to be of use. They love to help out. And when we are of service, we feel a quiet joy that only comes from being able to give generously. Indeed, a large body of research suggests that giving to others is much more satisfying than giving to oneself. In one study,[19] researchers found that people who spent more of their income on other people had higher levels of happiness than those who spent less. In this study, the researchers also conducted an experiment in which they gave participants money. The researchers then asked some of the participants to spend the money on themselves and asked some participants to spend the money on other people. Those participants who were asked to spend money on other people reported higher levels of happiness than those asked to spend money on themselves. Doing good for others is also doing well for ourselves.

Importantly, as children develop, finding opportunities for doing good that align with their own interests and skill set is key. Jana, my (Stacey's) friend, describes her son's experience:

> My 12-year-old is a computer geek. He loves all things electronic. And so, for him, when he's helping the elderly learn how to "double click" [yes, many need to be taught that!] or designing a website for a nonprofit organization, he gets a lot of pleasure and purpose from it. It doesn't feel like a burden to him or something he has to do.

In other words, by matching "service" with the "skills" our children already have, we can potentiate both, leading to more passion for giving as well as appreciation for their own skills and talents. We also give them a sense that they can make a difference in the world. We give them a sense of purpose.

In addition to generating positive events, seek to prolong the positive emotion even before the event occurs. Before an event happens, discuss the event to create a sense of anticipation. Involve your child in the planning of a trip or a birthday party. Give them a sense of autonomy by letting them make decisions. Anticipation is more evocative and can be more powerful than retrospection (thinking about past events).[20] By anticipating a positive event happening, we can get a different kind of joy from it.

Being happy and wanting our children to be happy might, at first blush, be universal. But some people are frightened or uncomfortable in the presence of certain positive emotions and seek to dampen or minimize the experience of those emotions. The tendency to engage in these dampening or downregulating strategies is associated with negative outcomes, including lower levels of life satisfaction and higher levels of depression.[21-23] Relatedly, when parents pick up a book to learn about child development, they are often focused on things like reducing negative behavior or learning strategies to foster success (e.g., academic achievement). We argue for the importance of looking at the whole child. The absence of negative behavior or even the presence of desirable behavior (e.g., excellent grades) are not markers of well-being. Lucy, a friend of mine (Stacey) and a mother of two, shares her story:

> My father was very authoritarian when I was growing up. He was very focused on academic achievement and demanded utmost respect from us. I was a very obedient kid and did very well in school, and that seemed enough for my father. Similarly, my son is a good kid. He's excelling in school, follows all the rules. I should have known from my own experience, but I never

guessed that my son wasn't happy despite all of his successes. I don't want it to be either–or. I think he can both be successful and happy.

And we can have both. Like most things, cultivating positive emotional experiences requires practice. By fostering positive emotions in children, we are, in essence, creating an individual who can experience maximum joy and meaning in life. In the next section, we dive a little bit deeper into the idea of cultivating positive emotions in the context of parent–child relationships.

HOW TO CAPITALIZE ON CHILDREN'S POSITIVITY

Childhood is typically a time full of unbridled delight. Well, let us restate that: Childhood is a time full of unfiltered emotions such that all feelings are expressed in their raw, true, unprocessed form. Thus, when a child is experiencing true joy, there is nothing quite as pure as that joy. The squeal of delight a 2-year-old emits when they find a roly-poly [sweet dough] behind the refrigerator and manage to stuff it into their mouth before their watchful parent swipes the child's hand away—it's something to behold. As parents, we have the option of entering into our child's emotion and coregulating it. Specifically, with respect to children's positive emotion displays, we can choose to upregulate their emotion to join into the positive emotion. We can choose to share in the experience and contribute to it, prolong it, and maybe even increase it, or we can choose to dampen it and discourage their positive emotion display. Whenever possible, choose to upregulate; that is, never let a happy moment go to waste.

Savoring is the process by which we attempt to hold onto, extend, or intensify positive emotions.[24] We can do this by sharing the event with others or allowing ourselves to express joy (e.g., laugh), and we can congratulate ourselves or give ourselves space to acknowledge our success. While the moment is happening, we can use mindfulness strategies to focus on the moment, to bring all our senses to bear on the situation, and to stop our mind from wandering. And we can use these strategies with our children. Savoring can transpire when a parent snuggles in deeper to a hug with a toddler, holds on, and closes their eyes to really take in the moment and make it last a little longer. Savoring can mean taking a new experience and highlighting it for all the senses. I (Stacey) tried this savoring strategy when introducing my daughter, Eliana, to the amazingness that is cotton candy. Our conversation went something like this:

> *Stacey:* I got you a surprise!
>
> *Eliana:* (*Squeals*) What is it?!
>
> *Stacey:* Something you never had before, a special type of candy!
>
> *Eliana:* What is it?! I want to see it!
>
> *Stacey:* (*Speaks excitedly*) It's cotton candy!
>
> *Eliana:* (*Picks up on my excitement*) Oh, my gosh! I never had cotton candy before!
>
> *Stacey:* Well, what do you think of it?
>
> *Eliana:* It's like a cloud!
>
> *Stacey:* Yes, it's like a cloud! Take a look at it and feel it.
>
> *Eliana:* It's pink, my favorite color, and it's so soft. It is like a cloud!
>
> *Stacey:* But it tastes sweet. Try it!
>
> *Eliana:* (*Tastes the candy*) It is candy!
>
> *Stacey:* Do you notice how it feels on your tongue?
>
> *Eliana:* It just melts in your mouth. It's amazing!
>
> *Stacey:* Now can Mommy have some? Oh my, it's so delicious! Let's share it with Papa!

Parents often tell us that one of the things they love about having children is getting to relive experiences like eating cotton candy for

the first time. It is such a pleasure and an honor to shepherd our children through these positive spaces. We can use savoring strategies to both amplify our own and our children's joy.

Savoring is also something that we can do by ourselves or with our partners. Savoring can mean sitting at our office, pulling out a picture of our child, and reflecting on a moment where we felt great as parents. For parents, savoring their children can frequently occur, maybe too frequently! Dean, a father of two, comments,

> Every time we go on a date, we are without the kids, but all we talk about are the kids. I sometimes feel maybe we should talk about something else. But I work so much, and I love hearing

about their antics. It is also fun to laugh together again about something silly that one of the kids said or something ridiculous that they did.

Related to savoring, *capitalization* is a specific strategy for savoring that is of great relevance to parents and partners. It refers to the idea of amplifying the positive experience that someone else had.[25] Consider, for example, after receiving a promotion from work, you come home to your partner and share the exciting news. Your partner can say with enthusiasm, "That is amazing! Tell me more! I want to hear all about the new position! Heck, I want to hear exactly how the news was delivered. What did your boss say exactly?" Alternatively, your partner can say, "Oh, that's nice. The extra money can pay down the mortgage. What are we doing for dinner?" When your partner expresses joy at your success, they are allowing you to relive the experience, to prolong a positive moment. But even more importantly, their very reactions to your retelling can extend, upregulate, and amplify the emotional experience. The experience becomes more real and more important when it is shared within the context of this relationship.

In the realm of parenting, capitalizing can occur when we invite our children to share with us their small achievements, their joys, and their successes. By sharing in their joy, we amplify it. You can also do this by reliving positive events that you two have engaged in together. In other words, memory sharing is a great context for capitalization. My colleagues and I (Stacey) have found that there is variability in how parents talk to their children.[26] There is individual and cultural variability in what parents focus on when they share stories about their past. Some parents focus on the details of the event. "What happened? Where? How?" Other parents focus on the child's emotional experience: "What did you like best?" They affirm their child's positive emotion by saying things like, "It was fun, wasn't it?"

They even extend that positive moment to the past—"Riding that horse is kinda like riding that truck last summer, right?"—and the future—"When do you think we should do it again?" Parents who highlight the centrality of emotions tend to have kids with better memories[27] as well as better emotion understanding.[26,28]

Imagine, for example, your daughter comes home from school extremely excited about an upcoming field trip her school is taking to a science museum. She is telling you all about the field trip with a look of adventure in her eyes. If you were going to upregulate her positive emotion, you would ask her more questions with high-pitched excitement in your voice that matches or even pushes the envelope on her excitement. You might say things like, "I'm so excited for you that you get to go there!" or "What do you think will be the best part of your field trip?" "Who else do you think is excited about this?" "I wonder what all you will get to see while you're there!" "I bet it will be amazing!"

If, instead, you were interested in downregulating her excitement, you could do so in myriad ways. You could dampen her excitement by not responding to her statements at all or by responding with less enthusiasm or vigor than she was offering. You could also dampen by issuing warnings about her excitement. So, for example, you could say things like, "Well, don't get your hopes up, because it might not be as good as you're expecting" or "I just want to warn you that sometimes the museum exhibits are closed for repair, so you might want to know that before you go." And, if you really wanted to burst her bubble, you could say,

> You know, things are never as good as you think they're going to be. Remember the last field trip? You thought it was going to be so great, but then you went, and it was incredibly disappointing when you actually got there. Well, you might want to rethink getting so excited about this one because then it will just be a big letdown. Just trying to protect you.

Ostensibly meant to be helpful, these downregulating responses put a damper on children's positive emotion and are ultimately a big downer. What do children want from their parents when they come to them with excitement? They want what anyone wants when they share emotion: They want the other person to meet them where they are, to connect with them, to join their emotional experience, and to give a little emotion back. They don't want to be told that they aren't seeing things clearly or that they really shouldn't feel the way that they feel.

Evidence suggests that parents who engage in upregulation of children's positive emotion have children who show better psychological adjustment. Specifically, compared to parents who engage in dampening strategies, parents who upregulate positive emotion have children with fewer depressive symptoms, fewer behavior problems, and better cardiovascular regulation.[29-32] Parents who are less likely to encourage children to engage in elaborative emotional processing of positive events (savoring)—in other words, those parents who are more likely to disengage or to dampen during these conversations—report being avoidant of or anxious regarding emotional intimacy within close relationships.[33] In a recent study my colleagues and I (Stacey) did in the lab, we staged a positive event that allowed a child to win a game against an adult experimenter and to knock down a tower of blocks (what can be more fun for a 4-year-old?).[34] After this positive event, we asked the parent (who was observing the entire time) to discuss the event with the child. What we found was that there was significant variability in parents' responses. Some parents really tried to draw details from their child, and some parents gave up quickly after they found that the child was not responsive. We also used electrodes to measure the children's vagal tone, a physiological marker of better emotion regulation. What we found was that even after controlling for how parents respond to children's negative emotions, parents who upregulated children's positive emotions had higher levels of physiological regulation.

RELATIONAL SAVORING

There is a specific type of strategy for cultivating positive emotions in the context of parent–child relationships that has particular relevance. We have conducted research on something called *relational savoring*, which involves focusing on positive moments of closeness and connectedness with another person. High-quality relational savoring involves deeply attending to moments of felt attachment security or moments in which one was providing to or receiving sensitive care from another person.[35] Scholars argue that people naturally engage in this type of savoring, and indeed, research shows that parents who demonstrate the capacity to do this type of savoring have greater attachment security,[33] fewer depressive symptoms,[29] and higher parental reflective functioning[29] (i.e., the ability to reflect on their mental states as a parent and their child's mental states; see Chapter 6). Relational savoring is thought to have an impact on people via its incorporation of a focus on positive emotion, which, according to theory, broadens attention and builds resources,[5] and its focus on attachment content, which enhances feelings of security.[35] Relational savoring has also been developed and tested as an intervention tool that is taught to parents, adults, and children as a way to help them get the most benefit from their relationships.[35]

The explicit goal of this technique is to help people slow down and become aware of the positive meaning and significance of their attachment relationships. The exercise is designed specifically for people who have had a history of negative experiences in attachment relationships (such as a history of rejection, neglect, or abuse) and who may have trouble accepting or receiving support from others and instead readily notice relationship threats. Our brains are hardwired to be attentive to threat, including threats originating from within relationships, which can make it difficult to savor positive moments occurring in relationships. So, relational savoring is a way of purposefully turning one's mind to the moments of positive connection within a relationship and making the most out of those moments. Relational savoring can be done individually (in one's mind), with a counselor in a therapy session, or between people. The intervention has been found to help parents increase their parenting satisfaction and emotional state,[36] to improve the emotional state of males in a residential treatment facility,[37] to help long-distance relationship partners enhance their emotional state,[32] and to reduce the physiological reactivity of older adults.[38]

One central aim of relational savoring is to help people (in this case, parents) extract the maximum benefits from positive experiences they have in relationships that might otherwise pass by unnoticed or that might receive less attention than they deserve. By shining a mental spotlight on these experiences and magnifying their significance, we can help parents create meaning from moments that might have gone unconsidered. The relational savoring protocol, as developed and tested in our (Stacey and Jessie's) research laboratory and clinical practice, involves a series of steps that move from identifying memories, selecting one memory to focus on, immersing oneself in sensory aspects of the memory, identifying the emotions associated with the memory, identifying cognitions/creating meaning from memory, and looking to the future. In brief, you select a memory of a time when you provided loving care to your child, recalling the details of the experience, focusing on how you felt during the experience, recalling what you were thinking during the experience, and thinking about what this memory means about your relationship with your child in the future.

Allow us to use an example to illustrate from a parent who participated in a study conducted in my (Jessie's) laboratory. This mother chose to savor a memory of a time when her child got upset because of something his sibling had done, and the child came to her to share his feelings with her. She was moved that he trusted her enough to share his feelings, and she reflected on what this trust means to her. When asked to think about what her memory meant for her and for her child in the future, she said,

> So, I guess flashing forward in the future, I would say because of that connection, perhaps he'll be more inclined to want to talk to me about something. Maybe our communication will really open, and he won't be afraid to talk to me about things. . . . It can be something that maybe—that will stay the same up until his adulthood, right. He'll like, you know, come in front of my face and make eye contact with me and say, "Hi, Mom." If he feels like he can talk to me about things, it has to do with trust and being connected, and, you know, being present, like he feels, like, I'll listen in the way that he needs me to or hopes me to. That moment can translate into so many things that I'm not even aware of.[35]

This example illustrates how this parent used the savoring exercise to magnify the significance of the memory she was recalling. She had spent time thinking about this memory, and she then chose to imbue the memory with more meaning. She ended this reflection by saying that the connection she and her child had together in that moment meant that her child will be able to trust her in the future, and it will enable him to feel he can talk to her about things and that she will listen to him. The end goal of the reflection is for parents to use the meaning they have created out of these positive experiences they have had to inform their understanding of their current and future relationship with their child. For step-by-step instructions on how to use the exercise with respect to your own experiences as a parent, check out Exhibit 8.1, which provides foolproof guidance on how to engage in relational savoring.

Relational savoring can also be done with children to maximize the benefits they receive from their caregiving experiences.

EXHIBIT 8.1. **The Practice of Relational Savoring**

Relational Savoring involves deeply reflecting on a moment of close connection between you and your child.

First, select a memory to savor. Pick one in which you felt close or in sync with your child. You can savor a memory of a time when you found joy in helping your child grow, or a time when your child needed you and you were there for them. It may be a time when you felt like you comforted, soothed, protected, or supported your child.

Then, using the memory you have chosen, follow these five steps:

1. Bring the memory to mind at a time when you are feeling calm and are able to reflect deeply on it.
2. Recall as many of the details of the experience as you can.
3. Focus on how you felt at the time, and try to recreate those feelings in your body.
4. Recall what you were thinking about the experience.
5. Reflect on how the bond you have with your child will impact your relationship in the future.

To have memories to savor, you need to pay attention to these moments of close connection as they occur between you and your child throughout the day.

To further illustrate the steps of relational savoring and what relational savoring can look like, see Exhibit 8.2 for a transcript of a relational savoring session conducted by me (Jessie) and my 6-year-old daughter, Talia. That excerpt of Talia sharing her positive memory illustrates the principles of how you can use this type of dialogue with your child to help them extract the maximum benefit and meaning from their experiences in relationships (and in general). It helps children get in the practice of recognizing the positive in situations and making meaning out of their experiences.

> **EXHIBIT 8.2. Talia, Age 6, Savors a Memory of Her Dad**
>
> *Jessie (the mom interviewer):* So, I want you to think of a time when you felt that somebody in your life was, really, really there for you to support you or show you that they loved you or really took care of you in a way that really made you feel safe or loved or special or taken care of. Or a time when someone really showed you that they believed in you or something like that.
>
> *Talia:* It was with Daddy. (*Jessie:* Yeah?)
>
> *Talia:* Yeah, um. I was at hockey (*Jessie:* Uh-huh.) and I was, um, getting on my stuff. Well, I was coming in, and they went to a room (*Jessie:* Yeah.) when I was, um, like, rollerblading around, and I didn't know where they were (*Jessie:* Yeah.), and then I didn't know. And then Daddy, um, saw me and—and I—I felt better.
>
> *Jessie:* Okay, so first you didn't know where Daddy was and you didn't know where your brother and sister were. (*Talia:* Mm-hmm.) So, you didn't know where anybody was. (*Talia:* Yeah.) And then Daddy saw you? (*Talia:* Mm-hmm.) And what did Daddy do when he saw you?
>
> *Talia:* He, um, I came to him (*Jessie:* Uh-huh.), and then we cuddled for a little bit.
>
> *Jessie:* Okay, yeah. And how did you feel when you saw him?
>
> *Talia:* I felt, um, better.
>
> *Jessie:* Mm-hmm. Tell me more about that.
>
> *Talia:* I was scared at first, and then I felt better.
>
> *Jessie:* Mm-hmm, that was a really strong, safe feeling?
>
> *Talia:* Yeah.
>
> *Jessie:* Okay, so I want you to think, um, really, um, a lot about that memory, okay? So, you were at the—it was at, uh, a hockey rink, right? (*Talia:* Uh-huh.) Okay, so you were at the hockey rink. And can you tell me a little about what that day was like? Do you remember what the temperature was like? Or do remember what you were looking at or what you saw? Or, like, who else was there.
>
> *Talia:* Um, my brother and sister were there. (*Jessie:* Mm-hmm.) And— and outside, it was pretty cold because it was, like, 5 o'clock.
>
> *Jessie:* Mm-hmm, it was 5 o'clock. Was it winter? Was it . . .

(continues)

EXHIBIT 8.2. Talia, Age 6, Savors a Memory
of Her Dad (*Continued*)

Talia: It was fall.

Jessie: Fall, okay. And do remember what you were wearing or . . .?

Talia: I remember that I—when I got scared, I was wearing all my hockey gear.

Jessie: Do you remember what you could see or what you could smell or . . .?

Talia: I smelled the air.

Jessie: Okay, and that was the part when you were scared. Did he hug you? (*Talia:* Yeah.) Yeah, he hugged you?

Talia: And my heart—my heart was, like, beating really fast (*makes fast tapping noises*) when I didn't know where he was. (*Jessie:* Mm-hmm.) Then, when I did, it was like this (*makes slow tapping noises*). It was like that (*makes fast tapping noises*), then it slowly (*makes slow tapping noises*). . . .

Jessie: So, at first it was beating superfast, and then it started (*Talia:* Like [*makes fast beating noises with voice*]. . . .) Ooh, really fast. (*Talia: And then [makes slow beating noises with voice*]. . . .) Then it started slowing down. Yeah, slower and slower, okay. And, okay, so—that—those were all the details of that. And if you could try to tell me what you were feeling and try to even make your body feel that way now, but you were already doing that. (*Talia: I did it!*) Yeah! So, your heart was beating superfast. And what else were you feeling?

Talia: Um, I was feeling, like, it was like I found a home to live in.

Jessie: Like you found a home to live in? (*Talia: Uh-huh.*) And that home, was that home your daddy? (*Talia: Yeah.*) Yeah? Yeah, that's lovely. Tell me what else were you feeling.

Talia: I was feeling really happy and better about being scared.

Jessie: Mm-hmm. How did it make you feel better about being scared?

Talia: It made me feel fine. (*Jessie: Feel fine.*) And not like I was, like, lost.

> **EXHIBIT 8.2. Talia, Age 6, Savors a Memory of Her Dad (*Continued*)**
>
> *Jessie:* Okay, and not like you were lost anymore because you found your home. (*Talia: Mm-hmm.*) Mm-hmm. Um, okay, and what kinds of, like, thoughts were you thinking. Were you thinking, my daddy will always be there for me? Or my daddy really loves me? Or I can really trust my daddy? (*Talia: Trust, the trust.*) The trust one, yeah. What does that mean for you—for you—for your future?
>
> *Talia:* It means that he always has my back.
>
> *Jessie:* That he always has your back? (*Talia: Uh-huh.*) Yeah, what does that mean?
>
> *Talia:* It means that he won't let me get lost. He'll always look for me.
>
> *Jessie:* Yeah, that's really nice that you have a daddy that will always look for you.
>
> *Talia:* He'll look—he'll look after me.
>
> *Jessie:* Okay, this is really nice one. Thank you for sharing it with me. (*Talia: Mm-hmm.*)

A WORD ON THE DON'TS OF POSITIVE EMOTION

We want to pause for a minute to say a bit on the don'ts of positivity. One message that can sometimes be mistakenly heard from people when psychologists speak about the importance of positivity is that people should experience and express positive emotion even when they are not actually feeling positive emotion. So, we want to be clear that we are not saying any such thing. Our message, first and foremost, is never to express anything you don't feel. Similarly, you should never deny a feeling you do feel. You should be genuine with yourself and with your child. Children are quite good at telling when people aren't genuine, so they will know if you are faking it. Plus, it's simply not good practice to act happy when you are not feeling it.

Suppressing emotions can lead to deleterious outcomes and affect the quality of parent–child interactions. In one study, researchers found that when parents suppressed their negative emotions in front of their children after having to do a stressful task, they were less warm and engaged with their children.[39] While it might feel intuitive to suppress our feelings of stress and negative affect so that we don't spread these feelings to our children, it can be detrimental in two ways. First, when we suppress our emotions and experience, it makes us less authentic and less able to genuinely interact with our children, and children may pick up on this and react accordingly. Second, when we suppress our emotions, we deprive our children of the opportunity to understand the complex emotional lives we have as parents and lose the opportunity to model for them how to respond to these negative emotions.

Not suppressing your negative emotions is different from saying that you shouldn't try to see the positive side of things, which can be a useful practice. Trying to see the positive side of things involves an intentional act in which you are being honest about your goal of effortfully working to envision a good outcome or silver lining. That is wholly different from denying the bad or negative part of something. One of the core skills of controlling and regulating emotions is to *reappraise*,[40] that is, interpret the situation in a light that allows for growth when it is possible to do so. Positive reappraisal is different from negative reappraisal. In negative reappraisal, we reframe an event so that it is less negative, but with positive reappraisal, we try to reframe an event so that it has a positive bent. Consider the following scenario: My (Stacey's) daughter, Eliana, comes home from school upset that the school will be closed on her birthday, and she will be unable to celebrate with her class. If I were to help her positively reappraise the situation, I might say, "I am sorry you won't be able to celebrate with your friends on your birthday, but that means we can have an extra day to bake some special goodies for your class!" Negative reappraisal might mean saying something like, "Well, at least you will still get to celebrate with your family."

We ask that you extend the same kindness and respect to your child. By this, we mean that if your child is struggling and shares with you that they are feeling some kind of negative emotion, we do not recommend responding by asking them to look on the bright side or to just be happy about the situation. This type of response is typically experienced as invalidating by the receiver. Instead, it is far preferable to express empathy and concern for the child, who ultimately is in a state of pain; this may be all the child is able to receive at this moment. Once the child's pain has been soothed by the parent, it is possible the child may then be able to consider silver linings or take another point of view on the situation, but only at this later point.

CONCLUSION

It is easy to get caught up in cycles of negativity; distress is eye-catching and lends itself to rumination. However, there is ample research out there suggesting the benefits of positive emotion. It goes without saying that it is natural for parents to want to create positive experiences and moments for their children. In this chapter, we highlighted strategies for doing so and for maximizing these positive experiences. In particular, people who savor the good parts of their experiences and who are grateful for those positive aspects of their lives tend to lead lives that are more fulfilling and meaningful. They are also more resilient. Our children feed on the emotions of those around them, so if you give off a vibe of positive emotionality, they will observe that within you, soak that energy up, and give it right back to you. We hope that the tools we presented in this chapter will give you some ideas for how to approach these topics with your children and with yourself. You deserve to savor the positive moments you have with your child and as a parent.

TL, DR

- Helping children downregulate their emotions is important, but the absence of negative emotion does not mean the presence of positive emotion.
- A host of research studies suggest that positive emotions help us be creative, promote well-being, and recover from stress.
- We can use strategies to upregulate our children's positive emotions, teach them gratitude, give them opportunities to help others, and help them to capitalize and savor positive experiences.

CHAPTER 9

NURTURING YOUR CHILD'S NATURE

William James, the brilliant philosopher known as the "father of modern psychology," wrote in his famous 1890 book *The Principles of Psychology* that infants were born as a "blooming, buzzing, confusion" to describe the idea that infants enter this loud, chaotic world with little tools to make sense of it all.[1] Indeed, when we look at a hopeless newborn, born naked and almost blind, it does seem that they know very little and understand virtually nothing. Moreover, newborns look similar to one another with their mostly bald heads, squinty eyes, and pursed lips. At the same time, ask any midwife or ob–gyn, and they can tell you that at birth there is already tremendous variation among infants.

Some babies come into this world screaming, their faces red and their hands clenched in fists. Others come quietly into this world with a beatific smile. Some babies seem born ready to connect (like my [Jessie's] first baby), making eye contact with me for an amazing 2 hours following birth. Like my (Stacey's) second baby, some just looked resentful and angry for having been taken out of the womb. Parents of twins can tell you that within weeks, if not days, each twin has their quirks and personality tendencies.

Tabula rasa is the Latin phrase that is translated as "blank slate" in English. The term was used to describe the way that infants were thought to enter the world. The phrase echoes an old debate in psychology: Are children born as a *tabula rasa*, molded by experiences around them, or do they come with their own predispositions and prescribed competencies? Unlike many things in psychology in which the current state of the research requires us to answer often with the phrase "it depends" or "we don't know yet," it is definitive that for the question of whether children are born as blank slates, we can answer with a resounding *no*.

Parents with multiple children often express surprise at how *different* their children are from one another. As trite as it may sound, every child is indeed different, with their own likes and dislikes, levels of fussiness, and preferences for varying levels of activity and social interaction. These differences can be evident pretty early on in life. As Caitlyn, a mother of twins remarked,

> As early as 6 months, if not before, I can tell the twins are already very different. Vanessa is easygoing and still is. She prefers Mommy, can listen to directions, and rarely cries. Becca, on the other hand, has always been prone to temper tantrums. She has difficulty sharing and with transitions. I get nervous every time I have to interrupt her when she is focused on a task because I'll never know how she'll respond.

"Temperament" is often confused with the term "personality," and you will often hear them used interchangeably. However, there is a difference between the two. *Temperament* is considered the origin or precursor of personality. It emerges early in life and refers to individual differences in emotional and behavioral reactivity, soothability, and regulation that is somewhat consistent across situations as the result of genetics or prenatal experiences.[2] Temperament describes how emotional the child is, how active they are, how easy they can be calmed, and how much they need routine. Consider, for example, a baby who can sleep anywhere, is generally happy, and is eager to approach new things. Contrast this baby with a baby who cries frequently, dislikes novelty or transitions, and is difficult to soothe. Temperament is relatively stable across time; it plus the experiences that the child will go through during life together form the basis of adult personality.

Parents of more than one child know that the effects of their parenting interventions on their child's behavior likely depend on their child's temperament. This can be infuriating for parents because the tried-and-true methods that parents have perfected with one child may crash and burn with another. As Jennifer, a mother of two, told us,

> We thought we were terrible parents because none of the parenting advice—for example, just give him two choices!—worked with our strong-willed oldest son. He was irritable and demanding. Sleep training was an absolute disaster. He cried for 4 weeks straight for hours. We gave up on that. We gave him different foods to try; he resolutely refused and ate only chicken nuggets and drank Kool-Aid for years. It took us many years before deciding to have a second child because we didn't think we could handle another child. But then our second was a piece of cake! We suddenly realized maybe we weren't so bad at parenting after all!

Similarly, I (Jessie) used to think that the infants who slept through the night early in life were either miracle babies or myths. When I heard such tales of these babies from friends, I became so jealous, I could barely see through my sleep-deprived eyes. I just couldn't fathom such a creature existing when I was caring for my 4-month-old, who was still waking up three, four, sometimes five times a night. But then, it happened—I had my own mythical child. My third child miraculously slept through the night on her own at 5 weeks old. It wasn't anything special I was doing because I was no better by that time at the perfect swaddling method; her body just knew how to sleep. My body, on the other hand, was woefully unprepared for this type of transition, so for weeks after this, I still kept waking up throughout the night, thinking there must be something wrong with her. But, no, she just came to us like this. Temperament!

Like most complexity in life, children's temperaments are not determined by a single factor. While genetics are likely essential and explain 20% to 60% of the variability, there is no clear evidence yet that a specific pattern of inheritance or specific genes confer specific character traits. In addition to genetics, some evidence suggests that prenatal experiences can affect children's temperament. As we discuss in Chapter 4, maternal emotions may affect children's levels of emotional reactivity.

At birth, children are already 9 months old and have all sorts of intuition and innate understanding and expectations of the world around them. Their biological history, a combination of their mother's and father's genetic makeup, experiences of prior generations, and their own prenatal experiences shape who they are at birth. Although the environment in which they are born can certainly exert a significant effect, it is not acting on a blank slate. Instead, children's nature influences and shapes how they experience the world around them. In other words, as we illustrate throughout this book, genes and the environment constantly interact to influence and shape the development of our children. In the next section, we describe how genes and the environment are intricately related and how they relate to children's temperament.

GENE–ENVIRONMENT CORRELATIONS

When psychologists say that something is *correlated*, we mean that they are related in such a way that when one changes, the other tends to change, too. Take, for example, height and weight. These two characteristics tend to be positively correlated. By *positive*, we mean when one goes up the other also goes up. The correlation is pretty strong, indicating that, in general, as height goes up, so does weight. Like most things in life, however, it is not a perfect correlation. There are tall, skinny people who don't weigh very much. Two things can also be negatively correlated: When one goes up, the other goes down. For example, the more massages I (Stacey) get, the lower my levels of negative mood!

Genes and the environment are also correlated. But the correlations between genes and environment are complicated. Scientists describe them as passive, evocative, and active. We can use these gene–environment correlations as a framework to understand how children's genes shape the way they experience the world around them.

Passive Gene–Environment Correlations

Passive gene–environment correlations refer to the idea that the child's genes inherited from each parent are also related to the environment in which they grow up. Keep in mind our constant refrain that the environment is often created by the parent in early childhood. You may have heard of the amazing rock-climbing baby who was scaling walls before she could talk. Ellie Farmer's video on YouTube has received thousands of views.[3] She climbed her first wall at 8 months. Now, is Ellie genetically inclined to climb, or was there something about her early environment? As you should know by now, having read our book in detail, it's challenging to know. Because, you see, her parents are competitive climbers; they have passed on whatever genes may be associated with climbing. But because they are climbers, they also were very much concerned with her motor development. Her father built an 8-foot climbing wall that was next to her crib. She visited the climbing gym with her parents nearly every day, hanging, gripping, and scrambling up walls. So, the environment in which she was born has also contributed to her ability to climb. But before you allow this climbing-baby prodigy to make you feel inferior about your own baby, rest assured: Babies come in all shapes and sizes with all kinds of capabilities, and these may say nothing about their motor skills later in life. (My [Stacey's] first baby at 8 months was standing and taking steps, but my second could barely sit at this same point in development. My [Jessie's] youngest, now her most physically agile, didn't walk until 13 months).

This passive correlation between genes and the environment is evident in myriad ways. Parents who love to read may pass on those reader-loving genes, but they are also likely to pass on an environment full of books. Parents who have an antisocial personality are also more likely to exhibit a harsh parenting style, which can also lead to higher levels of antisocial behaviors in their children. Even when parents do not pass on their genes, because of their own genetic predispositions, they create an environment that nurtures a specific trait—a phenomenon called *genetic nurturing*. In other words, a parent's nature affects the way they nurture. To illustrate, a parent may have the gene that predisposes them to anxiety. They may not pass on the anxiety gene to their children, but in their behavior—the way that they express fear to their child, their overcautious nature—they may create an environment that makes the child anxious.

Evocative Gene–Environment Correlation

The second type of gene–environment correlation is called *evocative correlation*. In this case, the relationship between genes and the environment occurs because certain heritable characteristics elicit or evoke a certain type of environment. In other words, certain inherited traits can evoke qualities or characteristics from the environment. Beautiful people may be more outgoing and social in part because people are more likely to talk to and be nice to them as babies. Children who are hyperactive and noncompliant are more likely to elicit more controlling behaviors from their caregivers. Individuals who are depressed may also lead their partners to interact with them in certain ways, leading to more marital distress.

Our own inherited characteristics shape and influence the behaviors of others around us, which, in turn, can lead to better or worse outcomes. To illustrate, my (Stacey's) second daughter, Samara ("Sama"), is a happy baby. Sama smiles and waves at strangers; stops to pet everybody's dog; and tries to engage in conversation with every leaf, rock, and tree. Because of this, she gets a lot of social interaction from the college students and elderly adults who live in our college/retirement town. Through the years, these varied interactions will likely increase her comfort with strangers and foster joy in chatting and connecting with people, and she likely will grow up to be an extroverted adult.

Active Gene–Environment Correlations

The third type of gene-environment correlation is *active*. Here, the association between genetically influenced traits on the environment operates through a process whereby the individual picks the environment that is consistent with those traits. For example, extroverts are more likely to seek out different social settings than introverts. They are more likely to become involved in theater or obtain a job in which there is a lot of interaction with other people. Those environments, then, also reinforce their extraversion. In contrast, introverts may choose activities, such as chess club, cross-country running, and tennis, in which there is less interaction with other people. They may end up in a career that involves relatively less interaction with people. These environments would strengthen the introvert's inherited characteristic so that it becomes even stronger.

The idea of niche-picking is intriguing and consistent with the notion that, to change (if this is indeed our goal), we have to put ourselves in uncomfortable situations. For an introvert to learn to be more outgoing, it would help to put themselves out there—to join a dance group or other activities that offer social interaction. Importantly, this is also consistent with the ideas behind cognitive behavior therapy approaches to the treatment of anxiety and depression, which hold that to make progress, clients must "lean into" their discomfort and gradually work to challenge the situations or circumstances they avoid.

STRENGTH OF GENE–ENVIRONMENT CORRELATIONS

The relative power or strength of these gene–environment correlations is likely to depend on age. Passive correlation, for example, is stronger in early childhood when parents exert a significant impact on children's daily lives as well as on their physical and social-emotional environments. Active correlations are likely to matter more when children are older and more capable of choosing their environments. In the context of parenting, it is helpful to think about which of our child's characteristics and traits are more innate and consider the characteristics that we might want to foster. Knowing about these gene–environment correlations gives us the power to be able to disrupt them should we wish to do so.

Let us give you an example of a case in which we might wish to break the gene–environment correlation. Anxious parents, for example, may pass on genes that lead to higher anxiety. They also may create an environment and parent in such a way that fosters anxiety. For children who are naturally anxious and temperamentally fearful, the path of least resistance might be to always try to protect them from things in the environment that will frighten them, but if we want them to learn to be brave, we have to create opportunities for them to face their fears. This approach is consistent with how psychologists treat clinical anxiety in children and adults: We help clients face their fears in a progressive way by slowly exposing them to the situations or experiences that are frightening for them and helping them gain the confidence that they can tolerate the situations themselves or the distress they experience when they encounter these situations. But you, as a parent, have the tools to essentially inoculate your temperamentally fearful child against anxiety early in life by helping them work against the vulnerability that is baked into their temperament, so to speak. Temperamentally fearful children are much more prone to develop anxiety-related problems later in life.[4-6] Still, parents can help them by encouraging them bit by bit to explore their environments and gain confidence in facing risks in safe ways.

Here's the example. I (Jessie) am a temperamentally fearful person, which may be one reason why I am also good at treating anxiety disorders in children and adults. Although I do not have an anxiety disorder, I can easily understand the way that anxiety works. My instincts as a person and a parent are frequently to avoid risk or harm. Fortunately, my partner is not temperamentally fearful. Quite the opposite is true: He is a thrill-seeker who has repeatedly sought out occupations designed to activate his typically underaroused autonomic nervous system (or so his psychologist wife says). First, he was a combat rescue helicopter pilot, then a police officer in Watts, and now a police officer helicopter pilot. He likes to jump out of planes or helicopters, deploy to war zones, and generally do hero's work.

I (Jessie) remember this one interaction in which differences in our temperament affected how we wanted to parent. Our eldest was about 24 months (in other words, fairly new to walking). We were visiting a friend's house. She had climbed up a carpeted, four-stair ledge in their home and was poised to jump off of it. I drew in my breath sharply, leaned forward, and yelled her name, about to tell her to stop, when my husband put his arm out and told me to let her do it. "What's the worst that can happen there? It's carpeted. It's four stairs," he said. I responded, "Well, she could get hurt," expecting that to end the conversation. However, he replied, "She's not going to break anything. She will be totally fine. Plus, she'll probably learn that she shouldn't jump from that high again. That seems like an important thing to learn to me. Let her do it." I paused, totally stunned because, in that instant, I knew he was right! What he said was everything I had learned about in my clinical training and my training as a parenting researcher, but it also was completely against the grain of what my biology and my fierce mama bear instinct was telling me.

This is what safe exploration is about: being safe to fail and figuring out that failing (and in this case, falling) is okay. This child, in particular, needed that kind of parenting because this was my (Jessie's) careful, cautious kid—the kid who always knew her limits and didn't need any limits set on her by others. Needless to say, we let her jump, and she did fall. She didn't get hurt. She cried for a few minutes and then decided to get back up and jump from the second step rather than the fourth step of the ledge. Over the next few years, I watched my husband as he parented from a place of confidence regarding his children's ability to overcome stress and obstacles, and I attempted to embody that approach, too. Today, this child can fearlessly climb tall trees and rock-climbing walls, and I credit my husband for that fearlessness.

Many parents have the instinct to protect and shelter the children—who seem more vulnerable to stress—from experiences in the outside world that cause stress. It makes perfect sense: If you are a kind, caring person and you have a child who is particularly prone to fear, anxiety, or sadness, wouldn't you want to protect that child from experiencing undue distress? On the immediate, short-term, the answer is always going to be a resounding *yes*. The problem is that on the scale of years, children need to develop hardiness, or resilience, to the ups and downs of life, and nobody needs this more than these temperamentally fearful children. So, whereas our nurturing parenting instinct might tell us to protect these children from stress more than their tougher-seeming siblings, we actually should be working harder than usual to expose these temperamentally fearful children to manageable amounts of stress. By doing so, we can build up their ability to withstand this type of insult in the future. Just as we inoculate children against viruses, we have to inoculate them against stress, and the only way to do that is to let them experience these difficult life situations and allow them to witness themselves living through these situations and building up their metaphorical muscles (and coping skills) to do it again.

But remember that it is all about the match between the child (and their temperament) and the environment. Not all children need or would benefit from a parenting approach that pushes them to face challenges. My (Stacey's) first child is fearful and needs encouragement to explore. We used to joke that she would never get kidnapped because she was always attached to me like an extra appendage. However, once we went camping, and I let our second child wander, trying to get a sense of how far she would go, the kid kept walking. It was dark, and eventually my fear outweighed her fear, and I had to go running after her. To this day, Sama will walk outside if the door is open and she is not being supervised. Unlike with Eliana, my focus is more on placing boundaries than encouraging her to push them.

MEASUREMENT OF TEMPERAMENT

In this section, we lay out several different ways in which child development researchers have measured and defined children's temperament. We also urge you to think about your children's personality along these dimensions. Understanding your child's temperament is important because there is no universal way of parenting. The best parenting style is one that is sensitive and responsive to your child's needs and personality. This argument is similar to the idea of equality versus equity. Young children tend to think that being good and fair means that everyone should be treated the same. But, as adults, we know that there is much variability in what each individual may need to thrive. Some of us need 8 to 9 hours of sleep; others can function on 6 to 7. Some children need more encouragement to try something new; others jump right in. Understanding your children's temperament will give insight into how to parent them in a way that allows your children to get what they need.

The ancient philosopher Hippocrates was the one who began the crusade of looking into how to classify temperament. Around 400 BC, he developed a theory on the different characteristics of people based on fluids in the body, which was further detailed by the physician Galen in the 2nd century. For example, if you had an excess of phlegm, you were thought to be of a calm disposition. If you had an excess of blood, you were thought to be cheerful.[7,8] We don't necessarily judge kids' temperaments today on things like bodily fluids, but the theory sparked an interest in this field of research that continues today.

On a typical weekday, our student researchers visit with two to three families in our laboratory. Because temperament influences how children respond to a wide range of tasks, it is one thing we measure often. Using questionnaires,[9] we ask parents to rate their children on items, such as how restless they are, the extent to which they respond to an adult's request, how often they are worried and sad, and the extent to which they offer to help others. In addition to this questionnaire data, we look at their behavior, including their energy levels ("Are they constantly fidgeting, running around?"), frequency and intensity of different emotions ("Are they often irritable? How easily do they control their emotions?"), reactions to events ("Do they avoid new situations or embrace them?"), and how good their self-control is. We often observe children as they go through several everyday tasks—some pleasant, like playing with bubbles, and some not so pleasant, like being surprised by a realistic-looking toy spider. The goal of these tasks is to try to elicit emotional and behavioral responses in the children for us to assess how reactive they are. Does the child cry aloud, scream, and start kicking and throwing things? Do they laugh after realizing the spider is fake or persist in fretting and being upset? These measures help us assess the beginnings of personality: children's temperament.

In general, children's temperament can be characterized along three dimensions: (a) activity level, (b) mood, and (c) distractibility/persistence. *Activity level* refers to how active your child is. Can they sit still? Do they like to run around? There are some gender differences: Boys, for example, tend to have higher levels of activity level. *Mood* characterizes the intensity of children's emotional experiences, both positive and negative, as well as how reactive they are. Does a sudden loud noise phase your child? Do they get nervous when encountering a new adult? *Distractibility/persistence* refers to the extent to which your child can exert some modicum of self-control. Can they focus on a task? Do they keep trying despite failing? These aspects of temperaments are associated with later outcomes. Highly emotional kids tend to be shy, and less reactive kids tend to be more outgoing and fearless.[10] Kids who are persistent and less distractive have better self-control, more empathy, and less aggression later in life.[11,12]

Should you be afraid if your child starts to cry in the park or gets angry when their big brother grabs their toy? No. Crying or yelling, or even tantrums, are normal (and healthy!). You only start to see these trends as temperament, and later as personality, if your child does them consistently—if their aggression is worse than other kids their age, shows up in many different contexts (e.g., at home, at day care, on the playground), and persists across time. What if they are on the extreme end consistently, though? You might be thinking, "Should I, as a parent, worry about things like mental illness later on?" Not necessarily. Researchers have guesses that some temperament traits share the same brain and hormone pathways as mental disorders. However, these systems are complex, and there are many other conditions that have to be met for a disorder to develop.

Environmental factors, including parenting nurturance and life expe-riences, all continue to matter.

The key point is having a sense of your child's temperament because it is crucial to tailoring your parenting style. The following is a list of variables developed by temperament researchers to con-sider when thinking about your child's temperament:[13,14]

- activity level (how much they walk, sleep, and so on)
- predictability (how consistent their sleep or eating schedule is)
- approachability (how much they approach or avoid something new)
- adaptability (how easily they are able to change their response in a new situation)
- responsiveness (how easily they respond to something new)
- intensity (the energy behind their response to something)
- mood (how often they have positive or negative emotions)
- distractibility (how easily they change their behavior because of something new)
- persistence (how long they are able to pay attention to an activity)

When considering where your child falls along this continuum, it is important to keep in mind how they respond across different situa-tions and times. It can be challenging for parents because parents are unable to compare their behavior with that of other children. Thus, we recommend getting input from your child's teacher or pediatrician.

PARENTING AND CHILDREN'S TEMPERAMENT

Temperament is not destiny. Children's temperament matures and may change over the course of development. During this process of change, environmental factors, such as parenting, matter. Parenting, however, varies significantly across cultures and across time. While the universal goal of parenting is to ensure that our offspring not only survive but thrive, how parents get children to that place varies. In Chapter 5, we discuss the idea of metaparenting and how individual factors like socioeconomic status and parental histories all shape how we parent. In this section, we argue that, in addition to these factors, a serious consideration of best parenting practices needs to factor in who is being parented. Our parenting behaviors affect our children, but our children's behaviors also affect our parenting; it is transactional.

This model of transactional relations is consistent with the empirical research that has demonstrated a surprising number of child characteristics that influence parenting. Gender is one, but birth order and especially the child's temperament matter.[15] For example, parents seem to be harsher with boys[16] and more controlling with girls.[17] The effects of gender on parenting, however, does seem to depend on age. Parents don't treat infants differently, but as the child grows up, gender differences increase.[18] Parents are more anxious with their firstborn—for instance, parents are more likely to take their firstborn to an emergency room in the case of illness as compared with later children.[19] There is even some evidence to suggest that children may be treated differently based on their levels of attractiveness with more attractive infants and toddlers receiving more attention![20] But perhaps most important is children's own temperament. Children's temperament shapes their behavior, moods, and habits. This individual variability, in turn, can affect how parents react to their children. Next, we lay out three important ideas for parents to consider regarding the role of children's temperament.

Idea 1: Understand That Your Children's Temperament Can Affect the Way You Parent

Sometimes we like to think that parenting is a one-way street, but the research is pretty definitive: Child behavior and temperament influence how we parent, and parenting behaviors also affect children. Children who are more easily irritated, for example, are likely to have parents who are inconsistent with regard to discipline; this inconsistency, in turn, leads to more child irritation.[21] On the other hand, the same study shows that children who are more fearful or happier have mothers who are accepting. Also, children who are easily frustrated, impulsive, and are less able to exert self-control are more susceptible to the negative influences of parenting.[22] For me (Stacey), it is much easier for me to be patient with my second daughter, who rarely cries, and when she does, it is usually for a reason that most people can understand. I am much more impatient with my eldest child. I *know* I should be more patient with Eliana, but she is very thin-skinned. She takes everything personally, and I find I have to be more thoughtful, to slow down, and to be more considerate of her emotions.

Some of the most convincing evidence for the evocative role of child temperament in the context of parenting is experimental and quasi-experimental studies in which the researchers are able to change child characteristics. What?! How is this possible, you may ask! In one study, the researchers capitalized on children with attention-deficit/hyperactivity disorder. They found that when these children were medicated (likely improving their ability to self-regulate), mothers also responded differently and became less negative toward their children when working on a specific task together.[23] Most of the studies have looked at only mothers, but, of course, child temperament also affects fathers (although the type of trait also matters). For example, high child activity is associated with less maternal positive parenting behavior but not paternal behavior.[24] Children who are more difficult (often conceptualized as high on negative emotions and high on activity level), however, do tend to elicit less affection from fathers.[25]

Idea 2: Consider Your Own Temperament

It is essential to note that we, as parents, have our own temperaments. Reflecting on our personality and, in particular, being aware of how it may clash with our children's temperament can help us to create healthier parent–child interactions. For the extroverted parent, it may be more difficult for us to understand why our child may be so painfully shy. Understanding this difference means that it may take more empathy and perspective-taking on our part to relate to our children and to create a nurturing context. And we may have to teach this perspective-taking to their siblings, too, especially if there's a mismatch. For example, a scheduled and orderly family may have a hard time understanding an energetic, impulsive member, and vice versa.

The concept of *goodness of fit* refers to a match or mismatch between an individual's temperament and personality and the environment around them. Consider, for example, differing levels of preference for activity between couples. If one partner loves to travel, be out and about, and always on the go, it would be challenging for them to have a partner who prefers slow, leisurely days at home. Similarly, your child's temperament may or may not match your own. This difference will affect how the child adjusts, how you parent, and the stress and friction within a family. Understanding how your temperament and your children's temperament may match or may not match may help shed insight into children's behavior. For example, if you are an early riser, and, at 6 a.m. your child is crying, whining, and acting out because they are expected to get out of bed but they are a late riser, the issue may not be so much that your child is acting out but, rather, that there is a mismatch between your circadian rhythm and your child's. Rather than pathologizing your child's behavior or your behavior, conceiving of this as an issue of mismatch might be more helpful.

237

This is one of those areas in which having other parent friends is really helpful. It can be extremely useful to be able to talk about your child's behavior with other parents so that you can have a sense of whether your child is exhibiting behavior that is outside the norm of what can be expected for their age. I (Jessie) remember worrying a ton about how much help my daughter was requiring from me to complete her homework in the fourth grade. I kept thinking that my daughter wasn't developing age-appropriate independence and study skills (and that this was my fault, of course). However, I then talked to two of my mom friends and realized that their kids were similar to my daughter. I suddenly felt grateful for all of the ways in which Sam was able to manage things on her own (and reassured as to the normative nature of Sam's help-seeking behavior).

Idea 3: Tailor Your Parenting Styles to Your Children's Personality

When trying to catch a fish, there are many factors to consider. We need to know where this type of fish lives. Does it live in the oceans? Or rivers? When does it eat? What does this type of fish like to eat? The type of bait matters. Do these fish prefer live bait to artificial bait? What is the best hook size for this type of fish? The better we know the fish, their likes and dislikes, their habits and behaviors, the better equipped we are to catch that fish. Children are similar. Understanding that children are born with innate differences in how they respond and approach the world is important for parents to be able to guide their children and shift their parenting strategies and behaviors so that there is a good fit.

Parents often tell us that one set of parenting practices may work fantastically with one child but then fail spectacularly with a second child. One couple had this experience. Shayla was Peter and Sarah's firstborn child. Both Peter and Sarah worked full-time, and Sarah expected to return to work within 6 weeks of Shayla's birth. Thus, like most people, they were very concerned with sleep disruptions. At birth, they quickly implemented a schedule for Shayla. They provided lots of light and stimulation during the day. At dusk, they dimmed all lights and spoke in hushed tones. Shayla was sleeping through the night at 3 weeks. And when Shayla was 3 years old, they gave birth to a bubbly, blond baby boy named Doug. They tried the same sleep training strategy that they had used with Shayla, but 8 months later, Doug was still insistent on sleeping with his mom in her bed, and he was still waking up multiple times to nurse. As Sarah told us,

> Before Doug, when people tell me they can't get their kid to sleep, I used to think, "You are clearly doing something wrong." After Doug, I realized we were just lucky with Shayla. She was just a good sleeper. We didn't have anything to do with it.

Ken, a father of three, also put it succinctly:

> We had read all our books and taken a ton of classes. We thought we were prepared, and it seemed that way. Our first son never threw a tantrum. He ate anything from octopus to blue cheese. We thought we were amazing parents. Then, we had number two. We learned we were not amazing parents.

Instead of thinking of parenting as a static style, think about it as a toolbox. The more tools you have in your box, the more strategies you can try. This is particularly important because children change. What works for a 3-year-old is not necessarily going to work for a 17-year-old. Thus, parents also have to change and develop.

The best parenting is dynamic. Overall, we encourage parents to be aware, empathetic, reflective, and flexible. Throughout this book, we discuss extensively the importance of awareness regarding where your child is in both their physical needs (e.g., "Are they tired?" "Did they eat?") and their more stable, temperamental psychological characteristics (e.g., "Is my child easygoing and flexible, or will they need time to adjust?") as well as their moment-to-moment mental states (e.g., "Is my child feeling rejected, or is my child scared of something?"). Awareness is the first stage of being able to parent mindfully. If, for example, you are introducing some new activity, knowing whether your child is more likely to be fearful will shape how much preparation, time, and soothing you must be willing to do. This preparation will, in turn, affect the success of that endeavor.

The second stage of parenting mindfully is empathy. Empathy can be hard because it requires you to understand the world from another's perspective. But having empathy that your youngest, for example, may find something extremely scary (say going on a roller coaster) that you and your oldest child experience as a fun activity may help you to be more patient (and as every parent knows, patience is worth its weight in gold). Understanding that in some ways, especially early in life, some children are just built more fearful than others may allow you to more empathetic to your anxious child. In other words, they are not choosing to be scared.

Third, be reflective and flexible. Nothing changes immediately. Reflecting on your successes and challenges as parents creates room for growth and flexibility. One child may prefer elaborate explanations for why their behavior led to a time-out. For another child, these elaborations may simply be reinforcing because they are receiving your attention. Thus, it is important to be flexible between children. This switching in parenting style may lead to some resentment if children are old enough to see that they are being treated differently. Children (and many adults) think that being fair is every-one getting the same thing. But if everyone gets the same thing, many will not get what they need.

I (Stacey) remember one time when I was on a short plane ride with my two daughters, a 6-year-old and an 8-month-old. Both were tired and hungry. "When are they going to bring us a snack?" the 6-year-old wailed. "Soon, once the plane takes off," I said, as the baby started to bawl. I started nursing the baby only to hear my older child complain, "That's not fair! How come Sama gets a snack first? Why doesn't she have to wait?" In my frustration, I yelled, "Do you want the other breast?" Needless to say, the other passengers raised their eyebrows. A more appropriate response would have been to explain why the baby's needs can and should be met first.

Remember that your family and your situation may be very different. The research studies mentioned earlier in this chapter were trying to characterize hundreds of families rather than any one family alone. Our goal is not to state precisely *how* children's tempera-ments affect your parenting but, rather, that they do. In understand-ing this, we hope parents will then be aware of and consider how children's temperaments change the way they parent. The effect of children on their parents' parenting is neither inherently negative nor positive. Children whose behavior is more difficult may need more control. Knowing this, parents might be aware not to exert too much control lest they compromise the autonomy of their children. Importantly, the extent to which the evocative effects of child tem-perament exert their impact, however, is not universal. The specific contexts also matter. It is likely the case that when parents have a lot of support, are not stressed, and are simply engaging in free play with their children, they are more able to be calm, positive, and nur-turing no matter how difficult the child is being. Families that are fortunate to have multiple adults may assign specific tasks to certain adults. In my (Stacey's) family, for example, my husband does the bedtime routine because he is much better able to resist the whining and complaints and to be consistent.

To be an effective parent, we need to know our children. Each of your children may respond differently to types of parenting interventions. Some children respond best to clear, simple directives (e.g., commands directly given to them), whereas others respond better when all distractions are removed from their attention and they have eye contact with their parent. Others are more responsive when they have physical contact with their parent. Other children respond better when they are given two different options and get to pick which of those options they like better. From years of parenting your child, you may be able to identify what types of strategies work best with your child and under what circumstances.

STRESS, PARENTING, AND THE "DIFFICULT" CHILD

For those with easygoing, happy children, you may feel free to skip this last section. For those with what some researchers have described as *difficult temperament*—those children with high levels of negative affect, poor emotional or behavioral regulation, and few positive emotions—stick with us for a little longer. As we discussed earlier, children's temperament can be influential in outcomes later in life.

In particular, a certain class of children, the ones with "difficult temperaments" are the ones about whom parents are most often worried. Given a warm, nurturing environment, most children, regardless of their temperament, will grow up to be successful, productive, and happy adults. But it is impossible to lead a stress-free life. So how does temperament interact with stress? Here we discuss two main models that describe these relationships. The diathesis-stress model of temperament generally conceives of children who fall on the more negative or difficult side of temperament as more vulnerable to adversity. When comparing the two types of children, this model holds that, in stressful contexts, children who are emotionally reactive will do worse.

New research in developmental psychology, however, suggests that the diathesis-stress model is not completely accurate. The differential susceptibility model of temperament[26] argues that, yes, children who are easygoing and mellow thrive in many different contexts; however, their counterparts, the so-called "difficult" ones, also have some unique advantages. These researchers argue that, in essence, emotionality is not a marker for vulnerability but is a marker of how susceptible you are to environmental influences. To put it in other words, *differential susceptibility* refers to the idea that the environment is likely to affect some people more than others. As an example, some of us can sleep anywhere, and others, like my (Stacey's) husband, require noise-canceling headphones, a mask, a noise machine, and blackout curtains.

These theorists have often talked about two types of children: dandelions and orchids. Dandelions are the easygoing children. They grow in lots of different environments. Emotionally, they are happy, they sleep regularly, and they have great attention and behavioral control. They are easy to soothe and easy to parent. These children are often contrasted with orchid children, who cry a lot, get upset at change, and have an irregular sleep schedule. These are the emotionally temperamental, moody, active kids. Rather than conceiving the orchid children as more vulnerable, these researchers[26] argue that these children are more susceptible to environmental influences for better or worse. That is, they are more emotionally reactive because they are more sensitive. And being more sensitive means that they are more likely to be influenced by the environment. In other words, parents' behaviors and words matter more to these children.

My (Stacey's) daughter, Eliana, was challenging even before she was born. She would punch my stomach from the inside to express her dissatisfaction when the noise levels got too loud or if

I ate something spicy or stood up too fast. I could feel what I thought were the telltale signs of crying: hiccups and an almost imperceptible shaking every time we went to see a loud movie or concert. After she was born, Eliana continued her tirade. She screamed when the breast milk flowed too fast or slow, when we changed her diaper, or when her car seat strap was too tight—and it was always too tight, or too rough, or too hot.

When she turned 18 months, if I (Stacey) raised my voice, even slightly, she would look away, her lips would tremble, and the tears would flow. By the time she was 4, it dawned on me that Eliana had cried almost every single day during day care drop-off. Compare this with my second child, who cried three times and then got over it. By 6 years of age, Eliana still has not slept through the night. She cries because of bad dreams, and nearly every single day, we have to discuss how some social interaction at school has led to hurt feelings.

Eliana is what developmental psychologists would describe as high on "emotionality," negative emotionality, in particular, and "difficult." According to traditional models of personality and health, that is, the diathesis-stress model discussed earlier, children high on emotionality are at increased risk for behavioral problems, such as anxiety and depression. This is particularly true if there is stress in the child's environment (be it low-quality child care, harsh parents, or poverty). However, Eliana also laughs easily and loves being tickled. She loves food and enjoys intense flavors like goat cheese and brie. She can sit still and pay attention if she is interested in what her father is reading to her. Here is one more thing about Eliana: She really loves anything soft and fuzzy. She is sensitive.

Differential susceptibility argues that, yes, children who are high on emotionality are more likely to be negatively affected by the environment, but they also benefit more when the environment is positive. Specifically, these children are better described as sensitive rather than emotional. But being sensitive doesn't just mean that you are more likely to be affected by negative factors in the environment. It also means that you are also more likely to benefit if the environment is warm and supportive. Orchid and dandelion children are different in how susceptible they are to outside influences. Orchid children in the right environment may grow up to be the poets and artists of the world.

Because of having a child like Eliana, I (Stacey) set out to test this hypothesis. Results of the study[27] demonstrated that children who were more emotional had higher levels of biological stress when mothers scored low on warmth and supportiveness, but they actually benefited more from a warm, nurturing parenting style compared with the children who were low on emotional reactivity. Those who were low on emotional reactivity were somewhat unaffected by parenting style. Another example of the benefits of high negative emotionality is the data demonstrating that emotional children are more likely to survive famines! One possibility may be that those kids crying their butts off may be more likely to be fed. The squeaky

245

wheel does get the grease! And if that grease is warm and loving, that wheel is just going to keep on rolling. Our research, as well as that of others, has demonstrated that in the context of warm, responsive care, orchid children thrive and benefit more than their easygoing peers.

What does this mean if you have an orchid child? For me (Stacey), it meant being aware that Eliana is sensitive to a variety of things, including people, objects, noise, touch. It was simply understanding that things that may not bother me or any other baby may affect her strongly. She did not choose this; she wasn't being difficult. She wasn't being a crybaby. After this understanding, the next step was for us to capitalize on that. We gave room for her to express her wishes within reason, and we focused just as much on creating experiences that made her smile and laugh as we did on minimizing things that made her cry.

Some days, every child is an orchid child—moody, teary eyed, and reactive. Next, we detail several concrete strategies for parenting that are particularly relevant to orchid children. While all children can benefit from these strategies, orchid children may need a little more help.

Take Care of the Basics

When we think about children's development and well-being, we don't often zero in on the basics. Physiological needs are fundamental. To learn well, to feel well, children need to have their basic needs met. When you have emotionally reactive children, it is essential to remember that they are sensitive to a wide range of things—not just disappointments or stress but hunger and fatigue, too. I (Stacey), for one, am notorious for being hangry. My hunger manifests as a stress response. I get tense and easily irritated, and I lose the ability to think rationally. Even as an adult, I sometimes forget this, lashing out at my husband for something minor. For emotional children, we cannot underscore the importance of making sure your child gets enough sleep, that they are eating healthy, and, just as importantly, regularly. These children need to have a context to work out their intense emotions. Dance class, swimming, or simply outside play can be a lifeline for these children. Ensuring that their basic needs are met is a means of preventing them from getting emotionally out of balance.

Prioritize Routine, Prepare for Novelty

Routine helps all children and adults alike to know what to expect. Children have so little control over their daily lives that knowing what is going to happen and when are even more important for them. Routines are also fundamentally helpful for reactive children. Consider that each time we experience something new, most of us feel a little bit nervous and anxious, but after experiencing the same thing over and over, we habituate. For reactive children, keeping a routine reduces the frequency of reacting. If you must deviate from routine (and we all have to from time to time), it is important to prepare your child well in advance and explain the when and why of the deviation—but also knowing when and if things return to normal are important. Reading books and role-playing are extremely helpful because they give children a concrete way of imagining what will happen and also assist them in knowing how to respond. For the first day at a new school, you might read books, have your child imagine what their first day would look like, or take your child to visit the school. Just as important, engage your child in simple role-playing. For example, I (Stacey) started the following conversation with Eliana when she was 3 to 4 years old: "Okay, Eliana, let's talk about what tomorrow is going to look like. I am going to drop you off. Your new teacher might say, 'Hi, Eliana!' What are you going to say next?"

Empathize, Then Respond

Perhaps one of the most important things we can do for our emotionally reactive child is to stop being judgmental. For me (Stacey) this meant I had to stop asking, "Why are you crying?" in my exasperated, annoyed tone. Instead, I had to learn to accept my daughter's feelings as true expressions of her internal experience rather than toddler manipulations. I don't always succeed, though. It's hard because I am not as sensitive, and I don't always understand her perspective. Like this morning, when Eliana was upset that we only had regular Cheerios instead of Honey-Nut Cheerios, it was difficult for me to maintain my level of equanimity, especially because I couldn't care less about what kind of cereal I eat!

But emotional children are built that way, and although their experiences and feelings may not always be easy to understand, they are not any less real. Thus, acknowledging their feelings will help downregulate their reactivity. Once calm, it is much easier for you both to problem solve: "How about toast instead? Or maybe I can add a little honey to the cereal?" In addition to acknowledging their emotions and responding, uplifting the positive ones that we discussed in past chapters is pivotal.

Repent and Repair

Inevitably, there will be times when we lose our patience, when we raise our voices, or we do some things of which we are not proud. I (Stacey) have lost count of the number of times I have yelled and regretted it. Once I put a screaming Eliana into her room and stood outside the door, holding onto the doorknob so she couldn't get out. In these circumstances, it's okay to later apologize to your child and repair your relationship. In these contexts, nonverbal behavior is oh so important. Touching your child and getting down to their level will go a long way toward conveying your sincerity.

Accept and Acknowledge

Parenting is difficult, and parenting orchid children effectively can be even more draining. While it is taboo for parents to admit that they don't like parenting, not acknowledging it can mean that we don't seek help and support when we need it. To be good parents, parents need to be well. So, sometimes, it's okay to let your child cry a little longer than necessary. Other times, it's okay to say to your child, "Mommy loves you, but she didn't get enough sleep last night, so she is too tired to play right now." Taking care of yourself is not selfish if it will allow you to be your best self as a parent.

Children who are more emotional or just more reactive are more susceptible to outside influences. They are more likely to have negative outcomes if faced with adversity. But just as importantly, they benefit more and sometimes exclusively from our efforts to provide a positive and nurturing developmental context. Orchid children are more vulnerable and need more from their parents, yes. But they also thrive in warm, supportive contexts, and, as a parent, the rewards are also incredible. Overall, in parenting Eliana, my (Stacey's) focus has shifted more on softening the edges of the world and highlighting the colors, taste, and feel of things Eliana loves. And the wonderful thing about orchid children is that they respond. Just as much as an orchid child will likely throw a tantrum and cry if their mother raises her voice, the child will respond positively when their mother affirms her love for them. In addition to love and affirmation, the effects of having their physical needs met are just as strong. Eliana is easygoing, conversational, and friendly on days when she has slept well, gone swimming, and had plenty of snacks compared to days when none of those needs was met.

CONCLUSION

Perhaps the key message to remember from this chapter is that children come into the world with their own quirks and characteristics. These characteristics, whether high levels of emotion or higher levels of activity, mean children need different things and benefit from different types of parenting styles, activities, and enrichment. This sometimes can be hard to understand, especially if our own personalities are different from those of our children.

At the same time, understanding our own personality and our children's temperament allows us to more precisely tailor our parenting strategies so that they are more effective. Perhaps even more important, by understanding our children's temperament, we are able to be more empathetic.

TL, DR

- Children are born with innate characteristics and quirks that affect their development and how people respond to them.
- Temperament can be described along three main dimensions: (a) activity level, (b) moodiness or emotional reactivity, and (c) distractibility/persistence. Understanding where your child falls along these dimensions is helpful for your understanding of how you should parent.
- Your temperament (nature) and your child's temperament affect how you parent (nurture)!

CHAPTER 10

THE COPARENT

It's a dreary Friday afternoon in March, and I (Jessie) am leading a therapy group for new parents struggling with the transition to parenthood. Today, the parents are talking about the ways they feel misunderstood or unsupported in their roles as parents. Trisha, a mom of a 5-month-old boy, starts out by saying that she feels like nobody understands what she's going through. She's felt really distant from just about everyone in her life since her son was born—but most especially her husband, who seems to be trying to be useful but only gets in Trisha's way. He makes lots of little suggestions to Trisha about how to do things (e.g., how to hold their son when she's feeding him, how she should dress him, whether it's warm enough for him to leave the house). Most of the time, Trisha wishes he would just go away and that she could just be on her own with her son. She finds that she feels calmer and happier when her husband's not around.

Across the room is Max, a young father who says his experience is the opposite of what Trisha has been feeling. If anything, he feels completely dependent on his wife. He feels like nothing he does for his baby girl, Olivia, is quite right. He can't hold her as well as his wife can, and he doesn't know how to make her stop crying as quickly. It's gotten to the point at which he is worried about being alone with his daughter. He feels like he's going to mess up and let both Olivia and his wife down. His wife is desperate for alone time; she's always begging Max to step up and take charge in parenting—to gain confidence and be able to do more things with Olivia. How does he tell her he just can't do it? Will she understand?

A third person speaks up: It's Maryam, who shares that everything would be okay in her family if it weren't for her in-laws. She feels like she's managing parenting fine, and her baby, a 2-month-old little girl named Sara, is also fine, but things get really complicated because her in-laws want to be over at the house most days. When they're there, they are constantly criticizing everything about the family's life—from her parenting to her cooking to the way her floors look. She can't stand the way it makes her feel. And her husband won't say anything to them. She's asked him one hundred times to put them in line or tell them they can't come visit, but he just won't. She's at the point at which she just can't take it anymore. Could it possibly be that something as simple as this could crumble their marriage?

I (Jessie) take a deep breath in, realizing that all of the clients who have just spoken have articulated struggles illustrating the most difficult part of parenting: Figuring out how to parent alongside another person. And I breathe out and sigh because it's not that surprising.

BEYOND THE PAIR: CONSIDERING THE COPARENTING RELATIONSHIP

Human children are unique in many ways compared with other species. And one of those ways is that with human children, other adults—both related and unrelated—are involved in child-rearing, likely because human children take so long to mature. Consider the turquoise killifish, which live in little pools of water in Mozambique. By 14 days, they have matured and can start procreating. By 14 days, my (Stacey's) babies had mastered the art of crying continuously every night from 6 p.m. to 8 p.m. Human children can't really walk until about 12 months, whereas a foal is up and walking in a couple of hours. Because human development is so slow and costly, having multiple adults invested and involved in raising human children increases our chance for survival. But the more people who are involved, the trickier it is to manage (as every single parent who has spent significant time with their in-laws knows).

While research has long recognized the impact of individual parents on a wide range of children's behaviors and development[1,2] as well as the influence of the couple relationship quality on children's development,[3] it has only been within the past 25 years that researchers have begun to recognize the distinct effects of the coparenting relationship on children, or even to identify that such a thing as a coparenting relationship exists. So, what, you ask, is the coparenting relationship? The *coparenting relationship* is the relationship that exists between two people who are committed to caring for a child; it typically (but not always) emerges before the first child's birth.[4] It is

co-perenting

Eliana, 7

often (but not always) rooted in biological relatedness or a stated commitment to raise a child together.[5] The coparenting relationship can occur between two members of a couple or between family members (e.g., adult daughter and mother), but the majority of the research on coparenting has been conducted on romantic partners who are coparents. So, in this discussion of coparenting, we primarily discuss coparenting among couples.

The coparenting relationship and the couple relationship are separable, albeit related, even from the beginning of couples' transition to parenthood.[6–10] In other words, the coparenting relationship refers to how you and your partner parent together and the qualities that characterize the ways in which you engage in this process, whereas the couple relationship focuses on the relationship between the two adults. Although the quality of coparenting can be related to the quality of the overall couple or marital relationship, it is not the same thing. Many couple relationships are going along just fine until a child is introduced into the mix, and the couple needs to quickly adjust to being coparents as well as relationship partners. Things that used to be minor difficulties or quirks become major sources of conflict when people are parenting together. As just one illustration of this, I (Jessie) saw a couple for therapy, and nearly all of their conflicts centered around parenting. The couple would speak longingly of the days before they had children and when they would go on vacation as a couple and leave the kids at home. When they did so, nearly all of their problems would melt away. Before they had children, these seemingly minor issues—that one partner was forgetful and sometimes a bit inconsiderate and that the other partner could be prone to being a bit emotional—stayed minor, but after the kids had arrived, they hit a boiling point.

For many couples, the birth of the first child is the harbinger of the steepest decline in marital satisfaction.[10–12] This is unsurprising given that this is when the most changes occur in a couple's life cycle. When partners become parents, they transition to a new way of relating to one another: They have to operate as a team because they are now engaged in an activity (parenting) that works better when they work together. The coparenting relationship consists of internal components, which includes such things as parents' experiences of coparenting (e.g., the extent to which a parent feels as though their coparent validates and respects their method of parenting, the extent to which a parent feels their coparent helps to support their parenting)[13,14] and external components of coparenting, which include those aspects of coparenting that are observable to the outside world (e.g., observable division of labor, observable discrepancy in coparenting values among coparents).[15]

Before we begin discussing the discrete impacts of coparenting on children, let's pause to make a couple of asides. First, although the majority of the research thus far on the topic of coparenting has been conducted on heterosexual couples, it is essential to remember that coparenting relationships are diverse and include those of partnered but nonmarried parents, same-sex partners, separated or divorced parents of a child, adoptive parents, and a parent and other extended family caregivers (e.g., maternal or paternal grandmother or grandfather, sibling). For many families, parents juggle multiple coparenting relationships (e.g., with the child's other biological parent—with whom parent used to be romantically involved but is now separated, with the individual's new romantic partner, and with the individual's partner's former partner, who is the biological parent of the partner's children). The impact and the complexity of the coparenting relationship in these different configurations may be similarly important to in terms of how they affect children. Many scholars argue that in the truest sense of the word, every child is coparented in that they are raised by a network of people;[16] we just have less knowledge about the processes governing these systems of coparenting in other networks of relationships.

Second, the experiences of single parents are also important to understand. Research is always a bit slow to catch up to the diversity of people's experiences, but this does not mean our thinking on these topics needs to necessarily be delayed. Single parenting, either by choice or by circumstance, is on the rise in the United States, especially among low-income or ethnic minority families.[17] And single parents may be different than coupled parents in important ways. Data from a large-scale, nationally representative study of 4,176 lower income families (the Fragile Families Study) found that mothers of young children (ages 5 and under) who exited stable coresidential partnerships with biological fathers reported higher levels of parenting stress than mothers who remained in stable coresidential partnerships with biological fathers.[18] Importantly, this study also found that for mothers with higher levels of education, the stress increase was not as large.

Furthermore, *single-by-choice parents*, that is, parents who are not divorced or widowed but who choose to become parents on their own, are also on the rise within the United States and other Western societies.[19-22] As a group, these single-by-choice parents tend to be more highly educated, wealthier, and older than other parents.[23-25] Single parents face a unique set of challenges and also opportunities in parenting. In terms of challenges, single parents never or rarely get a parenting break unless they share physical custody with another parent. They typically have to engineer breaks by hiring babysitters or drawing on family support. This might result in higher levels of stress because these parents shoulder large burdens in both the parenting and the work domains.[26,27] Furthermore, among single parents whose child has another parent, the coparenting relationship may still be important. One particularly interesting study of separated parents found that coparenting quality was linked to children's externalizing behavior (things like aggression) and that coparenting quality among separated parents was associated with number of partners each person had during the study period.[28]

Thus, research from two separate streams of data suggest that single parents may face higher levels of stress regardless of how they became single (whether they started out that way when they first became a parent or became single after having a child). Because we know that parenting stress is likely to have an appreciable effect on parents and on children (see Chapter 2 for more details), paying attention to single parents may be especially important in this respect. Research is catching up in this area,[29–34] but it is still lacking.

It is now abundantly clear that children benefit when they have multiple adults who are involved in their lives.[35,36] Regardless of the form and dynamics of the relationships, if children are fortunate enough to have more than one adult invested and interested in their well-being, it behooves them to have these interrelationships function in harmonious ways. The couple's relationship affects the coparenting relationship but not always in the same way for everyone. One study found that fathers who were happier in their couple relationship were also more likely to be satisfied in their coparenting relationship; the same was not true for the mothers.[10] Furthermore, that study found that fathers who displayed more positive behavior during couple interactions before the child's birth were more likely to demonstrate higher quality coparenting after the child was born; this was not true for mothers. Another study found that mothers who displayed more positive behavior during a mock coparenting task conducted during pregnancy with an infant simulator (a lifelike infant doll programmed to cry for periods of time while the to-be parents work to soothe the baby together) were more likely to think about their partner's thoughts and feelings (in other words, they mentalized more) 6 months after the birth of the babies.[37]

WHAT IS COPARENTING?

When psychologists and sociologists use the term "coparenting," they are referring to something far more complex than simply the sharing or division of child-rearing responsibilities ("You do this, I'll do that"). Conceptualizations of everything that coparenting subsumes differ depending on who you ask, but most scholars agree that coparenting is a multifaceted construct that consists of the following four key components: (a) level of support and solidarity between the coparents, (b) degree of antagonism and disagreement in the coparents' goals, (c) the degree to which the coparents engage with the child, and (d) the ways and ease with which coparents distribute parenting tasks. Think back to the parents I (Jessie) was working with in my parenting group and the types of struggles they described having with their coparents. The coparental unit is the executive decision-making branch of the family that, together, enacts orders that children must follow.[38-40] The coparenting relationship is thought to be present prenatally—when the mother is pregnant—and to develop over time, although as of yet, the ways in which coparenting relationships develop over time are still poorly understood.[7] It's rare for first-time pregnant couples to be able to accurately anticipate what parenting will be like, making it difficult to have conversations in which couples discuss their expectations for the coparenting relationship beyond generalities. For instance, a member of a couple may be able to articulate that they want their coparent to play an equal role in parenting, but ideas about what an "equal role" looks like may differ between the two members of the couple.

We asked Franz, the new father of a baby girl whom we introduced in Chapter 3, to tell us what his coparenting relationship was like with his wife:

> In some ways, my perspective is unique from the father's perspective. But because of the different roles [mothers and fathers] play,

the time spent with the baby, even if the hours are the same, is not equal.

For example, because the mother can automatically soothe with breastfeeding, I get resentful sometimes that the "time" my wife has with the baby is of a fundamentally different quality than the "time" I have with her. By definition, when I have the baby, my job is to engage and entertain, and largely field and find solutions to fussing. I essentially never get to snuggle her, whereas my wife often gets to snuggle her. Of course, we both have her at difficult periods. I'm not saying this is an all-or-nothing thing. But when my wife and I bicker about who's not helping enough, I can't help but think that if we split a day exactly like 6 hours with Mom and 6 hours with Dad, my 6 hours are basically harder than my wife's because during so much of our time, the baby *just wants her mom*, which makes her difficult. And the opposite is not true: When my wife has her, my wife is not regularly coping with a child who *just wants her dad*.

On a related point—I often get to sleep in until about 7:00 a.m., 7:30 sometimes, even if the baby wakes up at 5:30. *But* . . . my wife basically spends that 60 to 90 minutes just letting her nurse while they both doze in and out. I would gladly swap places, if you catch my drift.

Franz's perspective clearly highlights that although multiple people may be engaged in "parenting the baby," what this looks likes and how it feels is very different across people. Thus, we emphasize that it is important not to just talk generalities but to dive deep into the specifics.

Coparenting can be measured via self-report questionnaires that tap into these different dimensions of the coparenting relationship quality, or it can be measured by having coparents complete an actual or simulated coparenting task (using a preprogrammed doll that is set to behave in a certain way) and measuring how the two parents behave in concert with one another (in other words, to what extent do they coordinate they parenting behavior? What behavioral strategies do they use to coordinate their parenting behavior? And what are the situations/topics/parenting challenges in which they are unable to effectively support one another in their parenting?).

These different measures of coparenting tell us different things. The survey measures of coparenting tell us what parents perceive about their coparenting relationship in terms of its characteristics and quality, which provides an important window into the experienced quality of the relationship. On a survey measure, a parent will respond to a series of items about their relationship with their coparent (e.g., "My partner asks my opinion on issues related to parenting," "It is easier and more fun to play with the child alone than it is when my partner is present too"; Coparenting Relationship Scale).[41] The behavioral tasks in which parents participate provide important observational data; these tasks are typically videotaped and later rated by trained observers who assign numerical scores to the parents' behaviors and can compare parents across a large sample. This type of assessment tool can provide a more objective assessment parents' coparenting behavior, but it does not say much of anything about the coparents' subjective experience of coparenting.

THE INFLUENCE OF THE COPARENTING RELATIONSHIP ON CHILDREN

The quality of the coparenting relationship is associated with children's developmental outcomes. These associations are statistically significant after accounting for other important variables, such as the quality of the couple or marital relationship and the quality of parenting behavior.[42–44] Studies such as these suggest that coparenting contributes something unique to children's development; this is akin to the idea that the whole is greater than the sum of its parts. Children learn and acquire something valuable from watching the inner workings of parents collaborating on their parenting that ultimately amounts to more than what they glean from each parent individually.

Positive Impacts of Coparenting on Children

Let's start with the positive. Children stand to benefit tremendously from being exposed to your coparenting relationship. First off, they gain a lot from seeing you work collaboratively with your partner to compromise, work through relationship challenges, air grievances, and resolve conflicts. The psychological principle of modeling[45] demonstrates that people learn through watching others perform an action. For instance, children may learn how to become effective communicators by watching you and your coparent communicate calmly with one another.

One of the major areas of child functioning with which the coparenting relationship is associated is children's psychological adjustment, specifically their internalizing and externalizing symptoms. *Internalizing symptoms* are those that primarily manifest or express themselves internally and consist of symptoms, such as anxiety, depression, and bodily complaints like complaining about a stomachache. *Externalizing symptoms* consist of symptoms that have their primary expression in the external world and consist of symptoms like aggression, disruptive behaviors, impulsivity, and inattention. In one recent study that combined the results of many other studies that had been conducted on this topic in a meta-analysis,[46] researchers found that the association between coparenting quality and children's psychological internalizing and externalizing symptoms was significant but small in size after controlling for marital quality and parenting quality. Furthermore, the associations between coparenting and child outcomes appeared to be stronger in samples with larger percentages of male children. So, children whose parents had more positive coparenting relationships had fewer internalizing and externalizing symptoms, and these links appear strong among male children. It is important to remember that these studies are correlational, so they aren't saying that higher quality coparenting promotes better mental health in children but, rather, that higher quality coparenting and better mental health in children tend to be found alongside one another. However, many of the studies were "longitudinal," meaning that they followed families over time, and the measures of coparenting preceded the measures of children's mental health, which provides a more compelling argument than a single measure of the two constructs at one point in time.

There is something about the how parents work together that has an additive effect on children's outcomes. It is clear that children have an awareness of how we interact with them and how we interact together. My (Stacey's) daughter, Eliana, for example, is an expert at knowing which parent to come to when she wants extra screen time. Eliana's dad is much more lenient and relaxed. Once, when I came home from work, I saw that Eliana was playing on the iPad. I said, "What are you doing? You know, we have a rule that there's no technology on the weekdays." Eliana's response was, "Well, Papa said I could!" When my husband came into the room, there was a silent standoff between both parents. Evet at 5 years of age, Eliana was sitting there and watching carefully how the two would respond. By observing, she was learning how adults handle conflict and also learning about the quality of that relationship. Would the two turn toward each other to solve their problems? Would they punish and demean one another? How these interactions play out are just as important as the direct interactions we have with our children.

Disagreement in the Coparenting Relationship and Its Impact on Children

Many potential problems can arise in the coparenting relationship. One such problem is quite commonplace: disagreement among parents regarding how to handle a parenting situation. Parents arrive at the stage of being a parent with their own set of experiences and expectations about what it means to be a parent, and these experiences and expectations differ across parents. Quite often, parents carry with them a set of things they wish to replicate from their own experiences and a set of things they wish to avoid. Many times, these wish lists are not consciously held beliefs but may, instead, be implicit assumptions that are only made apparent when they are threatened or challenged. When these parenting values contrast between coparents, there is the opportunity for coparents to disagree and experience conflict as a result. Coparents then must use their conflict resolution skills to resolve the differences in their parenting values and expectations.

My (Jessie's) husband, for example, grew up eating donuts every Sunday after church. It was a routine his family did every weekend. In my family, eating donuts was a highly restricted activity that maybe occurred twice a year, if that. So, imagine my shock when my husband assumed that he would feed our children donuts once a week! It completely clashed with my assumption that our children would, under no circumstances, eat donuts more than twice a year. This example is a relatively low-stakes example of a parenting values/expectations clash, that is, neither parent actually cared too deeply about their children's donut-eating habits. In fact, both could sit back and laugh at themselves for the reactions they had to these situations. And, yet, for each of them, these donut-eating values were sort of baked into the daily rituals of family life in a way they had not previously questioned until the different approaches collided in the course of their coparenting relationship.

My husband and I (Jessie) ended up having more than a few heated conversations about our children's donut consumption before landing on a resolution, which was for them to eat donuts after they went to church (which occurs almost weekly) but for that to be the kids' one and only dessert of the day. This issue was likely resolved easily because it was fairly low stakes, and both my husband and I were willing to acknowledge how our differences in backgrounds contributed to our parenting behavior, and we both were willing to compromise.

Other coparenting conflicts have been more challenging to work through. Over the course of the past pandemic period, for example, we heard stories from families that had debated how strictly they should adhere to social distancing guidelines, we heard about conflicts arising from embedding values that were perceived as being tied to political parties, and we even heard about what types of things children need to have to thrive (e.g., "No, they do not need new clothes, or toys" vs. "My children are unable to see their friends, so I want to shower them with all the toys they want!"). Disagreements are inevitable, but it is how we handle these disagreements that matters.

Conflict in the Coparenting Relationship and Its Impact on Children

Disagreement in the coparenting relationship can lead to conflict if parents cannot resolve the issue through discussion and compromise. Sometimes unresolved disagreements can lead to other negative outcomes within the coparenting relationship, such as distance between the coparents or gatekeeping of one parent by another parent. However, quite often, disagreements that are not resolved escalate via negative emotionality into coparenting conflicts. Witnessing conflict between parents can evoke feelings of anxiety and uncertainty within children.[47] Children feel more confidence when their parents appear to be in charge and coexist in a harmonious way. In contrast, when children grow up in a family in which there is a high degree of conflict between the coparents, they may experience a high level of anxiety regarding the stability of family unit and their place in it.

Higher levels of conflict are associated with less nurturing and involvement from parents.[48] Coparenting conflict also predicts adolescents' psychological adjustment as strongly or, in some cases, even more strongly than marital quality.[49] Some evidence suggests that higher levels of conflict may arise when fathers show early signs of being more involved in infant care when children are young.[50] This effect may seem ironic in the sense that higher paternal involvement seems, on its face, like a positive thing, so why would it lead to more conflict? Although this is true, more involvement from both caregivers may mean that there is a greater need for the two caregivers to work more collaboratively as coparents, which also means there are more opportunities for coparenting conflict. When one parent is more disengaged from the parenting role, it creates fewer opportunities for coparenting conflict while simultaneously creating other potential challenges.

Triangulation in the Coparenting Relationship and Its Impact on Children

As conflict rises in families, *triangulation* can occur when a child faces pressure to form an alliance, or an especially close relationship, with one parent against another parent. An example would be if a father and his daughter become close and align in their negative perceptions of the mother. Imagine a father a daughter who have a series of inside jokes about the mother in the family. Their relationship creates a triangle in which the daughter and the father are on two corners of the short side of the triangle, and the mother is on the angle at the end of the long side of the triangle. This depiction conveys the idea that the daughter and father have a close relationship while the daughter and the father are both relationally distant from the mother. The triangle

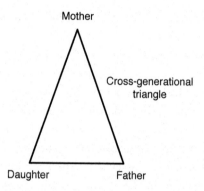

is problematic because in a family system, parents are supposed to have especially close relationships, and children are not supposed to break through those relationships and become closer to one parent and squeeze another parent out.

The concept of triangulation derives from family systems theory,[51] which holds that the family is a system that consists of different subsystems, such as the parent subsystem and the sibling subsystem. According to family systems theory, there are supposed to be metaphorical boundaries in place that separate each subsystem from the other subsystems. The degree of permeability across the different subsystems differs from family to family. There can be different types of triangles within the family system (such as the triangle just discussed in which the father and daughter are close, and the mother is pushed to the outside; this is called a cross-generational triangle). One study[52] compared children in families with these kinds of cross-generational triangles with children in families in which children were blamed for the problems in the family and with children in cohesive families. Findings showed that children in families with cross-generational triangles were in families with higher marital conflict.

The results of a meta-analysis found that children in families with any kind of triangulation have more externalizing symptoms (e.g., aggression, inattention).[46] This meta-analysis revealed that these associations were stronger in lower income families. The authors reasoned that having less income places a higher overall level of stress on the family and provides fewer resources for the family to be able to solve problems within the family, which could result in problems related to triangulation. This same meta-analysis also found that the association between triangulation and children's internalizing symptoms was stronger when parents were separated. The authors of the meta-analysis argued that parental separation may create additional opportunities for parents to form alliances with children against the other parent. This, in turn, can place the child in an uncomfortable position and can cause the child to experience internalizing distress, such as depression or anxiety.

Gatekeeping

Conflict can also lead to *maternal gatekeeping*, which occurs when mothers engage in behaviors that prevent collaborative parenting efforts between two parents from working and include things like taking care of the majority of the responsibilities related to child-rearing (without leaving room for the other parent to step in) and criticizing the other parent's involvement when they do attempt to contribute. The ultimate consequence of this behavior is that it keeps the other parent's involvement at bay. Gatekeeping may not always be conscious and deliberate. Parents are often anxious, stressed, and pressured to be the perfect parent. So, gatekeeping may be away in which they can exert control. However, in other cases, maternal gatekeeping is a way for the parent to remain the focal point for the child(ren)—to be the central figure to meet the child(ren)'s needs. Gatekeeping effectively keeps the parent as an intermediary between the other parent's interactions with the children such that the parent ends up controlling the other parent's access to the children.

Shawn, a father of two girls, is in a struggling relationship. He told us,

> I know I haven't been the best husband. I work too much. I am never around. But I try so hard to be a good father. However, it often seems like she [Shawn's wife] is turning the kids against me. I used to take the girls fishing and camping. Now that they are older, they sometimes complain about going, but instead of encouraging them to go with me, my wife will take their side. She tells them directly that they don't have to go if they don't want to or arranges their schedule so that they are busy when I am free.

In this sense, parents can only have access to the children on the other parent's own terms. If parents feel that what they believe regarding parenting doesn't matter, they will likely not have an impact. In support of this reasoning, studies have demonstrated that fathers' beliefs about coparenting are only associated with their parenting behavior when mothers report believing that fathers matter.[53,54]

The emphasis in this area of research has been on mothers' gatekeeping as an active and preemptive stance, but some scholars have noted that gatekeeping could just as well occur in reaction to disengaged fathering.[54] In this respect, mothers' behavior could be interpreted as protective toward their children in that they may be attempting to shield their children from the disappointment of unrealistic expectations from a caregiver who won't deliver. Alternatively, these so-called gatekeeping mothers could be engaging in this behavior in an attempt to protect themselves and their own expectations. If they have been repeatedly disappointed themselves by hoping their partners would be more involved than they were, mothers may engage in defensive, self-protective behavior to minimize their partner's engagement with their child.

We pause here to note that, thus far, the research on this topic has focused on heterosexual couples and on mothers as gatekeepers.

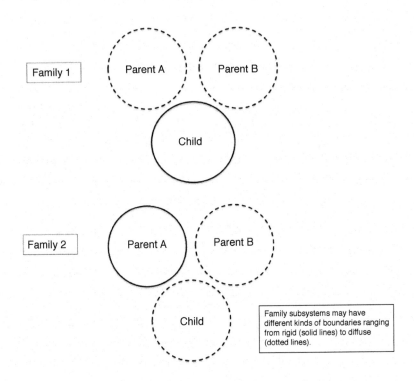

Family subsystems may have different kinds of boundaries ranging from rigid (solid lines) to diffuse (dotted lines).

However, it is possible that gatekeeping occurs among all kinds of couples and in all types of relationships.

Distance in the Coparenting Relationship and Its Impact on Children

Another coparenting challenge that can occur is that distance can creep into the coparenting relationship. Distance can take the form of a lack of communication or psychological distance; both of these types of distance can create other dynamics of import for children. When parents do not communicate about their coparenting, this can create challenges for children because they may then be forced to act as go-betweens for the parents, communicating messages from one parent to the other. The result can be some parentification (when children get treated as though they are parents) of the child, which creates opportunities for triangles to develop. Each of these dynamics poses risks for children. They provide the child with information that is too advanced for their maturity level and may also enable the child to feel more in control of their governance than is ideal. Each dynamic can also send a message to the child regarding the gap in closeness between the coparents; it effectively can result in a child's taking on the role of an additional coparent at times.

I (Stacey) recall a time when I was less than the ideal coparent with my mother-in-law. Eliana has a wonderful relationship with her grandmother. But, for a while during the pandemic, her grandmother ended up being stuck at our house. Although we had always gotten along, being stuck in a small house in the middle of the pandemic really bought out some negativity. But here we were, under "stay at home" orders. I couldn't take a break, so I dealt with it by retreating and not engaging. I would use Eliana to deliver messages to her grandma, even to tell her that dinner was ready. This led to all sorts of miscommunication and unnecessary pain.

RECOMMENDATIONS FOR IMPROVING THE COPARENTING RELATIONSHIP OR MAINTAINING HIGH-QUALITY COPARENTING RELATIONSHIPS

Just like there are best practices for maintaining a healthy romantic relationship, there are strategies we can use to foster a healthy coparenting relationship. In this section, we detail several crucial steps.

Cultivate an Intentional Mindset

The first step to promoting high-quality coparenting relationships is intentionality. Parents must approach this phase of their relationship with an intentional mindset, one aspect of which involves conceptualizing coparenting as separate from couple/marital relationship quality. Parents must tend to this aspect of their relationship separately and deliberately (e.g., set aside time to talk about it just like they set aside time to talk about their couple relationship or to talk about parenting). Couple therapists are well known for advising couples to stop talking about their children when they go on dates or have alone time. The wisdom behind this advice is that couples need to create a space in which they can exist for one another outside of their role as coparents. Although this advice is undoubtedly sound, there is also wisdom on the other end of the continuum—that coparents must also ensure that they make space in their relationship to discuss the ways in which they are parenting together as a couple. Note that this is different than simply discussing their children (e.g., their children's interests, their children's struggles) because it involves an intentional focus on the ways in which parents coordinate and align their efforts as a team to raise their children.

These conversations should not take the place of other conversations about the couple relationship or each parent as individuals; rather, each of these conversations has its place within a healthily functioning family. Parents overlap in at least two aspects of their identities: They identify as members of the same couple relationship and also as parents of the same child. They need to spend time on both topics. In addition, discussing nonshared aspects of their identities—for instance, aspects about their individual or personal selves—can serve to strengthen the other aspects of their shared identities.

One way in which parents can engage in discussions about coparenting can be to identify what their shared and unique values are for parenting. These values can be based in culture, religion, history, politics, science, literature, intuition, morality, education, personal beliefs or history, or any other belief system that the parent holds. To begin this process, you may wish to first ask yourself and your coparent, "What are your top three to five goals in parenting? What type of child are you trying to raise, and how are you trying to do it? For instance, are you trying to raise a child who is self-sufficient and driven or a child who is compassionate and sensitive to the needs of others? Are you trying to raise a child who is egalitarian and antiracist? Are you trying to cultivate curiosity and wonder about the world in your child?"

After you have identified your own parenting values, share these with your coparent. Acknowledging that something is a parenting value helps parents to both identify that something matters to them and to gain a bit of distance from the value (rather than to be completely fused with it). Only by gaining some distance and recognizing that it is possible for others to have different parenting values can parents begin to question whether they want to have that value in particular. This value grounding exercise helps parents be explicit about what they want in their parenting practice so that they are not reacting to their coparent's parenting from a place of emotionality without being aware of why they are having strong feelings about a topic (see Table 10.1). As a listener, when your coparent is discussing their coparenting values, it is appropriate to express interest, which can be accomplished through paying attention or by asking questions of the speaker. At the end of the speaker's turn in which they shared their parenting values, it is also appropriate for the listener to validate these as appropriate and worthwhile values to have as a parent. Your coparent needs to be told that it is clear that they have your child's best interests at heart. And know that they do, even if they disagree with you.

Next, you and your coparent should assign numerical values to the parenting values you have identified so that it's clear which ones are the most important. You can look together for points of convergence and divergence between the two lists. The points of

TABLE 10.1. Grounding Exercises With Your Coparent: Setting a Baseline

Guideline	Rationale
Identify personal parenting values you hold near and dear. State in terms of principles (e.g., "I value helping my children develop into self-sufficient, confident people") rather than behaviors.	This exercise takes you away from the nitty-gritty details and into thinking of the big picture.
Discuss this list with your coparent. Stay focused on the big-picture. Try to understand your partner's point of view in valuing each character trait/virtue/aspiration.	This discussion will help you understand the big picture principles your coparent holds near and dear to their heart.
Rate the values/priorities on a scale of 1 to 100 according to their importance and compare the lists.	This exercise helps you identify clear points of agreement and disagreement.
Discuss how to prioritize given that some values are shared and some are not shared.	This compromising step should help coparents come to a resolution.

convergence are easy: These are places where you are in alignment as coparents and should have relatively little disagreement (famous last words, we know). You and your coparent should discuss what to do about the points of divergence. How do you balance decisions as coparents when your beliefs about what is important for your child conflict? Coparents handle this in different ways: Some coparents find a middle ground, sometimes prioritizing what one parent wants to achieve in parenting and sometimes prioritizing what the other parent wants. Other coparents find it helpful to talk through the reasons why these parenting values matter to each parent so that the underlying meaning of the values becomes clear. In so doing, the other parent may understand and internalize their coparent's value.

Discuss How Coparenting Impacts Your Child

Another way in which parents can work on their coparenting is they can reflect on the impact of their coparenting relationship on their child. You can accomplish this by putting yourself in your child's shoes and thinking about how your child perceives the way you coparent. Taking this step can help you be proactive about preventing coparenting problems before they develop and adjusting your coparenting strategy so that it is beneficial to your child. Remember that what your child observes in you and your coparent creates a template for how your child will conceive of coparenting relationships in the future. Therefore, try to be aware of the messages you are sending your child about how people parent together, make decisions collaboratively, manage complex responsibilities, and share resources (see Table 10.2).

If you have a coparenting disagreement, you probably don't want to resolve it in front of your child unless you're confident you and your coparent can find your way to a resolution without too much wear and tear. The reason is that you don't want your child to observe too much tension or friction between you and your coparent about anything, especially about parenting-related topics, because it is easy for children to infer that they are the source of problems between their parents. Furthermore, it helps children to see that their parents are a united front, and that when they aren't united, they find a way

TABLE 10.2. Reflection on How Coparenting Affects Your Child

Guideline	Rationale
Reflect with your coparent regarding shared responsibilities.	This reflection helps you to be mindful of the messages you are sending to your child.
Ask your child what they notice about your relationship with your coparent.	Asking communicates to your child that this is a safe topic of discussion in your family, that thinking about the impact of family relationships is important, and that you value their input and will take it into consideration.
When you and your coparent disagree, take steps to resolve this disagreement. Work through this disagreement in private. Then share with the child that you have a resolution.	Doing so provides healthy modeling of conflict resolution and promotes healthy coparenting relationship quality.

to work through things productively. If a disagreement is likely to be a tough one to work through, it's a better strategy to table it until you have privacy to discuss it or to step out of the room to discuss it. Then make sure to follow up with your child and explain to them that you came to a resolution together and that you and your coparent are now aligned in terms of the best course of action moving forward. Much like with parenting missteps, many parents think that all is lost if they have a coparenting disagreement in front of their child. However, in reality, having this type of disagreement occur just creates an opportunity for you to teach your child another important life lesson: that disagreements between two reasonable people happen and can be productively resolved. In this way, you are modeling for your child how to handle and resolve a coparenting disagreement.

Become a More Effective Coparent With Your Ex

Children of divorce are at heightened risk for a range of psychological and behavioral problems, and yet studies suggest that it is not divorce itself that places children at risk but, rather, the problems attendant to the divorce that heightens children's risk.[55] The ways in which divorced parents coparent is one of those factors thought to have a profound influence on the ways in which divorce can affect the children. Contemporary wisdom holds that if separated parents can manage the divorce and develop a solid means of coparenting the children, the children will be a lot better off in terms of managing in response to the divorce.[56] Coparents with cooperative coparenting profiles have children with lower externalizing and internalizing symptoms as well as more positive family functioning.[56]

Well, easier said than done. What are the chances that you can parent well with a person after you've divorced? Coparenting following divorce can be incredibly challenging. Frequently the *last* thing a separated couple wants to do is have continued engagement with their former partner. However, if you are coparenting a child with someone, you may not have a choice about whether some form of continued engagement will persist. Oftentimes, divorced couples only have contact with one another related to issues regarding coparenting; thus, if conflict is to be had between the former couple, it transpires in the coparenting arena.

We do know some about what factors predict greater success in coparenting among divorced parents. Parents who show higher quality coparenting following divorce are more likely to have had a higher quality marriage before divorce[57] and are less likely to have had litigation involved in their divorce process.[58] Furthermore, lower life satisfaction, greater negative affect about the divorce, and more inconsistent parenting predicts coparenting that is more conflictual.[56] Coparenting effectively following divorce may have more to do with being able to focus on children's needs and to keep those in the foreground while being able to manage the emotional difficulties associated with interacting with one's former partner (the coparent). Children need for their parents to be coparenting them effectively, and when all coparenting conversations become stages on which conflicts about the former marital relationship can be enacted, children's needs get edged out of the situation.

Finding ways of managing this situation is essential. First, we recommend that you find an outlet to get your personal needs met so that you have someone to talk to about your unresolved feelings (e.g., anger, resentment, sadness, loss) regarding your former spouse. This outlet can be a person (e.g., friend, therapist, new partner), an activity (such as kickboxing, painting, singing), a social group (for instance, a support group), a place (such as the beach), or a spiritual connection. Any which way you cut it, nurturing something—a relationship, a hobby, time in a place—that helps you during this time will help you improve your parenting and your coparenting. This will help you find a place to go to get your emotional needs met (see Table 10.3).

Second, you should intentionally place your children's needs at the forefront of your interactions with your coparent. Remember that your children need you to be an effective coparent for them. Their needs are greater than your need to have the last word with your former partner. If conflicts need to be had with your partner, schedule separate times to talk through conflicts with your partner and separate times to talk through parenting issues. Your child needs you to do this. Your coparenting will benefit when, as you are making parenting decisions, you focus on your child's needs.

TABLE 10.3. Coparenting Through Divorce: Taking an Intentional Stance

Guideline	Rationale
Find an outlet for you to get your personal needs met.	Nurturing yourself will improve your parenting and your coparenting.
Place your child at the forefront of your mind when interacting with your coparent.	Focusing on your child's needs will benefit your coparenting.
Generate a list of coparenting values you wish to maintain through the divorce.	This exercise will ground you and your coparent in your parenting values and beliefs.
Seek backup: Find a neutral third party to help develop a coparenting plan.	Another person can help you put aside the conflicts that might emerge and assist you in staying focused.
Revise the coparenting plan.	Plans flex with children's needs.

Next, generate a list of coparenting values that you wish to maintain through the divorce. To do this, ask yourself, How do I wish to coparent through the separation and divorce? Ask your coparent to do the same, and then compare lists with your coparent. This exercise will help ground you in what your parenting values and beliefs are. It will take you away from the nitty-gritty details and into the space of thinking of big picture principles. Particularly in the context of the divorce/separation, this values-based work will aid you in focusing on what still unites you: your work as coparents. If working with your coparent becomes difficult and you are unable to use your coparenting values to ground you, it may be useful to find a neutral third party (such as a therapist or mediator). Developing a coparenting plan may be beneficial, and having a neutral third party assist you may help you put aside conflicts that might emerge between you and your coparent when discussing your coparenting without a third party present. A neutral third party can help you stay focused on what matters most now: coparenting your children effectively. And be prepared to revise the coparenting plan as needed. You can make these revisions directly with the coparent or with the neutral third party, if appropriate. Coparenting plans cannot be static because children's needs are not static and neither are parents' perspectives. Being flexible and ready to revise is key.

CONCLUSION

In physics, there is something called the *three-body problem*, which refers to the idea that, unlike the two-body problem, when three individual bodies interact with one another, the result is chaotic and difficult to predict. Our intuitions are scrambled. It makes the problem easier to solve if we make one of the bodies small and insignificant or if two of the bodies are standing still doing nothing.

In the context of coparenting, this would mean that we focus on two people in the relationship (the parents) and ignore the third (the child), or we focus all our energies on the child and ignore the exchange between the parents. These strategies may work for a short time, but they aren't real solutions, and they are likely to lead to the whole system falling apart. Coparenting is an important aspect of parenting, one that is hard but is important to get right—or, more accurately, one that is important to get "good enough." This is important not only for our children but also for ourselves as parents and for our partnerships with our coparents. Strong coparenting relationships make the whole family more resilient.

TL, DR

- Human children are often raised by multiple caregivers. While this is beneficial most of the time, it also requires much more cooperation and coordination.
- The coparenting relationship is distinct from the relationship between the two parents and also distinct from the relationship between parent and child. Although two individuals may have a fantastic relationship before children, or when children are not involved, the coparenting relationship (how the two work together on raising their child) can be strained. Data suggest that relationships undergo increased challenges and strain right after the birth of a child.
- The first step to promoting high-quality coparenting relationships is intentionality. One aspect of this intentional mindset involves conceptualizing coparenting as separate from couple/marital relationship quality. Parents must tend to this aspect of their relationship separately and deliberately (e.g., setting aside time to talk about it just like they set aside time to talk about their couple relationship or to talk about parenting).
- The second step is to identify what the coparents' shared and unique values are for parenting. These values can be based in culture, religion, history, politics, science, literature, intuition, morality, education, personal beliefs or history, or any other belief system that the parent holds.
- Prioritize your values. Check for overlap. Being explicit about the shared values and goals can help to navigate conflicts and to identify areas of compromise.

EPILOGUE

Parenting may well be one of the most challenging experiences of your life, but our hope is that it's also one of the most rewarding. Just as playing an instrument or any sport becomes truly rewarding only when we actually get good at it, becoming a good parent requires practice. As researchers in the field of child development, we have read hundreds if not thousands of articles and books on the topic, but nothing has taught us more than becoming parents. Our personal circumstances and training have allowed us to reflect on how theories of child development actually play out in the everyday lives of families.

One reason we started writing this book was to provide parents with a toolkit—with specific strategies—to use. We promised no shortcuts. To be good at this, practice is necessary. Our focus, though, is different from that of most current parenting books. Those books tend to focus on raising successful children, but our true belief is that you have to raise the whole child—that is, you have to consider their genes, their personality, their circumstances. Perhaps most important, we wanted to convey to this generation of stressed-out parents that, at the end of the day, your love is what is most integral to your child's happiness and well-being. And laying that foundation for your child—letting them know that they matter and that they are loved—is necessary for all great things.

We also wanted parents to know *that* they matter and *how* they matter as well as *which* concrete parenting strategies matter. So, we have taken you on a tour of many concepts that have great relevance for your relationship with your child: stress, empathy, reflective functioning, temperament, epigenetics, attachment, and parenting alongside a partner. Our hope is that you have emerged with an appreciation for the complexity of the bond you have created with your child, for the uniqueness of the child (or children) you have, and for the powerful role you play in shaping your children—and perhaps their children's(!) lives. In addition, we hope to have granted you insight into the dynamics of what is known regarding children's development as well as the myriad ways in which children's social worlds impact how they grow, learn, and love.

We'd like to leave you with six big takeaways from our book as they are embodied in the voices and perspectives of children we have seen in our lab and practice. In many ways, their voices convey what dozens of studies have shown: that parents matter.

OUR SIX BIG TAKEAWAYS FOR RAISING RESILIENT KIDS

Takeaway 1: Life Is Made of Small Moments

Even though it may be tempting to focus on "big moments" or milestones in parenting, in actuality, the day-to-day interactions paint the picture that is your child's life. How you respond to your child on a daily basis affects your child more than how or whether they experience big occasions or events (e.g., trips to Disneyland).

Here are the words of an 8-year-old-girl, a participant in one of our studies, who described her dad as being "fun":

> Every time when he plays with my stuffed bear because he makes it wave and hide some things. Like one time, he made it hide from my messy room. And he talks to it, and does, like, yes or no answers. So, he makes it nod like this and like that.

This little fun activity is something she remembers in great detail. It is in these little interactions with children that they learn their parents love them, care about them, and that they matter.

Takeaway 2: Children Learn From What They Observe

Children notice the behaviors they observe in you, their first and most important teachers. When you act in front of your child, ask yourself whether you want your child to use your behavior (e.g., if you yell at your partner, mistreat a service worker, or scowl disapprovingly at your image in the mirror) as a template for their future behavior. Think about the messages your behavior is sending to your child, who is learning how to view themselves from the way you view yourself.

When this 10-year-old was asked how she would like to be like her mom, she replied, "I'd like to be able to do things like my mom and know how to make dinner and stuff." When asked how she would *not* like to be like her mother, she answered, "I wouldn't have anyone to make me feel better—like anyone older than me to make me feel better when I was upset." These words are insightful. The child is aware that there are skill sets her mother has that she would hope to acquire. However, on some level, she also senses that, as an adult, it can be challenging because we are now the caretakers, and there may be no one we can rely on to take care of us. Children understand that parenting and adulting are challenging processes. They may be unable to express their concern, but, undoubtedly, they have great empathy toward us.

Takeaway 3: You Are the Chief Executive Officer

As brilliant as our children are, they are often incapable of regulating their emotions, biology, and behavior. Parents are crucial regulators of their children's body and mind with important implications for their children's long-term physical health and psychological well-being. Parents' kindness, caring, and empathy for their children, expressed through their behavior, their words, their emotions, and even their mere presence, have a soothing effect on children. This soothing effect is manifest at multiple levels of analysis—biological, behavioral, and experiential—and it begins in infancy and persists throughout development.

A 12-year-old girl told us the following story about her "calm" relationship with her mother:

> On the car ride here [to our research lab], I was all nervous and, "Geezayah!" (*She cringes.*) And she made me feel calm 'cause she was talking and listening to music. And, let's see. Any time before soccer games, when I'm really nervous and antsy, she makes me feel calm. Whenever I get sick with the stomach virus where I'm throwing up and everything, she'll rub my back and brush my hair, and it makes me feel calm.

In this story, note that, again, it's the little things like having one's hair brushed or back rubbed that matter. For the child, they simply feel better; that is the most important outcome. But we know from research that, over time, these little behaviors shape how their body will react to stress. And just as important, long after our children have grown up and moved from the house, the mark or signature we have left remains.

Much like the rodents that lick and groom their pups, we have central roles in helping our children contain, make sense of, and learn to express their emotions. We can also help them discover means of knowing how to channel their emotions into productive energy.

Takeaway 4: We Will Make Mistakes— and Our Children Will Forgive Us for Them

At some parent point in our children's lives, we will make a mistake. We will get angry, or we will lose our patience. We may be aware of our mistake immediately, or that knowledge may not come until years later. At the same time, perfection is an impossible goal.

The key when we make mistakes with our children is to make amends. We should have enough respect for our children that we can apologize. At the same time, it is important to acknowledge that our mistake is seen and experienced as a part of a larger picture. If, as parents, we are patient, warm, and understanding most of the time, our children will forgive us for the rest.

To prove it to you, here's my (Stacey's) daughter, Eliana (a frequent victim of my yelling), talking about why I yell:

> The baby cries a lot at night, so Mom is tired a lot, and when she's tired, she will yell, especially when she thinks I am not listening. But she'll say sorry, and we'll talk about what to do to help her not yell so much. Even though I don't like when she yells, I still love her the mostest!

Parenting is hard, so it is unfair to expect parents to be perfect. Yet, knowing this, many of us still feel a tremendous amount of guilt—for not being around enough, for losing our tempers, for working too much—but if our children can forgive us, we should forgive ourselves.

Takeaway 5: Parenting Is Hard, and Showing Up Is What Matters Most

We have spent our careers studying how children think about their relationships with their parents and what messages they internalize from their parents' actions, and we know that hands down what matters most is knowing that their parents have their back and are there for them when the chips are down. To be honest, we have to acknowledge that there are many times we don't love parenting. This was true especially during the early years, when the sheer physicality of keeping our children alive, making sure they were fed, guessing and second-guessing their wants, striving to make sure their demands were being heard, and desperately figuring out how best to cultivate these young beings so they would have a chance at being their best selves occupied our hands, heart, and minds. Changes in society—for example, jobs that make us move far away from our families—have stripped us from the social support that was more typical of the past. In addition, over the past 40 years, we have transitioned from being a society in which children were meant to be seen and not heard to a society in which children are meant to be seen, heard, understood, entertained, and paid attention to every minute of the day. Both children and parents have become overscheduled creatures—overscheduling has become the new "ideal." In addition, parents' behavior is now under a microscope both by other parents and by nonparents. Although it may be a good thing that we now understand that parenting matters and that children's development is consequential, we may have traded one set of problems for another.

We refuse to accept the hyperfocus on parenting, this insistence that there is only one right way to parent. In this book, we argue that what is best for one child is not necessarily best for another. What is best for one parent is not necessarily best for another. Furthermore, we advocate for the adoption of general "best practice" principles that will help parents guide their parenting in a certain direction that privileges their child's emotional needs for connection with the parent—all while honoring the child's uniqueness and the parent's needs.

The core skill of all parenting is to love our children but to have it be an action that emanates in being fully present for as many moments as possible. It is through love that something as challenging and as hard as parenting can take on meaning and can bring us joy. And it's through small acts of love that our children come to know their value.

As an 8-year-old participant in our lab stated, "I know they love me even when they're mad at me because you [just] know." For the child to "just know," the parent has to have spent many a night rubbing backs or have showed up at countless plays and competitions. They have had to wipe away tears, kiss skinned knees, and also take away screens and force their child to eat "just one piece of broccoli, please!" Parenting is not for the faint of heart. But, at the end of the day, know that.

Takeaway 6: You Are Loved

For most young children, their parents *are* their worlds. It would be impossible to overstate the impact that parents have on young children. Of course, this changes a bit as children age, but even for school-age children and adolescents, their relationship with their parents is extremely important. We often forget how much our children love us, but remembering that it is love that underlies their connection to us can be grounding. They look to us for affection and information and attention (oh, so much attention) because they love us.

Use this to motivate you as a parent. That we are loved and are often the ones they love most make it one of the biggest joys and challenges of being a parent. As soon as we have children, it's like a part of us has split off from us—a part of us that, for many early years, wants to be reunited, to be in touch, to be close. While endearing, this intense desire for connection can also be draining. Thus, we reiterate that part of loving our children is taking care of ourselves.

We asked one 8-year-old boy why he says he "loves, loves his mom": "Can you think of a specific time when you felt that way—that like you really liked her?" Let's take a little tour through his reasons:

> Almost every day, pretty much, but I'll just think of one. Like, once, I got a really bad splinter, and she helped me take it out. . . . That's why I really love them. There're other reasons, too. Like

they borned me and stuff. Well, actually, that my mom did, but my dad helped a bit with the birth thing, you know. Because, if they didn't marry, then—then I might have not been born by them. 'Cause I could've been born by somebody else, but, you know.

On some level, kids know that we gave them life, but that is only the beginning.

Little eyes are watching, and they are admiring. They love and adore you. They love you for the big things, like being there for them to hold them when they hurt, and they also love you for the simple fact that you are their parents. Remember that and hold it near your heart when parenting drags you down.

We wish for you that you can love and admire yourself the same way they love and admire you.

NOTES

CHAPTER 1

1. American Psychological Association. (2020, May). *Stress in America*™ *2020: Stress in the time of COVID-19, volume one* [Press release]. https://www.apa.org/news/press/releases/stress/2020/report

2. Lopes, L., Muñana, C., & Hamel, L. (2020, August 6). *It's back-to-school amid COVID-19, and mothers especially are feeling the strain.* Kaiser Family Foundation. https://www.kff.org/policy-watch/its-back-to-school-amid-covid-19-and-mothers-especially-are-feeling-the-strain/

3. Munsey, C. (2010, January). The kids aren't all right. *Monitor on Psychology, 41*(1), 22. https://www.apa.org/monitor/2010/01/stress-kids

4. Levine, S., & Mody, T. (2003). The long-term psychobiological consequences of intermittent postnatal separation in the squirrel monkey. *Neuroscience & Biobehavioral Reviews, 27*(1–2), 83–89. https://doi.org/10.1016/S0149-7634(03)00011-3

5. Lehmann, J., & Feldon, J. (2000). Long-term biobehavioral effects of maternal separation in the rat: Consistent or confusing? *Reviews in the Neurosciences, 11*(4), 383–408. https://doi.org/10.1515/REVNEURO.2000.11.4.383

6. Liu, D., Diorio, J., Tannenbaum, B., Caldji, C., Francis, D., Freedman, A., Sharma, S., Pearson, D., Plotsky, P. M., & Meaney, M. J. (1997). Maternal care, hippocampal glucocorticoid receptors, and hypothalamic-pituitary-adrenal responses to stress. *National Science, 277*(5332), 1659–1662. https://doi.org/10.1126/science.277.5332.1659

7. Caldji, C., Tannenbaum, B., Sharma, S., Francis, D., Plotsky, P. M., & Meaney, M. J. (1998). Maternal care during infancy regulates the development of neural systems mediating the expression of fearfulness in the rat. *Proceedings of the National Academy of Sciences, 95*(9), 5335–5340. https://doi.org/10.1073/pnas.95.9.5335

8. Camacho, L., & Pogribny, I. P. (2017). Epigenetic effects of bisphenol A (BPA): A literature review in the context of human dietary exposure. In V. Patel & V. Preedy (Eds.), *Handbook of nutrition, diet, and epigenetics* (pp. 1–20). Springer. https://doi.org/10.1007/978-3-319-31143-2_32-1

9. Anderson, O. S., Sant, K. E., & Dolinoy, D. C. (2012). Nutrition and epigenetics: An interplay of dietary methyl donors, one-carbon metabolism and DNA methylation. *Journal of Nutritional Biochemistry, 23*(8), 853–859. https://doi.org/10.1016/j.jnutbio.2012.03.003

10. Weaver, I. C. G., Cervoni, N., Champagne, F. A., D'Alessio, A. C., Sharma, S., Seckl, J. R., Dymov, S., Szyf, M., & Meaney, M. J. (2004). Epigenetic programming by maternal behavior. *Nature Neuroscience, 7*, 847–854. https://doi.org/10.1038/nn1276

11. Wang, J., Wu, Z., Li, D., Li, N., Dindot, S. V., Satterfield, M. C., Bazer, F. W., & Wu, G. (2012). Nutrition, epigenetics, and metabolic syndrome. *Antioxidants & Redox Signaling, 17*(2), 282–301. https://doi.org/10.1089/ars.2011.4381

12. Liu, C. H., & Doan, S. N. (2019). Innovations in biological assessments of chronic stress through hair and nail cortisol: Conceptual, developmental, and methodological issues. *Developmental Psychobiology, 61*(3), 465–476. https://doi.org/10.1002/dev.21830

13. Weiner, H. (1992). *Perturbing the organism: The biology of stressful experience*. University of Chicago Press.

14. McEwen, B. S. (2002). *The end of stress as we know it*. Joseph Henry Press.

15. Chrousos, G. P. (2009). Stress and disorders of the stress system. *Nature Reviews Endocrinology, 5*, 374–381. https://doi.org/10.1038/nrendo.2009.106

16. Juster, R. P., McEwen, B. S., & Lupien, S. J. (2010). Allostatic load biomarkers of chronic stress and impact on health and cognition. *Neuroscience and Biobehavioral Reviews, 35*(1), 2–16. https://doi.org/10.1016/j.neubiorev.2009.10.002

17. Henry, J. P. (1992). Biological basis of the stress response. *Integrative Physiological and Behavioral Science, 27*, 66–83. https://doi.org/ 10.1007/BF02691093

18. Sapolsky, R. M. (1994). *Why zebras don't get ulcers: A guide to stress, stress related diseases, and coping.* W. H. Freeman.

19. Coan, J. A., Schaefer, H. S., & Davidson, R. J. (2006). Lending a hand: Social regulation of the neural response to threat. *Psychological Science, 17*(12), 1032–1039. https://doi.org/10.1111/j.1467-9280. 2006.01832.x

20. Cohen, S. (2004). Social relationships and health. *American Psychologist, 59*(8), 676–684. https://doi.org/10.1037/0003-066X.59.8.676

21. Cacioppo, J. T., Rourke, P. A., Marshall-Goodell, B. S., Tassinary, L. G., & Baron, R. S. (1990). Rudimentary physiological effects of mere observation. *Psychophysiology, 27*(2), 177–186. https://doi.org/ 10.1111/j.1469-8986.1990.tb00368.x

22. Coyne, J. C., Rohrbaugh, M. J., Shoham, V., Sonnega, J. S., Nicklas, J. M., & Cranford, J. A. (2001). Prognostic importance of marital quality for survival of congestive heart failure. *American Journal of Cardiology, 88*(5), 526–529. https://doi.org/10.1016/s0002-9149(01)01731-3

23. Robles, T. F., & Kiecolt-Glaser, J. K. (2003). The physiology of marriage: Pathways to health. *Physiology & Behavior, 79*(3), 409–416. https://doi.org/10.1016/s0031-9384(03)00160-4

24. Berscheid, E. (2003). The human's greatest strength: Other humans. In L. G. Aspinwall & U. M. Staudinger (Eds.), *A psychology of human strengths: Fundamental questions and future directions for a positive psychology* (pp. 37–47). American Psychological Association. https:// doi.org/10.1037/10566-003

25. Hostinar, C. E., & Gunnar, M. R. (2015). Social support can buffer against stress and shape brain activity. *AJOB Neuroscience, 6*(3), 34–42. https://doi.org/10.1080/21507740.2015.1047054

26. Gunnar, M. R., & Donzella, B. (2002). Social regulation of the cortisol levels in early human development. *Psychoneuroendocrinology, 27*(1–2), 199–220. https://doi.org/10.1016/s0306-4530(01)00045-2

27. Engert, V., Buss, C., Khalili-Mahani, N., Wadiwalla, M., Dedovic, K., & Pruessner, J. C. (2010). Investigating the association between early life parental care and stress responsivity in adulthood. *Developmental*

Neuropsychology, 35(5), 570–581. https://doi.org/10.1080/87565641.
2010.494752

28. Felitti, V. J., Anda, R. F., Nordenberg, D., Williamson, D. F., Spitz, A. M., Edwards, V., Koss, M. P., & Marks, J. S. (1998). Relationship of childhood abuse and household dysfunction to many of the leading causes of death in adults: The Adverse Childhood Experiences (ACE) Study. *American Journal of Preventive Medicine, 14*(4), 245–258. https://doi.org/10.1016/s0749-3797(98)00017-8

29. Dube, S. R., Fairweather, D., Pearson, W. S., Felitti, V. J., Anda, R. F., & Croft, J. B. (2009). Cumulative childhood stress and autoimmune diseases in adults. *Psychosomatic Medicine, 71*(2), 243–250. https://doi.org/10.1097/PSY.0b013e3181907888

30. Brown, M. J., Thacker, L. R., & Cohen, S. A. (2013). Association between adverse childhood experiences and diagnosis of cancer. *PLOS ONE, 8*(6), Article e65524. https://doi.org/10.1371/journal.pone.0065524

31. Schüssler-Fiorenza Rose, S. M., Xie, D., & Stineman, M. (2014). Adverse childhood experiences and disability in U.S. adults. *PM&R, 6*(8), 670–680. https://doi.org/10.1016/j.pmrj.2014.01.013

32. Chapman, D. P., Whitfield, C. L., Felitti, V. J., Dube, S. R., Edwards, V. J., & Anda, R. F. (2004). Adverse childhood experiences and the risk of depressive disorders in adulthood. *Journal of Affective Disorders, 82*(2), 217–225. https://doi.org/10.1016/j.jad.2003.12.013

33. Dube, S. R., Miller, J. W., Brown, D. W., Giles, W. H., Felitti, V. J., Dong, M., & Anda, R. F. (2006). Adverse childhood experiences and the association with ever using alcohol and initiating alcohol use during adolescence. *Journal of Adolescent Health, 38*(4), 444E1–444E10. https://doi.org/10.1016/j.jadohealth.2005.06.006

34. Anda, R. F., Brown, D. W., Felitti, V. J., Dube, S. R., & Giles, W. H. (2008). Adverse childhood experiences and prescription drug use in a cohort study of adult HMO patients. *BMC Public Health, 8*, Article198. https://doi.org/10.1186/1471-2458-8-198

35. Lang, J., McKie, J., Smith, H., McLaughlin, A., Gillberg, C., Shiels, P. G., & Minnis, H. (2020). Adverse childhood experiences, epigenetics and telomere length variation in childhood and beyond: A systematic review of the literature. *European Child & Adolescent Psychiatry, 29*(10), 1329–1338. https://doi.org/10.1007/s00787-019-01329-1

36. Perroud, N., Paoloni-Giacobino, A., Prada, P., Olié, E., Salzmann, A., Nicastro, R., Guillaume, S., Mouthon, D., Stouder, C., Dieben, K., Huguelet, P., Courtet, P., & Malafosse, A. (2011). Increased methylation of glucocorticoid receptor gene (*NR3C1*) in adults with a history of childhood maltreatment: A link with the severity and type of trauma. *Translational Psychiatry*, *1*(12), Article e59. https://doi.org/10.1038/tp.2011.60

37. Tyrka, A. R., Ridout, K. K., Parade, S. H., Paquette, A., Marsit, C. J., & Seifer, R. (2015). Childhood maltreatment and methylation of FK506 binding protein 5 gene (*FKBP5*). *Development and Psychopathology*, *27*(4 Pt. 2), 1637–1645. https://doi.org/10.1017/S0954579415000991

38. McGowan, P. O., Sasaki, A., D'Alessio, A. C., Dymov, S., Labonté, B., Szyf, M., Turecki, G., & Meaney, M. J. (2009). Epigenetic regulation of the glucocorticoid receptor in human brain associates with childhood abuse. *Nature Neuroscience*, *12*(3), 342–348. https://doi.org/10.1038/nn.2270

39. King, S., Dancause, K., Turcotte-Tremblay, A.-M., Veru, F., & Laplante, D. P. (2012). Using natural disasters to study the effects of prenatal maternal stress on child health and development. *Birth Defects Research, Part C*, *96*(4), 273–288. https://doi.org/10.1002/bdrc.21026

40. Laplante, D. P., Barr, R. G., Brunet, A., Galbaud du Fort, G., Meaney, M. L., Saucier, J. F., Zelazo, P. R., & King, S. (2004). Stress during pregnancy affects general intellectual and language functioning in human toddlers. *Pediatric Research*, *56*(3), 400–410. https://doi.org/10.1203/01.PDR.0000136281.34035.44

41. Dancause, K. N., Laplante, D. P., Fraser, S., Brunet, A., Ciampi, A., Schmitz, N., & King, S. (2012). Prenatal exposure to a natural disaster increases risk for obesity in 5½-year-old children. *Pediatric Research*, *71*(1), 126–131. https://doi.org/10.1038/pr.2011.18

42. Cao-Lei, L., Massart, R., Suderman, M. J., Machnes, Z., Elgbeili, G., Laplante, D. P., Szyf, M., & King, S. (2014). DNA methylation signatures triggered by prenatal maternal stress exposure to a natural disaster: Project Ice Storm. *PLOS ONE*, *9*(9), Article e107653. https://doi.org/10.1371/journal.pone.0107653

43. Lebans, J. (2020, May 8). *What the ice storm can teach us about the prenatal impacts of pandemic stress*. CBC Radio. https://www.cbc.ca/

radio/quirks/may-9-covid-stress-and-pregnancy-a-black-hole-in-our-backyard-and-more-1.5561112/what-the-ice-storm-can-teach-us-about-the-prenatal-impacts-of-pandemic-stress-1.5561123

44. Yehuda, R., Daskalakis, N. P., Bierer, L. M., Bader, H. N., Klengel, T., Holsboer, F., & Binder, E. B. (2016). Holocaust exposure induced intergenerational effects on *FKBP5* methylation. *Biological Psychiatry*, *80*(5), 372–380. https://doi.org/10.1016/j.biopsych.2015.08.005

45. Danieli, Y., Norris, F. H., & Engdahl, B. (2017). A question of who, not if: Psychological disorders in Holocaust survivors' children. *Psychological Trauma: Theory, Research, Practice, and Policy*, *9*(Suppl. 1), 98–106. https://doi.org/10.1037/tra0000192

46. Piacentini, J., Langley, A., & Roblek, T. (2007). *Cognitive-behavioral treatment of childhood OCD: It's only a false alarm—Therapist guide*. Oxford University Press.

CHAPTER 2

1. Connelly, J., & Mosher, B. (Executive Producers). (1957–1963). *Leave it to Beaver* [TV series]. Revue Studios, MCA TV, Gomalco Productions.

2. Reitman, C., Fox, P., & Young, A. (Directors). (2017–present). *Workin' moms* [TV series]. Wolf & Rabbit Entertainment.

3. Nomaguchi, K., & Milkie, M. A. (2020). Parenthood and well-being: A decade in review. *Journal of Marriage and Family*, *82*(1), 198–223. https://doi.org/10.1111/jomf.12646

4. Nomaguchi, K., & Fettro, M. N. (2018). Cohort differences in mothers' perceptions of neighborhood quality, child well-being, and parental strain, 1976–2002. *Family Relations*, *67*(4), 449–466. https://doi.org/10.1111/fare.12327

5. LeMoyne, T., & Buchanan, T. (2011). Does "hovering" matter? Helicopter parenting and its effect on well-being. *Sociological Spectrum*, *31*(4), 399–418. https://doi.org/10.1080/02732173.2011.574038

6. Segrin, C., Woszidlo, A., Givertz, M., & Montgomery, N. (2013). Parent and child traits associated with overparenting. *Journal of Social and Clinical Psychology*, *32*(6), 569–595. https://doi.org/10.1521/jscp.2013.32.6.569

7. Lareau, A. (2011). *Unequal childhoods: Class, race, and family life.* University of California Press.

8. Dotti Sani, G. M., & Treas, J. (2016). Educational gradients in parents' child-care time across countries, 1965–2012. *Journal of Marriage and Family, 78*(4), 1083–1096. https://doi.org/10.1111/jomf.12305

9. Elliott, S., & Reid, M. (2019). Low-income Black mothers parenting adolescents in the mass incarceration era: The long reach of criminalization. *American Sociological Review, 84*(2), 197–219. https://doi.org/10.1177/0003122419833386

10. Villalobos, A. (2014). *Motherload: Making it all better in insecure times.* University of California Press.

11. Wall, G. (2018). "Love builds brains": Representations of attachment and children's brain development in parenting education material. *Sociology of Health & Illness, 40*(3), 395–409. https://doi.org/10.1111/1467-9566.12632

12. Lee, E., Bristow, J., Faircloth, C., & Macvarish, J. (2014). *Parenting culture studies.* Palgrave Macmillan.

13. Hays, S. (1996). *The cultural contradictions of motherhood.* Yale University Press.

14. McGinley, M. (2018). Can hovering hinder helping? Examining the joint effects of helicopter parenting and attachment on prosocial behaviors and empathy in emerging adults. *Journal of Genetic Psychology, 179*(2), 102–115. https://doi.org/10.1080/00221325.2018.1438985

15. Reed, K., Duncan, J. M., Lucier-Greer, M., Fixelle, C., & Ferraro, A. J. (2016). Helicopter parenting and emerging adult self-efficacy: Implications for mental and physical health. *Journal of Child and Family Studies, 25*, 3136–3149. https://doi.org/10.1007/s10826-016-0466-x

16. Rousseau, S., & Scharf, M. (2015). "I will guide you": The indirect link between overparenting and young adults' adjustment. *Psychiatry Research, 228*(3), 826–834. https://doi.org/10.1016/j.psychres.2015.05.016

17. Borelli, J. L., Margolin, G., & Rasmussen, H. F. (2015). Parental overcontrol as a mechanism explaining the longitudinal association between parent and child anxiety. *Journal of Child and Family Studies, 24*(6), 1559–1574. https://doi.org/10.1007/s10826-014-9960-1

18. Borelli, J. L., Burkhart, M., Rasmussen, H. F., Smiley, P. A., & Hellemann, G. (2018). Children's and mothers' cardiovascular reactivity

to a standardized laboratory stressor: Unique relations with maternal anxiety and overcontrol. *Emotion, 18*(3), 369–385. https://doi.org/10.1037/emo0000320

19. Gunderson, J., & Barrett, A. E. (2017). Emotional cost of emotional support? The association between intensive mothering and psychological well-being in midlife. *Journal of Family Issues, 38*(7), 992–1009. https://doi.org/10.1177/0192513X15579502

20. Rizzo, K. M., Schiffrin, H. H., & Liss, M. (2013). Insight into the parenthood paradox: Mental health outcomes of intensive mothering. *Journal of Child and Family Studies, 22*(5), 614–620. https://doi.org/10.1007/s10826-012-9615-z

21. Nelson, M. K. (2010). *Parenting out of control: Anxious parents in uncertain times.* New York University Press.

22. Milkie, M. A., Nomaguchi, K., & Schieman, S. (2019). Time deficits with children: The link to parents' mental and physical health. *Society and Mental Health, 9*(3), 277–295. https://doi.org/10.1177/2156869318767488

23. Offer, S. (2014). Time with children and employed parents' emotional well-being. *Social Science Research, 47,* 192–203. https://doi.org/10.1016/j.ssresearch.2014.05.003

24. Kotila, L. E., & Kamp Dush, C. M. (2013). Involvement with children and low-income fathers' psychological well-being. *Fathering, 11*(3), 306–326.

25. Milkie, M. A., & Warner, C. H. (2014). Status safeguarding: Mothering work as safety net. In L. Ennis (Ed.), *Intensive mothering: The cultural contradictions of modern motherhood* (pp. 66–85). Demeter.

26. Connelly, R., & Kimmel, J. (2015). If you're happy and you know it: How do mothers and fathers in the US really feel about caring for their children? *Feminist Economics, 21*(1), 1–34. https://doi.org/10.1080/13545701.2014.970210

27. Alon, T., Doepke, M., Olmstead-Rumsey, J., & Tertilt, M. (2020). *This time it's different: The role of women's employment in a pandemic recession.* National Bureau of Economic Research. http://www.nber.org/papers/w27660

28. Liu, N., Zhang, F., Wei, C., Jia, Y., Shang, Z., Sun, L., Wu, L., Sun, Z., Zhou, Y., Wang, Y, & Liu, W. (2020). Prevalence and predictors of PTSS during COVID-19 outbreak in China hardest-hit areas: Gender

differences matter. *Psychiatry Research*, *287*, Article 112921. https://doi.org/10.1016/j.psychres.2020.112921

29. Greenhaus, J. H., & Beutell, N. J. (1985). Sources of conflict between work and family roles. *Academy of Management Review*, *10*(1), 76–88. https://doi.org/10.5465/amr.1985.4277352

30. Aycan, Z., & Eskin, M. (2005). Relative contributions of childcare, spousal support, and organizational support in reducing work–family conflict for men and women: The case of Turkey. *Sex Roles*, *53*(7–8), 453–471. https://doi.org/10.1007/s11199-005-7134-8

31. Borelli, J. L., Nelson-Coffey, K., River, L. M., Birken, S. A., & Moss-Racusin, C. (2017). Bringing work home: Gender differences in work-family guilt among parents of toddlers. *Journal of Child & Family Studies*, *26*(6), 1734–1745. https://doi.org/10.1007/s10826-017-0693-9

32. Frone, M. R., Russell, M., & Cooper, M. L. (1997). Relation of work–family conflict to health outcomes: A four-year longitudinal study of employed parents. *Journal of Occupational and Organizational Psychology*, *70*(4), 325–335. https://doi.org/10.1111/j.2044-8325.1997.tb00652.x

33. Geurts, S. A., Kompier, M. A., Roxburgh, S., & Houtman, I. L. (2003). Does work–home interference mediate the relationship between workload and well-being? *Journal of Vocational Behavior*, *63*(3), 532–559. https://doi.org/10.1016/S0001-8791(02)00025-8

34. Livingston, B. A., & Judge, T. A. (2008). Emotional responses to work–family conflict: An examination of gender role orientation among working men and women. *Journal of Applied Psychology*, *93*(1), 207–216. https://doi.org/10.1037/0021-9010.93.1.207

35. Shaw, E., & Burns, A. (1993). Guilt and the working parent. *Australian Journal of Marriage and Family*, *14*(1), 30–43. https://doi.org/10.1080/1034652X.1993.11004456

36. Ernst Kossek, E., & Ozeki, C. (1998). Work–family conflict, policies, and the job–life satisfaction relationship: A review and directions for organizational behavior–human resources research. *Journal of Applied Psychology*, *83*(2), 139–149. https://doi.org/10.1037/0021-9010.83.2.139

37. Borelli, J. L., Nelson, S. K., River, L. M., Birken, S. A., & Moss-Racusin, C. (2017). Gender differences in work–family guilt in parents

of young children. *Sex Roles, 76*(5–6), 356–368. https://doi.org/10.1007/s11199-016-0579-0

38. Mickelson, K., Chong, A., & Don, B. P. (2013). "To thine own self be true": Impact of gender role and attitude mismatch on new mothers' mental health. In J. Marich (Ed.), *The psychology of women: Diverse perspectives from the modern world* (pp. 1–16). Nova Science Publishers.

39. Aber, J. L., Jones, S., & Cohen, J. (2000). The impact of poverty on the mental health and development of very young children. In C. Zeanah (Ed.), *Handbook of infant mental health* (pp. 113–128). Guilford Press.

40. Cassells, R. C., & Evans, G. W. (2017). Ethnic variation in poverty and parenting stress. In K. Deater-Deckard & R. Panneton (Eds.), *Parental stress and early child development: Adaptive and maladaptive outcomes* (pp. 15–45). Springer International Publishing.

41. McLoyd, V. C. (1998). Socioeconomic disadvantage and child development. *American Psychologist, 53*(2), 185–204. https://doi.org/10.1037/0003-066X.53.2.185

42. Nam, Y., Wikoff, N., & Sherraden, M. (2015). Racial and ethnic differences in parenting stress: Evidence from a statewide sample of new mothers. *Journal of Child and Family Studies, 24*(2), 278–288. https://doi.org/10.1007/s10826-013-9833-z

43. Xu, Y., Wang, X., Ahn, H., & Harrington, D. (2018). Predictors of non-U.S. born mothers' parenting stress across early childhood in fragile families: A longitudinal analysis. *Children and Youth Services Review, 89*, 62–70. https://doi.org/10.1016/j.childyouth.2018.04.012

44. Rutherford, H. J., Wallace, N. S., Laurent, H. K., & Mayes, L. C. (2015). Emotion regulation in parenthood. *Developmental Review, 36*, 1–14. https://doi.org/10.1016/j.dr.2014.12.008

45. Sorce, J. F., Emde, R. N., Campos, J. J., & Klinnert, M. D. (1985). Maternal emotional signaling: Its effect on the visual cliff behavior of 1-year-olds. *Developmental Psychology, 21*(1), 195–200. https://doi.org/10.1037/0012-1649.21.1.195

46. Klinnert, M. D., Emde, R. N., Butterfield, P., & Campos, J. J. (1986). Social referencing: The infant's use of emotional signals from a friendly adult with mother present. *Developmental Psychology, 22*(4), 427–432. https://doi.org/10.1037/0012-1649.22.4.427

47. Boccia, M., & Campos, J. J. (1989). Maternal emotional signals, social referencing, and infants' reactions to strangers. *New Directions for*

Child and Adolescent Development, 1989(44), 25–49. https://doi.org/ 10.1002/cd.23219894404

48. Butler, E. A. (2011). Temporal interpersonal emotion systems: The "TIES" that form relationships. *Personality and Social Psychology Review, 15*(4), 367–393. https://doi.org/10.1177/1088868311411164

49. Butler, E. A., & Randall, A. K. (2013). Emotional coregulation in close relationships. *Emotion Review, 5*(2), 202–210. https://doi.org/ 10.1177/1754073912451630

50. Reed, R. G., Barnard, K., & Butler, E. A. (2015). Distinguishing emotional coregulation from codysregulation: An investigation of emotional dynamics and body weight in romantic couples. *Emotion, 15*(1), 45–60. https://doi.org/10.1037/a0038561

51. Borelli, J. L., Shai, D., Smiley, P. A., Boparai, S., Goldstein, A., Rasmussen, H. F., & Granger, D. A. (2019). Mother–child adrenocortical synchrony: Roles of maternal overcontrol and child developmental phase. *Developmental Psychobiology, 61*(8), 1120–1134. https://doi.org/10.1002/dev.21845

52. Hibel, L. C., Granger, D. A., Blair, C., & Finegood, E. D. (2015). Maternal–child adrenocortical attunement in early childhood: Continuity and change. *Developmental Psychobiology, 57*(1), 83–95. https:// doi.org/10.1002/dev.21266

53. LeMoult, J., Chen, M. C., Foland-Ross, L. C., Burley, H. W., & Gotlib, I. H. (2015). Concordance of mother–daughter diurnal cortisol production: Understanding the intergenerational transmission of risk for depression. *Biological Psychology, 108*, 98–104. https://doi.org/ 10.1016/j.biopsycho.2015.03.019

54. Papp, L. M., Pendry, P., & Adam, E. K. (2009). Mother–adolescent physiological synchrony in naturalistic settings: Within-family cortisol associations and moderators. *Journal of Family Psychology, 23*(6), 882–894. https://doi.org/10.1037/a0017147

55. Williams, S. R., Cash, E., Daup, M., Geronimi, E. M., Sephton, S. E., & Woodruff-Borden, J. (2013). Exploring patterns in cortisol synchrony among anxious and nonanxious mother and child dyads: A preliminary study. *Biological Psychology, 93*(2), 287–295. https://doi.org/ 10.1016/j.biopsycho.2013.02.015

56. Young, E. A., Vazquez, D., Jiang, H., & Pfeffer, C. R. (2006). Saliva cortisol and response to dexamethasone in children of depressed

parents. *Biological Psychiatry, 60*(8), 831–836. https://doi.org/10.1016/j.biopsych.2006.03.077

57. Anthony, L. G., Anthony, B. J., Glanville, D. N., Naiman, D. Q., Waanders, C., & Shaffer, S. (2005). The relationships between parenting stress, parenting behavior and preschoolers' social competence and behavior problems in the classroom. *Infant and Child Development, 14*(2), 133–154. https://doi.org/10.1002/icd.385

58. Deater-Deckard, K., & Scarr, S. (1996). Parenting stress among dual-earner mothers and fathers: Are there gender differences? *Journal of Family Psychology, 10*(1), 45–59. https://doi.org/10.1037/0893-3200.10.1.45

59. Reitman, D., Currier, R. O., Hupp, S. D. A., Rhode, P. C., Murphy, M. A., & O'Callaghan, P. M. (2001). Psychometric characteristics of the parenting scale in a head start population. *Journal of Clinical Child Psychology, 30*(4), 514–524. https://doi.org/10.1207/S15374424JCCP3004_08

60. Webster-Stratton, C. (1988). Mothers' and fathers' perceptions of child deviance: Roles of parent and child behaviors and parent adjustment. *Journal of Consulting and Clinical Psychology, 56*(6), 909–915. https://doi.org/10.1037/0022-006X.56.6.909

61. Crnic, K. A., Gaze, C., & Hoffman, C. (2005). Cumulative parenting stress across the preschool period: Relations to maternal parenting and child behaviour at age 5. *Infant and Child Development, 14*(2), 117–132. https://doi.org/10.1002/icd.384

62. Huth-Bocks, A. C., & Hughes, H. M. (2008). Parenting stress, parenting behavior, and children's adjustment in families experiencing intimate partner violence. *Journal of Family Violence, 23*, 243–251. https://doi.org/10.1007/s10896-007-9148-1

63. Doan, S. N., Venkatesh, S., Mendiola, I., Smiley, P., & Schmolze, D. (2021). *Stressed out and fed up: The effects of maternal stress on feeding behaviors* [Manuscript in preparation]. Department of Psychological Science, Claremont McKenna College.

64. Fonagy, P., & Target, M. (1997). Attachment and reflective function: Their role in self-organization. *Development and Psychopathology, 9*(4), 679–700. https://doi.org/10.1017/S0954579497001399

65. Slade, A. (2005). Parental reflective functioning: An introduction. *Attachment & Human Development, 7*(3), 269–281. https://doi.org/10.1080/14616730500245906

66. Fonagy, P., Gergely, G., Jurist, E. L., & Target, M. (2002). *Affect regulation, mentalization and the development of the self*. Other Press.

67. Mindell, J. A. (1997). *Sleeping through the night*. HarperCollins Publishers.

68. Bögels, S. M., Hoogstad, B., van Dun, L., de Schutter, S., & Restifo, K. (2008). Mindfulness training for adolescents with externalizing disorders, and their parents. *Behavioural and Cognitive Psychotherapy, 36*(2), 193–209. https://doi.org/10.1017/S1352465808004190

69. Bögels, S. M., Lehtonen, A., & Restifo, K. (2010). Mindful parenting in mental health care. *Mindfulness, 1*(2), 107–120. https://doi.org/10.1007/s12671-010-0014-5

70. Duncan, L. G., Coatsworth, J. D., & Greenberg, M. T. (2009). A model of mindful parenting: Implications for parent–child relationships and prevention research. *Clinical Child and Family Psychology Review, 12*(3), 255–270. https://doi.org/10.1007/s10567-009-0046-3

71. Bögels, S., & Restifo, K. (2014). *Mindful parenting: A guide for mental health practitioners*. Springer. https://doi.org/10.1007/978-1-4614-7406-7

72. Beer, M., Ward, L., & Moar, K. (2013). The relationship between mindful parenting and distress in parents of children with an autism spectrum disorder. *Mindfulness, 4*(2), 102–112. https://doi.org/10.1007/s12671-012-0192-4

73. Duncan, L. G., Coatsworth, J. D., Gayles, J. G., Geier, M. H., & Greenberg, M. T. (2015). Can mindful parenting be observed? Relations between observational ratings of mother–youth interactions and mothers' self-report of mindful parenting. *Journal of Family Psychology, 29*(2), 276–282. https://doi.org/10.1037/a0038857

74. Laurent, H. K., Duncan, L. G., Lightcap, A., & Khan, F. (2017). Mindful parenting predicts mothers' and infants' hypothalamic–pituitary–adrenal activity during a dyadic stressor. *Developmental Psychopathology, 53*(2), 417–424. https://doi.org/10.1037/dev0000258

75. Lippold, M. A., Duncan, L. G., Coatsworth, J. D., Nix, R. L., & Greenberg, M. T. (2015). Understanding how mindful parenting may be linked to mother–adolescent communication. *Journal of Youth and Adolescence, 44*(9), 1663–1673. https://doi.org/10.1007/s10964-015-0325-x

76. Parent, J., Garai, E., Forehand, R., Roland, E., Potts, J., Haker, K., Champion, J., & Compas, B. E. (2010). Parent mindfulness and child

outcome: The roles of parent depressive symptoms and parenting. *Mindfulness, 1*(4), 254–264. https://doi.org/10.1007/s12671-010-0034-1

77. Coatsworth, J. D., Duncan, L. G., Greenberg, M. T., & Nix, R. L. (2010). Changing parents' mindfulness, child management skills and relation-ship quality with their youth: Results from a randomized pilot intervention trial. *Journal of Child and Family Studies, 19*(2), 203–217. https://doi.org/10.1007/s10826-009-9304-8

78. Perez-Blasco, J., Viguer, P., & Rodrigo, M. F. (2013). Effects of a mindfulness-based intervention on psychological distress, well-being, and maternal self-efficacy in breast-feeding mothers: Results of a pilot study. *Archives of Women's Mental Health, 16*(3), 227–236. https://doi.org/10.1007/s00737-013-0337-z

79. Bögels, S. M., Hellemans, J., van Deursen, S., Römer, M., & van der Meulen, R. (2014). Mindful parenting in mental health care: Effects on parental and child psychopathology, parental stress, parenting, coparenting, and marital functioning. *Mindfulness, 5*(5), 1–16. https://doi.org/10.1007/s12671-013-0209-7

80. McDaniel, B. T. (2015). "Technoference": Everyday intrusions and interruptions of technology in couple and family relationships. In C. J. Bruess (Ed.), *Family communication in the age of digital and social media* (pp. 228–244). Peter Lang Publishing.

CHAPTER 3

1. Rowling, J. K. (1998). *Harry Potter and the sorcerer's stone*. A. A. Levine Books.

2. Tomasello, M. (2014). The ultra-social animal. *European Journal of Social Psychology, 44*(3), 187–194. https://doi.org/10.1002/ejsp.2015

3. Coan, J. A., & Sbarra, D. A. (2015). Social baseline theory: The social regulation of risk and effort. *Current Opinion in Psychology, 1*, 87–91. https://doi.org/10.1016/j.copsyc.2014.12.021

4. Bowlby, J. (1973). *Attachment and loss: Vol. 2. Separation, anxiety and anger*. The Hogarth Press and the Institute of Psycho-Analysis.

5. *Bucharest Early Intervention Project*. (n.d.). Bucharest Early Intervention Project [Home page]. http://www.bucharestearlyintervention project.org/

6. St. Petersburg–USA Orphanage Research Team. (2008). The effects of early social-emotional and relationship experience on the development of young orphanage children. *Monographs of the Society for Research in Child Development, 73*(3), vii–295. https://doi.org/10.1111/j.1540-5834.2008.00483.x

7. Fromm, E. (2008). *The art of loving* (Centennial ed., p. 51). The Continuum International Publishing Group. (Original work published 1956)

8. Zimmerman, E. (2020, June 18). What makes some people more resilient than others. *The New York Times.* https://www.nytimes.com/2020/06/18/health/resilience-relationships-trauma.html

9. Hostinar, C. E., & Gunnar, M. R. (2015). Social support can buffer against stress and shape brain activity. *AJOB Neuroscience, 6*(3), 34–42. https://doi.org/10.1080/21507740.2015.1047054

10. Taylor, S. E. (2011). *Social support: A review.* Oxford University Press. https://doi.org/10.1093/oxfordhb/9780195342819.013.0009

11. Uchino, B. N., Cacioppo, J. T., & Kiecolt-Glaser, J. K. (1996). The relationship between social support and physiological processes: A review with emphasis on underlying mechanisms and implications for health. *Psychological Bulletin, 119*(3), 488–531. https://doi.org/10.1037/0033-2909.119.3.488

12. Ozbay, F., Fitterling, H., Charney, D., & Southwick, S. (2008). Social support and resilience to stress across the life span: A neurobiologic framework. *Current Psychiatry Reports, 10*(4), 304–310. https://doi.org/10.1007/s11920-008-0049-7

13. Ozbay, F., Johnson, D. C., Dimoulas, E., Morgan, C. A., Charney, D., & Southwick, S. (2007). Social support and resilience to stress: From neurobiology to clinical practice. *Psychiatry, 4*(5), 35–40.

14. Barger, S. D., & Cribbet, M. R. (2016). Social support sources matter: Increased cellular aging among adults with unsupportive spouses. *Biological Psychology, 115*, 43–49. https://doi.org/10.1016/j.biopsycho.2016.01.003

15. Needham, B. L., Rehkopf, D., Adler, N., Gregorich, S., Lin, J., Blackburn, E. H., & Epel, E. S. (2015). Leukocyte telomere length and mortality in the National Health and Nutrition Examination Survey, 1999–2002. *Epidemiology, 26*(4), 528–535. https://doi.org/10.1097/EDE.0000000000000299

16. Brendtro, L. K. (2010). The vision of Urie Bronfenbrenner: Adults who are crazy about kids. *Reclaiming Children and Youth, 15*(3), 162–166.

17. Werner, E. E. (2013). What can we learn about resilience from large-scale longitudinal studies? In S. Goldstein & R. Brooks (Eds.), *Handbook of resilience in children* (pp. 87–102). Springer. https://doi.org/10.1007/978-1-4614-3661-4_6

18. Serbin, L., & Karp, J. (2003). Intergenerational studies of parenting and the transfer of risk from parent to child. *Current Directions in Psychological Science, 12*(4), 138–142. https://doi.org/10.1111/1467-8721.01249

19. Masten, A. S. (2001). Ordinary magic: Resilience processes in development. *American Psychologist, 56*(3), 227–238. https://doi.org/10.1037/0003-066X.56.3.227

20. Doan, S. N., & Evans, G. W. (2011). Maternal responsiveness moderates the relationship between allostatic load and working memory. *Development and Psychopathology, 23*(3), 873–880. https://doi.org/10.1017/S0954579411000368

21. Chen, E., Miller, G. E., Kobor, M. S., & Cole, S. W. (2011). Maternal warmth buffers the effects of low early-life socioeconomic status on pro-inflammatory signaling in adulthood. *Molecular Psychiatry, 16*(7), 729–737. https://doi.org/10.1038/mp.2010.53

22. Conradt, E., Hawes, K., Guerin, D., Armstrong, D. A., Marsit, C. J., Tronick, E., & Lester, B. M. (2016). The contributions of maternal sensitivity and maternal depressive symptoms to epigenetic processes and neuroendocrine functioning. *Child Development, 87*(1), 73–85. https://doi.org/10.1111/cdev.12483

23. Suomi, S. J. (2011). Risk, resilience, and gene-environment interplay in primates. *Journal of the Canadian Academy of Child and Adolescent Psychiatry, 20*(4), 289–297.

24. Rosenberg, M., & McCullough, B. C. (1981). Mattering: Inferred significance and mental health among adolescents. *Research in Community & Mental Health, 2,* 163–182.

25. Fonagy, P., Luyten, P., & Allison, E. (2015). Epistemic petrification and the restoration of epistemic trust: A new conceptualization of borderline personality disorder and its psychosocial treatment. *Journal of Personality Disorders, 29*(5), 575–609. https://doi.org/10.1521/pedi.2015.29.5.575

26. Thoits, P. A. (2011). Mechanisms linking social ties and support to physical and mental health. *Journal of Health and Social Behavior, 52*(2), 145–161. https://doi.org/10.1177/0022146510395592

27. Borelli, J. L., Ensink, K., Gillespie, M. L., Falasiri, E., Bernazzani, O., Fonagy, P., & Berthelot, N. (2021). Mothers' self-focused reflective functioning interacts with childhood experiences of rejection to predict current romantic relationship quality and parenting behavior. *Family Process*, *60*(3), 920–934. https://doi.org/10.1111/famp.12603

28. *Show them love without limits: Native American fathers share stories.* (n.d.). Native Hope. https://blog.nativehope.org/show-them-love-without-limits

29. Lereya, S. T., Samara, M., & Wolke, D. (2013). Parenting behavior and the risk of becoming a victim and a bully/victim: A meta-analysis study. *Child Abuse & Neglect*, *37*(12), 1091–1108. https://doi.org/10.1016/j.chiabu.2013.03.001

30. Lipscomb, S. T., Leve, L. D., Harold, G. T., Neiderhiser, J. M., Shaw, D. S., Ge, X., & Reiss, D. (2011). Trajectories of parenting and child negative emotionality during infancy and toddlerhood: A longitudinal analysis. *Child Development*, *82*(5), 1661–1675. https://doi.org/10.1111/j.1467-8624.2011.01639.x

31. Manczak, E. M., DeLongis, A., & Chen, E. (2016). Does empathy have a cost? Diverging psychological and physiological effects within families. *Health Psychology*, *35*(3), 211–218. https://doi.org/10.1037/hea0000281

CHAPTER 4

1. Lau, C., Rogers, J. M., Desai, M., & Ross, M. G. (2011). Fetal programming of adult disease: Implications for prenatal care. *Obstetrics and Gynecology*, *117*(4), 978–985. https://doi.org/10.1097/AOG.0b013e318212140e

2. Pesonen, A.-K., Räikkönen, K., Kajantie, E., Heinonen, K., Strandberg, T. E., & Järvenpää, A.-L. (2006). Fetal programming of temperamental negative affectivity among children born healthy at term. *Developmental Psychobiology*, *48*(8), 633–643. https://doi.org/10.1002/dev.20153

3. Benavides-Varela, S., Hochmann, J.-R., Macagno, F., Nespor, M., & Mehler, J. (2012). Newborn's brain activity signals the origin of word memories. *Proceedings of the National Academy of Sciences*, *109*(44), 17908–17913. https://doi.org/10.1073/pnas.1205413109

4. Webb, A. R., Heller, H. T., Benson, C. B., & Lahav, A. (2015). Mother's voice and heartbeat sounds elicit auditory plasticity in the human brain before full gestation. *Proceedings of the National Academy of Sciences, 112*(10), 3152–3157. https://doi.org/10.1073/pnas.1414924112

5. Rivera, M., Cealie, M. K., Hauber, M. E., Kleindorfer, S., & Liu, W. C. (2019). Neural activation in response to conspecific songs in zebra finch (*Taeniopygia guttata*) embryos and nestlings. *NeuroReport, 30*(3), 217–221. https://doi.org/10.1097/WNR.0000000000001187

6. Katsis, A. C., Davies, M. H., Buchanan, K. L., Kleindorfer, S., Hauber M. E., & Mariette, M. M. (2018). Prenatal exposure to incubation calls affects song learning in the zebra finch. *Scientific Reports, 8*, Article 15232. https://doi.org/10.1038/s41598-018-33301-5

7. Mampe, B., Friederici, A. D., Christophe, A., & Wermke, K. (2009). Newborns' cry melody is shaped by their native language. *Current Biology, 19*(23), 1994–1997. https://doi.org/10.1016/j.cub.2009.09.064

8. DeCasper, A. J., & Spence, M. J. (1991). Auditorily mediated behavior during the perinatal period: A cognitive view. In M. J. S. Weiss & P. R. Zelazo (Eds.), *Newborn attention: Biological constraints and the influence of experience* (pp. 142–176). Ablex Publishing.

9. Beauchemin, M., González-Frankenberger, B., Tremblay, J., Vannasing, P., Martínez-Montes, E., Belin, P., Béland, R., Francoeur, D., Carceller, A.-M., Wallois, F., & Lassonde, M. (2011). Mother and stranger: An electrophysiological study of voice processing in newborns. *Cerebral Cortex, 21*(8), 1705–1711. https://doi.org/10.1093/cercor/bhq242

10. Rauscher, F. H., Shaw, G. L., & Ky, K. N. (1993). Music and spatial task performance. *Nature, 365*, Article 611. https://doi.org/10.1038/365611a0

11. Chabris, C. F. (1999). Prelude or requiem for the "Mozart effect"? *Nature, 400*(6747), 826–828. https://doi.org/10.1038/23608

12. Pietschnig, J., Voracek, M., & Formann, A. K. (2010). Mozart effect–Shmozart effect: A meta-analysis. *Intelligence, 38*(3), 314–323. https://doi.org/10.1016/j.intell.2010.03.001

13. Nantais, K. M., & Schellenberg, E. G. (1999). The Mozart effect: An artifact of preference. *Psychological Science, 10*(4), 370–373. https://doi.org/10.1111/1467-9280.00170

14. Schellenberg, E. G., & Hallam, S. (2005). Music listening and cognitive abilities in 10- and 11-year-olds: The blur effect. *Annals of the*

New York Academy of Sciences, 1060(1), 202–209. https://doi.org/
10.1196/annals.1360.013

15. Stein, Z., Susser, M., Saenger, G., & Marolla, F. (1975). *Famine and human development: The Dutch Hunger Winter of 1944–1945*. Oxford University Press.

16. Garner, L. (1991, May 26). Lesley Garner meets the legendary actress as she prepares for this week's UNICEF gala performance. *The Sunday Telegraph*. https://web.archive.org/web/20050117094236/http:/ahepburn.com/article6.html

17. Kyle, U. G., & Pichard, C. (2006). The Dutch famine of 1944–1945: A pathophysiological model of long-term consequences of wasting disease. *Current Opinion in Clinical Nutrition and Metabolic Care, 9*(4), 388–394. https://doi.org/10.1097/01.mco.0000232898.74415.42

18. Ekamper, P., van Poppel, F., Stein, A. D., & Lumey, L. H. (2014). Independent and additive association of prenatal famine exposure and intermediary life conditions with adult mortality between age 18–63 years. *Social Science & Medicine, 119*, 232–239. https://doi.org/10.1016/j.socscimed.2013.10.027

19. St. Clair, D., Xu, M., Wang, P., Yu, Y., Fang, Y., Zhang, F., Zheng, X., Gu, N., Feng, G., Sham, P., & He, L. (2005). Rates of adult schizophrenia following prenatal exposure to the Chinese famine of 1959–1961. *JAMA, 294*(5), 557–562. https://doi.org/10.1001/jama.294.5.557

20. Tobi, E. W., Slieker, R. C., Luijk, R., Dekkers, K. F., Stein, A. D., Xu, K. M., Biobank-Based Integrative Omics Studies Consortium, Slagboom, P. E., Van Zwet, E. W., Lumey, L. H., & Heijmans, B. T. (2018). DNA methylation as a mediator of the association between prenatal adversity and risk factors for metabolic disease in adulthood. *Science. Advances, 4*(1), Article eaao4364. https://doi.org/10.1126/sciadv.aao4364

21. Painter, R. C., Osmond, C., Gluckman, P., Hanson, M., Phillips, D. I., & Roseboom, T. J. (2008). Transgenerational effects of prenatal exposure to the Dutch Famine on neonatal adiposity and health in later life. *BJOG, 115*(10), 1243–1249. https://doi.org/10.1111/j.1471-0528.2008.01822.x

22. Glynn, L. M., Wadhwa, P. D., Dunkel-Schetter, C., Chicz-Demet, A., & Sandman, C. A. (2001). When stress happens matters: Effects of earthquake timing on stress responsivity in pregnancy. *American*

Journal of Obstetrics and Gynecology, 184(4), 637–642. https://doi.org/
10.1067/mob.2001.111066

23. Mennella, J. A., Johnson, A., & Beauchamp, G. K. (1995). Garlic ingestion by pregnant women alters the odor of amniotic fluid. *Chemical Senses, 20*(2), 207–209. https://doi.org/10.1093/chemse/20.2.207

24. Mennella, J. A., Jagnow, C. P., & Beauchamp, G. K. (2001). Prenatal and postnatal flavor learning by human infants. *Pediatrics, 107*(6), Article E88. https://doi.org/10.1542/peds.107.6.e88

25. Gugusheff, J. R., Ong, Z. Y., & Muhlhausler, B. S. (2013). A maternal "junk-food" diet reduces sensitivity to the opioid antagonist naloxone in offspring postweaning. *FASEB Journal, 27*(3), 1275–1284. https://doi.org/10.1096/fj.12-217653

26. Spitzka, E. C. (1888). Maternal impressions, birth-marks, etc. *Medical Classics, 2*(2), 35.

27. Beydoun, H., & Saftlas, A. F. (2008). Physical and mental health outcomes of prenatal maternal stress in human and animal studies: A review of recent evidence. *Paediatric and Perinatal Epidemiology, 22*(5), 438–466. https://doi.org/10.1111/j.1365-3016.2008.00951.x

28. Gartstein, M. A., & Rothbart, M. K. (2003). Studying infant temperament via the Revised Infant Behavior Questionnaire. *Infant Behavior Development, 26*(1), 64–86. https://doi.org/10.1016/S0163-6383(02)00169-8

29. Eckstein, D., Aycock, K. J., Sperber, M. A., McDonald, J., Wiesner, V., III, Watts, R. E., & Ginsburg, P. (2010). A review of 200 birth-order studies: Lifestyle characteristics. *Journal of Individual Psychology, 66*(4), 408–434.

30. Davis, E. P., Snidman, N., Wadhwa, P. D., Glynn, L. M., Schetter, C. D., & Sandman, C. A. (2004). Prenatal maternal anxiety and depression predict negative behavioral reactivity in infancy. *Infancy, 6*(3), 319–331. https://doi.org/10.1207/s15327078in0603_1

31. O'Connor, T. G., Caprariello, P., Blackmore, E. R., Gregory, A. M., Glover, V., Fleming, P., & the ALSPAC Study Team. (2007). Prenatal mood disturbance predicts sleep problems in infancy and toddlerhood. *Early Human Development, 83*(7), 451–458. https://doi.org/10.1016/j.earlhumdev.2006.08.006

32. O'Connor, T. G., Heron, J., Golding, J., Glover, V., & the ALSPAC Study Team. (2003). Maternal antenatal anxiety and behavioural/

emotional problems in children: A test of a programming hypothesis. *Journal of Child Psychology and Psychiatry, 44*(7), 1025–1036. https://doi.org/10.1111/1469-7610.00187

33. Martin, R. P., Noyes, J., Wisenbaker, J., & Huttunen, M. O. (1999). Prediction of early childhood negative emotionality and inhibition from maternal distress during pregnancy. *Merrill-Palmer Quarterly, 45*(3), 370–391.

34. Rice, F., Harold, G. T., Boivin, J., van den Bree, M., Hay, D. F., & Thapar, A. (2010). The links between prenatal stress and offspring development and psychopathology: Disentangling environmental and inherited influences. *Psychological Medicine, 40*(2), 335–345. https://doi.org/10.1017/S0033291709005911

35. Glover, V. (2011). Annual research review: Prenatal stress and the origins of psychopathology—An evolutionary perspective. *Journal of Child Psychology and Psychiatry, 52*(4), 356–367. https://doi.org/10.1111/j.1469-7610.2011.02371.x

36. Bergman, K., Sarkar, P., Glover, V., & O'Connor, T. G. (2008). Quality of child–parent attachment moderates the impact of antenatal stress on child fearfulness. *Journal of Child Psychology and Psychiatry, 49*(10), 1089–1098. https://doi.org/10.1111/j.1469-7610.2008.01987.x

37. Endara, S. M., Ryan, M. A., Sevick, C. J., Conlin, A. M. S., Macera, C. A., & Smith, T. C. (2009). Does acute maternal stress in pregnancy affect infant health outcomes? Examination of a large cohort of infants born after the terrorist attacks of September 11, 2001. *BMC Public Health, 9*, Article 252. https://doi.org/10.1186/1471-2458-9-252

38. Catalano, R., & Hartig, T. (2001). Communal bereavement and the incidence of very low birthweight in Sweden. *Journal of Health and Social Behavior, 42*(4), 333–341. https://doi.org/10.2307/3090182

39. Brand, S. R., Engel, S. M., Canfield, R. L., & Yehuda, R. (2006). The effect of maternal PTSD following in utero trauma exposure on behavior and temperament in the 9-month-old infant. *Annals of the New York Academy of Sciences, 1071*(1), 454–458. https://doi.org/10.1196/annals.1364.041

40. Lauderdale, D. S. (2006). Birth outcomes for Arabic-named women in California before and after September 11. *Demography, 43*(1), 185–201. https://doi.org/10.1353/dem.2006.0008

41. Sandman, C. A., Glynn, L., Schetter, C. D., Wadhwa, P., Garite, T., Chicz-DeMet, A., & Hobel, C. (2006). Elevated maternal cortisol early

in pregnancy predicts third trimester levels of placental corticotropin releasing hormone (CRH): Priming the placental clock. *Peptides, 27*(6), 1457–1463. https://doi.org/10.1016/j.peptides.2005.10.002

42. Davis, E. P., & Sandman, C. A. (2010). The timing of prenatal exposure to maternal cortisol and psychosocial stress is associated with human infant cognitive development. *Child development, 81*(1), 131–148. https://doi.org/10.1111/j.1467-8624.2009.01385.x

43. Davis, E. P., Glynn, L. M., Schetter, C. D., Hobel, C., Chicz-Demet, A., & Sandman, C. A. (2007). Prenatal exposure to maternal depression and cortisol influences infant temperament. *Journal of the American Academy of Child and Adolescent Psychiatry, 46*(6), 737–746. https://doi.org/10.1097/chi.0b013e318047b775

44. Baibazarova, E., van de Beek, C., Cohen-Kettenis, P. T., Buitelaar, J., Shelton, K. H., & van Goozen, S. H. (2013). Influence of prenatal maternal stress, maternal plasma cortisol and cortisol in the amniotic fluid on birth outcomes and child temperament at 3 months. *Psychoneuroendocrinology, 38*(6), 907–915. https://doi.org/10.1016/j.psyneuen.2012.09.015

45. Raikkonen, K., Pesonen, A., Heinonen, K., Lahti, J., Komsi, N., Eriksson, J. G., Seckl, J. R., Järvenpää, A., & Strandberg, T. E. (2009). Maternal licorice consumption and detrimental cognitive and psychiatric outcomes in children. *American Journal of Epidemiology, 170*(9), 1137–1146. https://doi.org/10.1093/aje/kwp272

46. Räikkönen, K., Martikainen, S., Pesonen, A. K., Lahti, J., Heinonen, K., Pyhälä, R., Lahti, M., Tuovinen, S., Wehkalampi, K., Sammallahti, S., Kuula, L., Andersson, S., Eriksson, J. G., Ortega-Alonso, A., Reynolds, R. M., Strandberg, T. E., Seckl, J. R., & Kajantie, E. (2017). Maternal licorice consumption during pregnancy and pubertal, cognitive, and psychiatric outcomes in children. *American Journal of Epidemiology, 185*(5), 317–328. https://doi.org/10.1093/aje/kww172

47. Matthews, K. A., & Rodin, J. (1992). Pregnancy alters blood pressure responses to psychological and physical challenge. *Psychophysiology, 29*(2), 232–240. https://doi.org/10.1111/j.1469-8986.1992.tb01691.x

48. Costa, D. L., Yetter, N., & DeSomer, H. (2018). Intergenerational transmission of paternal trauma among US Civil War ex-POWs. *Proceedings of the National Academy of Sciences, 115*(44), 11215–11220. https://doi.org/10.1073/pnas.1803630115

49. Zalbahar, N., Najman, J., McIntrye, H. D., & Mamun, A. (2016). Parental pre-pregnancy BMI influences on offspring BMI and waist circumference at 21 years. *Australian and New Zealand Journal of Public Health, 40*(6), 572–578. https://doi.org/10.1111/1753-6405.12574

50. McPherson, N. O., Lane, M., Sandeman, L., Owens, J. A., & Fullston, T. (2017). An exercise only intervention in obese fathers restores glucose and insulin regulation in conjunction with the rescue of pancreatic islet cell morphology and microRNA expression in male offspring. *Nutrients, 9*(2), Article 122. https://doi.org/10.3390/nu9020122

51. Drake, A. J., & Walker, B. R. (2004). The intergenerational effects of fetal programming: Non-genomic mechanisms for the inheritance of low birth weight and cardiovascular risk. *Journal of Endocrinology, 180*(1), 1–16. https://doi.org/10.1677/joe.0.1800001

52. DiPietro, J. A., Novak, M. F., Costigan, K. A., Atella, L. D., & Reusing, S. P. (2006). Maternal psychological distress during pregnancy in relation to child development at age two. *Child Development, 77*(3), 573–587. https://doi.org/10.1111/j.1467-8624.2006.00891.x

53. DiPietro, J. A., Kivlighan, K. T., Costigan, K. A., Rubin, S. E., Shiffler, D. E., Henderson, J. L., & Pillion, J. P. (2010). Prenatal antecedents of newborn neurological maturation. *Child Development, 81*(1), 115–130. https://doi.org/10.1111/j.1467-8624.2009.01384.x

54. Ellman, L. M., Schetter, C. D., Hobel, C. J., Chicz-Demet, A., Glynn, L. M., & Sandman, C. A. (2008). Timing of fetal exposure to stress hormones: Effects on newborn physical and neuromuscular maturation. *Developmental Psychobiology, 50*(3), 232–241. https://doi.org/10.1002/dev.20293

55. LeWinn, K. Z., Stroud, L. R., Molnar, B. E., Ware, J. H., Koenen, K. C., & Buka, S. L. (2009). Elevated maternal cortisol levels during pregnancy are associated with reduced childhood IQ. *International Journal of Epidemiology, 38*(6), 1700–1710. https://doi.org/10.1093/ije/dyp200

CHAPTER 5

1. Barker, D. J., Forsén, T., Uutela, A., Osmond, C., & Eriksson, J. G. (2001). Size at birth and resilience to effects of poor living conditions in adult life: Longitudinal study. *BMJ, 323*(7324), 1273–1276. https://doi.org/10.1136/bmj.323.7324.1273

2. Julian, M. M. (2013). Age at adoption from institutional care as a window into the lasting effects of early experiences. *Clinical Child and Family Psychology Review, 16*(2), 101–145. https://doi.org/10.1007/s10567-013-0130-6
3. Parsons, C. E., Young, K. S., Joensson, M., Brattico, E., Hyam, J. A., Stein, A., Green, A. L., Aziz, T. Z., & Kringelbach, M. L. (2014). Ready for action: A role for the human midbrain in responding to infant vocalizations. *Social Cognitive and Affective Neuroscience, 9*(7), 977–984. https://doi.org/10.1093/scan/nst076
4. Kim, P., Strathearn, L., & Swain, J. E. (2016). The maternal brain and its plasticity in humans. *Hormones and Behavior, 77*, 113–123. https://doi.org/10.1016/j.yhbeh.2015.08.001
5. Luo, L., Ma, X., Zheng, X., Zhao, W., Xu, L., Becker, B., & Kendrick, K. M. (2015). Neural systems and hormones mediating attraction to infant and child faces. *Frontiers in Psychology, 6*, Article 970. https://doi.org/10.3389/fpsyg.2015.00970
6. Johnson, M. H., Dziurawiec, S., Ellis, H., & Morton, J. (1991). Newborns' preferential tracking of face-like stimuli and its subsequent decline. *Cognition, 40*(1–2), 1–19. https://doi.org/10.1016/0010-0277(91)90045-6
7. Suomi, S. J. (1995). Touch and the immune system in monkeys. In T. Field (Ed.), *Touch in early development* (pp. 89–104). Lawrence Erlbaum Associates.
8. Schanberg, S. M., & Field, T. M. (1987). Sensory deprivation stress and supplemental stimulation in the rat pup and preterm human neonate. *Child Development, 58*(6), 1431–1447. https://doi.org/10.2307/1130683
9. Field, T. M., Schanberg, S. M., Scafidi, F., Bauer, C. R., Vega-Lahr, N., Garcia, R., Nystrom, J., & Kuhn, C. M. (1986). Tactile/kinesthetic stimulation effects on preterm neonates. *Pediatrics, 77*(5), 654–658.
10. Ludington-Hoe, S. M., Anderson, G. C., Swinth, J. Y., Thompson, C., & Hadeed, A. J. (2004). Randomized controlled trial of kangaroo care: Cardiorespiratory and thermal effects on healthy preterm infants. *Neonatal Network, 23*(3), 39–48. https://doi.org/10.1891/0730-0832.23.3.39
11. Ferber, S. G., Feldman, R., & Makhoul, I. R. (2008). The development of maternal touch across the first year of life. *Early Human*

Development, 84(6), 363–370. https://doi.org/10.1016/j.earlhumdev. 2007.09.019

12. Feldman, R. (2007). Parent–infant synchrony: Biological foundations and developmental outcomes. *Current Directions in Psychological Science, 16*(6), 340–345. https://doi.org/10.1111/j.1467-8721.2007. 00532.x

13. Delgadillo, D., Boparai, S., Pressman, S. D., Goldstein, A., Bureau, J.-F., Schmiedel, S., Backer, M., Broekman, B., Hian Tan, K., Chong, Y.-S., Chen, H., Zalta, A. K., Meaney, M. J., Rifkin-Graboi, A., Tsotsi, S., & Borelli, J. L. (2021). Maternal expressions of positive emotion for children predicts children's respiratory sinus arrhythmia surrounding stress. *Developmental Psychobiology, 63*(5), 1225–1240. https:// doi.org/10.1002/dev.22082

14. Legerstee, M., & Varghese, J. (2001). The role of maternal affect mirroring on social expectancies in three-month-old infants. *Child Development, 72*(5), 1301–1313. https://doi.org/10.1111/1467-8624. 00349

15. Tschacher, W., Rees, G. M., & Ramseyer, F. (2014). Nonverbal synchrony and affect in dyadic interactions. *Frontiers in Psychology, 5,* Article 1323. https://doi.org/10.3389/fpsyg.2014.01323

16. Doan, S. N., & Wang, Q. (2010). Maternal discussions of mental states and behaviors: Relations to emotion situation knowledge in European American and immigrant Chinese children. *Child Development, 81*(5), 1490–1503. https://doi.org/10.1111/j.1467-8624. 2010.01487.x

17. Ruffman, T., Slade, L., & Crowe, E. (2002). The relation between children's and mothers' mental state language and theory-of-mind understanding. *Child Development, 73*(3), 734–751. https://doi.org/ 10.1111/1467-8624.00435

18. Tronick, E. Z., Als, H., Adamson, L., Wise, S., & Brazelton, T. B. (1978). The infant's response to entrapment between contradictory messages in face-to-face interaction. *Journal of the American Academy of Child Psychiatry, 17*(1), 1–13. https://doi.org/10.1016/ S0002-7138(09)62273-1

19. Weinberg, M. K., & Tronick, E. Z. (1996). Infant affective reactions to the resumption of maternal interaction after the still-face. *Child Development, 67*(3), 905–914. https://doi.org/10.1111/j.1467-8624.1996. tb01772.x

20. Evans, G. W., & Wachs, T. D. (Eds.). (2010). *Chaos and its influence on children's development: An ecological perspective.* American Psychological Association. https://doi.org/10.1037/12057-000

21. Davis, E. P., Stout, S. A., Molet, J., Vegetabile, B., Glynn, L. M., Sandman, C. A., Heins, K., Stern, H., & Baram, T. Z. (2017). Exposure to unpredictable maternal sensory signals influences cognitive development across species. *Proceedings of the National Academy of Sciences, 114*(39), 10390–10395. https://doi.org/10.1073/pnas.1703444114

22. Noroña-Zhou, A. N., Morgan, A., Glynn, L. M., Sandman, C. A., Baram, T. Z., Stern, H. A., & Poggi Davis, E. (2020). Unpredictable maternal behavior is associated with a blunted infant cortisol response. *Developmental Psychobiology, 62*(6), 882–888. https://doi.org/10.1002/dev.21964

23. Davis, E. P., Korja, R., Karlsson L., Glynn, L. M., Sandman, C. A., Vegetabile, B., Kataja, E. L., Nolvi, S., Sinervä, E., Pelto, J., Karlsson, H., Stern, H. S., & Baram, T. Z. (2019). Across continents and demographics, unpredictable maternal signals are associated with children's cognitive function. *EBioMedicine, 46,* 256–263. https://doi.org/10.1016/j.ebiom.2019.07.025

24. Beebe, B., Jaffe, J., Markese, S., Buck, K., Chen, H., Cohen, P., Bahrick, L., Andrews, H., & Feldstein, S. (2010). The origins of 12-month attachment: A microanalysis of 4-month mother–infant interaction. *Attachment & Human Development, 12*(1–2), 3–141. https://doi.org/10.1080/14616730903338985

25. Acker, M. M., & O'Leary, S. G. (1996). Inconsistency of mothers' feedback and toddlers' misbehavior and negative affect. *Journal of Abnormal Child Psychology, 24*(6), 703–714. https://doi.org/10.1007/BF01664735

26. Sawin, D. B., & Parke, R. D. (1979). Inconsistent discipline of aggression in young boys. *Journal of Experimental Child Psychology, 28*(3), 525–538. https://doi.org/10.1016/0022-0965(79)90079-1

27. Kidd, C., Palmeri, H., & Aslin, R. N. (2013). Rational snacking: Young children's decision-making on the marshmallow task is moderated by beliefs about environmental reliability. *Cognition, 126*(1), 109–114. https://doi.org/10.1016/j.cognition.2012.08.004

28. Howland, M. A., Sandman, C. A., Davis, E. P., Stern, H. S., Phelan, M., Baram, T. Z., & Glynn, L. M. (2021). Prenatal maternal mood entropy is associated with child neurodevelopment. *Emotion, 21*(3), 489–498. https://doi.org/10.1037/emo0000726

29. Macfie, J. (2009). Development in children and adolescents whose mothers have borderline personality disorder. *Child Development Perspectives, 3*(1), 66–71. https://doi.org/10.1111/j.1750-8606.2008.00079.x

30. Crandell, L. E., Patrick, M. P., & Hobson, R. P. (2003). "Still-face" interactions between mothers with borderline personality disorder and their 2-month-old infants. *British Journal of Psychiatry, 183*(3), 239–247. https://doi.org/10.1192/bjp.183.3.239

31. Carlson, V., Cicchetti, D., Barnett, D., & Braunwald, K. (1989). Finding order in disorganization: Lessons from research on maltreated infants' attachments to their caregivers. In D. Cicchetti & V. Carlson (Eds.), *Child maltreatment: Theory and research on the causes and consequences* (pp. 494–528). Cambridge University Press.

32. Staples, A. D., Bates, J. E., & Petersen, I. T. (2015). Bedtime routines in early childhood: Prevalence, consistency, and associations with nighttime sleep. *Monographs of the Society for Research in Child Development, 80*(1), 141–159. https://doi.org/10.1111/mono.12149

33. Anderson, S. E., Sacker, A., Whitaker, R. C., & Kelly, Y. (2017). Self-regulation and household routines at age three and obesity at age eleven: Longitudinal analysis of the UK Millennium Cohort Study. *International Journal of Obesity, 41*(10), 1459–1466. https://doi.org/10.1038/ijo.2017.94

34. Speirs, K. E., Liechty, J. M., Wu, C. F., & Strong Kids Research Team. (2014). Sleep, but not other daily routines, mediates the association between maternal employment and BMI for preschool children. *Sleep Medicine, 15*(12), 1590–1593. https://doi.org/10.1016/j.sleep.2014.08.006

35. Holden, G. W., & Hawk, C. K. (2002). Meta-parenting in the journey of child rearing. In L. Kuczynski (Ed.), *Handbook of dynamics in parent–child relations* (pp. 189–210). SAGE Publications.

CHAPTER 6

1. Fonagy, P., Steele, M., Steele, H., Moran, G. S., & Higgitt, A. C. (1991). The capacity for understanding mental states: The reflective self in parent and child and its significance for security of attachment. *Infant Mental Health Journal, 12*(3), 201–218. https://doi.org/10.1002/1097-0355(199123)12:3<201::AID-IMHJ2280120307>3.0.CO;2-7

2. Slade, A. (2005). Parental reflective functioning: An introduction. *Attachment & Human Development, 7*(3), 269–281. https://doi.org/10.1080/14616730500245906

3. Batson, C. D. (2011). *Altruism in humans*. Oxford University Press.

4. Decety, J., & Meyer, M. (2008). From emotion resonance to empathic understanding: A social developmental neuroscience account. *Development and Psychopathology, 20*(4), 1053–1080. https://doi.org/10.1017/S0954579408000503

5. Eisenberg, N. (2000). Emotion, regulation, and moral development. *Annual Review of Psychology, 51*(1), 665–697. https://doi.org/10.1146/annurev.psych.51.1.665

6. Eisenberg, N. (2018). Empathy-related responding and its relations to positive development. In N. Roughley & T. Schramme (Eds.), *Forms of fellow feeling: Empathy, sympathy, concern and moral agency* (pp. 165–183). Cambridge University Press. https://doi.org/10.1017/9781316271698.007

7. Zeegers, M. A., Colonnesi, C., Stams, G. J. J., & Meins, E. (2017). Mind matters: A meta-analysis on parental mentalization and sensitivity as predictors of infant–parent attachment. *Psychological Bulletin, 143*(12), 1245–1272. https://doi.org/10.1037/bul0000114

8. Bowlby, J. (1973). *Attachment and loss: Vol. 2. Separation, anxiety, and anger*. The Hogarth Press and the Institute of Psycho-Analysis.

9. Bretherton, I. (1985). Attachment theory: Retrospect and prospect. *Monographs of the Society for Research in Child Development, 50*(1/2), 3–35. https://doi.org/10.2307/3333824

10. Mikulincer, M., & Shaver, P. (2005). Mental representations and attachment security: Theoretical foundation for a positive social psychology. In M. W. Baldwin (Ed.), *Interpersonal cognition* (pp. 233–266). Guilford Press.

11. Dix, T. (1992). Parenting on behalf of the child: Empathic goals in the regulation of responsive parenting. In I. E. Sigel, A. V. McGillicuddy-

DeLisi, & J. J. Goodnow (Eds.), *Parental belief systems: The psychological consequences for children* (pp. 319–346). Lawrence Erlbaum Associates.

12. Stern, J. A., Borelli, J. L., & Smiley, P. A. (2015). Assessing parental empathy: A role for empathy in child attachment. *Attachment & Human Development, 17*(1), 1–22. https://doi.org/10.1080/14616734.2014. 969749

13. Fonagy, P., & Allison, E. (2012). What is mentalization? The concept and its foundations in developmental research. In N. Midgley & I. Vrouva (Eds.), *Minding the child: Mentalization-based interventions with children, young people, and their families* (pp. 11–34). Routledge/ Taylor & Francis Group.

14. Suchman, N. E., DeCoste, C., Leigh, D., & Borelli, J. (2010). Reflective functioning in mothers with drug use disorders: Implications for dyadic interactions with infants and toddlers. *Attachment & Human Development, 12*(6), 567–585. https://doi.org/10.1080/14616734. 2010.501988

15. Aureli, T., & Presaghi, F. (2010). Developmental trajectories for mother–infant coregulation in the second year of life. *Infancy, 15*(6), 557–585. https://doi.org/10.1111/j.1532-7078.2010.00034.x

16. Mikulincer, M., Shaver, P. R., & Pereg, D. (2003). Attachment theory and affect regulation: The dynamics, development, and cognitive consequences of attachment-related strategies. *Motivation and Emotion, 27*(2), 77–102. https://doi.org/10.1023/A:1024515519160

17. Raffaelli, M., Crockett, L. J., & Shen, Y. L. (2005). Developmental stability and change in self-regulation from childhood to adolescence. *Journal of Genetic Psychology, 166*(1), 54–76. https://doi.org/ 10.3200/GNTP.166.1.54-76

18. Saarni, C. (1984). An observational study of children's attempts to monitor their expressive behavior. *Child Development, 55*(4), 1504–1513. https://doi.org/10.2307/1130020

19. Decety, J. (2015). The neural pathways, development and functions of empathy. *Current Opinion in Behavioral Sciences, 3*, 1–6. https:// doi.org/10.1016/j.cobeha.2014.12.001

20. Zaki, J. (2017). Moving beyond stereotypes of empathy. *Trends in Cognitive Sciences, 21*(2), 59–60. https://doi.org/10.1016/j.tics.2016. 12.004

21. Kelly, K., Slade, A., & Grienenberger, J. F. (2005). Maternal reflective functioning, mother–infant affective communication, and infant attachment: Exploring the link between mental states and observed caregiving behavior in the intergenerational transmission of attachment. *Attachment & Human Development, 7*(3), 299–311. https://doi.org/10.1080/14616730500245963

22. Senehi, N., Brophy-Herb, H. E., & Vallotton, C. D. (2018). Effects of maternal mentalization-related parenting on toddlers' self-regulation. *Early Childhood Research Quarterly, 44*(3), 1–14. https://doi.org/10.1016/j.ecresq.2018.02.001

23. Gergely, G., & Watson, J. S. (1996). The social biofeedback theory of parental affect-mirroring: The development of emotional self-awareness and self-control in infancy. *International Journal of Psychoanalysis, 77*(6), 1181–1212.

24. Fonagy, P., Gergely, G., Jurist, E., & Target, M. (2002). *Affect regulation, mentalization and the development of the self.* Other Press.

25. Suchman, N. E., DeCoste, C., Borelli, J. L., & McMahon, T. J. (2018). Does improvement in maternal attachment representations predict greater maternal sensitivity, child attachment security and lower rates of relapse to substance use? A second test of Mothering From the Inside Out treatment mechanisms. *Journal of Substance Abuse Treatment, 85,* 21–30. https://doi.org/10.1016/j.jsat.2017.11.006

26. Manczak, E. M., DeLongis, A., & Chen, E. (2016). Does empathy have a cost? Diverging psychological and physiological effects within families. *Health Psychology, 35*(3), 211–218. https://doi.org/10.1037/hea0000281

27. Rasmussen, H. F., Borelli, J. L., Smiley, P. A., Cohen, C., Cheung, R. C. M., Fox, S., Marvin, M., & Blackard, B. (2017). Mother–child language style matching predicts children's and mothers' emotion reactivity. *Behavioural Brain Research, 325*(B), 203–213. https://doi.org/10.1016/j.bbr.2016.12.036

28. Kerr, M. L., Rasmussen, H. F., Buttitta, K. V., Smiley, P. A., & Borelli, J. L. (2021). Exploring the complexity of mothers' real-time emotions while caregiving. *Emotion, 21*(3), 545–556. https://doi.org/10.1037/emo0000719

29. Widen, S. C., & Russell, J. A. (2003). A closer look at preschoolers' freely produced labels for facial expressions. *Developmental Psychology, 39*(1), 114–128. https://doi.org/10.1037/0012-1649.39.1.114

30. Bosmans, G., & Kerns, K. A. (2015). Attachment in middle childhood: Progress and prospects. *New Directions for Child and Adolescent Development, 2015*(148), 1–14. https://doi.org/10.1002/cad.20100

31. Kerns, K. A., & Richardson, R. A. (2008). *Attachment in middle childhood*. The Guilford Press.

32. Mayseless, O. (2005). Ontogeny of attachment in middle childhood: Conceptualization of normative changes. In K. A. Kerns & R. A. Richardson (Eds.), *Attachment in middle childhood* (pp. 1–23). Guilford Press.

33. Rubin, K. H., Bukowski, W. M., & Parker, J. G. (1998). Peer interactions, relationships, and groups. In W. Damon & N. Eisenberg (Eds.), *Handbook of child psychology: Vol. 3. Social, emotional, and personality development* (5th ed., pp. 621–700). John Wiley and Sons.

34. Mayes, L. C. (2006). Arousal regulation, emotional flexibility, medial amygdala function, and the impact of early experience: Comments on the paper of Lewis et al. *Annals of the New York Academy of Sciences, 1094*(1), 178–192. https://doi.org/10.1196/annals.1376.018

35. Borelli, J., & Lai, J. (2019, June 25). How to decipher the emotions behind your child's behaviors. *Greater Good Magazine.* https://www.greatergood.berkeley.edu/article/item/how_to_decipher_the_emotions_behind_your_childs_behaviors

36. Eisenberg, N., Cumberland, A., & Spinrad, T. L. (1998). Parental socialization of emotion. *Psychological Inquiry, 9*(4), 241–273. https://doi.org/10.1207/s15327965pli0904_1

37. Klinnert, M. D. (1984). The regulation of infant behavior by maternal facial expression. *Infant Behavior and Development, 7*(4), 447–465. https://doi.org/10.1016/S0163-6383(84)80005-3

38. Sorce, J. F., Emde, R. N., Campos, J. J., & Klinnert, M. D. (1985). Maternal emotional signaling: Its effect on the visual cliff behavior of 1-year-olds. *Developmental Psychology, 21*(1), 195–200. https://doi.org/10.1037/0012-1649.21.1.195

39. Chaplin, T. M., Cole, P. M., & Zahn-Waxler, C. (2005). Parental socialization of emotion expression: Gender differences and relations to child adjustment. *Emotion, 5*(1), 80–88. https://doi.org/10.1037/1528-3542.5.1.80

40. Fivush, R. (1989). Exploring sex differences in the emotional content of mother–child conversations about the past. *Sex Roles, 20*(11–12), 675–691. https://doi.org/10.1007/BF00288079

41. Chaplin, T. M., Casey, J., Sinha, R., & Mayes, L. C. (2010). Gender differences in caregiver emotion socialization of low-income toddlers. *New Directions for Child and Adolescent Development, 2010*(128), 11–27. https://doi.org/10.1002/cd.266

42. Shai, D., & Fonagy, P. (2014). Beyond words: Parental embodied mentalizing and the parent-infant dance. In M. Mikulincer & P. R. Shaver (Eds.), *Mechanisms of social connection: From brain to group* (pp. 185–203). American Psychological Association. https://doi.org/10.1037/14250-011

43. Shai, D., & Belsky, J. (2011). When words just won't do: Introducing parental embodied mentalizing. *Child Development Perspectives, 5*(3), 173–180. https://doi.org/10.1111/j.1750-8606.2011.00181.x

CHAPTER 7

1. Grewen, K. M., Girdler, S. S., Amico, J., & Light, K. C. (2005). Effects of partner support on resting oxytocin, cortisol, norepinephrine, and blood pressure before and after warm partner contact. *Psychosomatic Medicine, 67*(4), 531–538. https://doi.org/10.1097/01.psy.0000170341.88395.47

2. Ditzen, B., Schaer, M., Gabriel, B., Bodenmann, G., Ehlert, U., & Heinrichs, M. (2009). Intranasal oxytocin increases positive communication and reduces cortisol levels during couple conflict. *Biological Psychiatry, 65*(9), 728–731. https://doi.org/10.1016/j.biopsych.2008.10.011

3. Folkman, S., & Lazarus, R. S. (1985). If it changes it must be a process: Study of emotion and coping during three stages of a college examination. *Journal of Personality and Social Psychology, 48*(1), 150–170. https://doi.org/10.1037//0022-3514.48.1.150

4. Lazarus, R. S., Kanner, A. D., & Folkman, S. (1980). Emotions: A cognitive–phenomenological analysis. In R. Plutchik & H. Kellerman (Eds.), *Theories of emotion* (pp. 189–217). Academic Press. https://doi.org/10.1016/B978-0-12-558701-3.50014-4

5. Dich, N., Doan, S. N., Kivimäki, M., Kumari, M., & Rod, N. H. (2014). A non-linear association between self-reported negative emotional response to stress and subsequent allostatic load: Prospective results from the Whitehall II cohort study. *Psychoneuroendocrinology, 49*, 54–61. https://doi.org/10.1016/j.psyneuen.2014.07.001

6. Gross, J. J., & John, O. P. (2003). Individual differences in two emotion regulation processes: Implications for affect, relationships, and well-being. *Journal of Personality and Social Psychology, 85*(2), 348–362. https://doi.org/10.1037/0022-3514.85.2.348

7. Richards, J. M., & Gross, J. J. (1999). Composure at any cost? The cognitive consequences of emotion suppression. *Personality and Social Psychology Bulletin, 25*(8), 1033–1044. https://doi.org/10.1177/01461672992511010

8. Doan, S. N., Dich, N., & Evans, G. W. (2016). Stress of stoicism: Low emotionality and high control lead to increases in allostatic load. *Applied Developmental Science, 20*(4), 310–317. https://doi.org/10.1080/10888691.2016.1171716

9. Gottman, J. M., Katz, L. F., & Hooven, C. (1996). Parental meta-emotion philosophy and the emotional life of families: Theoretical models and preliminary data. *Journal of Family Psychology, 10*(3), 243–268. https://doi.org/10.1037/0893-3200.10.3.243

10. Gottman, J. M., Katz, L. F., & Hooven, C. (1997). *Meta-emotion: How families communicate emotionally*. Routledge.

11. Gruber, J., & Borelli, J. L. (2017, December 12). The importance of fostering emotional diversity in boys. *Scientific American.* https://www.scientificamerican.com/article/the-importance-of-fostering-emotional-diversity-in-boys/

CHAPTER 8

1. Bowlby, J. (1979). *The making and breaking of affectional bonds.* Tavistock Publications.

2. Cassidy, J. (1994). Emotion regulation: Influences of attachment relationships. *Monographs of the Society for Research in Child Development, 59*(2–3), 228–249. https://doi.org/10.1111/j.1540-5834.1994.tb01287.x

3. Porges, S. W. (1995). Orienting in a defensive world: Mammalian modifications of our evolutionary heritage—A polyvagal theory. *Psychophysiology, 32*(4), 301–318. https://doi.org/10.1111/j.1469-8986.1995.tb01213.x

4. Lyons-Ruth, K. (2007). The interface between attachment and intersubjectivity: Perspective from the longitudinal study of disorganized

attachment. *Psychoanalytic Inquiry, 26*(4), 595–616. https://doi.org/10.1080/07351690701310656

5. Fredrickson, B. L. (1998). What good are positive emotions? *Review of General Psychology, 2*(3), 300–319. https://doi.org/10.1037/1089-2680.2.3.300

6. Fredrickson, B. L. (2001). The role of positive emotions in positive psychology: The broaden-and-build theory of positive emotions. *American Psychologist, 56*(3), 218–226. https://doi.org/10.1037/0003-066X.56.3.218

7. Fredrickson, B. L. (2013). Positive emotions broaden and build. In P. Devine & A. Plant (Eds.), *Advances in experimental social psychology* (Vol. 47, pp. 1–53). Academic Press.

8. Isen, A. M. (1990). The influence of positive and negative affect on cognitive organization: Some implications for development. In N. L. Stein, B. Leventhal, & T. Trabasso (Eds.), *Psychological and biological approaches to emotion* (pp. 75–94). Lawrence Erlbaum Associates.

9. Isen, A. M., Daubman, K. A., & Nowicki, G. P. (1987). Positive affect facilitates creative problem solving. *Journal of Personality and Social Psychology, 52*(6),1122–1131. https://doi.org/10.1037/0022-3514.52.6.1122

10. Kok, B. E., & Fredrickson, B. L. (2010). Upward spirals of the heart: Autonomic flexibility, as indexed by vagal tone, reciprocally and prospectively predicts positive emotions and social connectedness. *Biological Psychology, 85*(3), 432–436. https://doi.org/10.1016/j.biopsycho.2010.09.005

11. Denollet, J., Schiffer, A. A., & Spek, V. (2010). A general propensity to psychological distress affects cardiovascular outcomes: Evidence from research on the Type D (distressed) personality profile. *Circulation: Cardiovascular Quality and Outcomes, 3*(5), 546–557. https://doi.org/10.1161/CIRCOUTCOMES.109.934406

12. Thorn, B. E., Pence, L. B., Ward, L. C., Kilgo, G., Clements, K. L., Cross, T. H., Davis, A. M., & Tsui, P. W. (2007). A randomized clinical trial of targeted cognitive behavioral treatment to reduce catastrophizing in chronic headache sufferers. *Journal of Pain, 8*(12), 938–949. https://doi.org/10.1016/j.jpain.2007.06.010

13. Segerstrom, S. C., & Miller, G. E. (2006). Psychological stress and the human immune system: A meta-analytic study of 30 years inquiry.

Psychological Bulletin, 130(4), 601–630. https://doi.org/10.1037/
0033-2909.130.4.601

14. Fredrickson, B. L., & Levenson, R. W. (1998). Positive emotions speed recovery from the cardiovascular sequelae of negative emotions. *Cognition and Emotion, 12*(2), 191–220. https://doi.org/10.1080/026999398379718

15. Fredrickson, B. L., Mancuso, R. A., Branigan, C., & Tugade, M. M. (2000). The undoing effect of positive emotions. *Motivation and Emotion, 24*, 237–258. https://doi.org/10.1023/A:1010796329158

16. Fredrickson, B. L., Tugade, M. M., Waugh, C. E., & Larkin, G. (2003). What good are positive emotions in crises? A prospective study of resilience and emotions following the terrorist attacks on the United States on September 11th, 2001. *Journal of Personality and Social Psychology, 84*(2), 365–376. https://doi.org/10.1037/0022-3514.84.2.365

17. Jans-Beken, L., Jacobs, N., Janssens, M., Peeters, S., Reijnders, J., Lechner, L., & Lataster, J. (2020). Gratitude and health: An updated review. *Journal of Positive Psychology, 15*(6), 743–782. https://doi.org/10.1080/17439760.2019.1651888

18. Bartlett, M. Y., & DeSteno, D. (2006). Gratitude and prosocial behavior: Helping when it costs you. *Psychological Science, 17*(4), 319–325. https://doi.org/10.1111/j.1467-9280.2006.01705.x

19. Dunn, E. W., Aknin, L. B., & Norton, M. I. (2008). Spending money on others promotes happiness. *Science, 319*(5870), 1687–1688. https://doi.org/10.1126/science.1150952

20. Van Boven, L., & Ashworth, L. (2007). Looking forward, looking back: Anticipation is more evocative than retrospection. *Journal of Experimental Psychology: General, 136*(2), 289–300. https://doi.org/10.1037/0096-3445.136.2.289

21. Raes, F., Smets, J., Nelis, S., & Schoofs, H. (2012). Dampening of positive affect prospectively predicts depressive symptoms in non-clinical samples. *Cognition and Emotion, 26*(1), 75–82. https://doi.org/10.1080/02699931.2011.555474

22. Calkins, S. D., Smith, C. L., Gill, K., & Johnson, M. C. (1998). Maternal interactive style across contexts: Relations to emotional, behavioral and physiological regulation during toddlerhood. *Social Development, 7*(3), 350–369. https://doi.org/10.1111/1467-9507.00072

23. Yap, M. B., Allen, N. B., & Ladouceur, C. D. (2008). Maternal socialization of positive affect: The impact of invalidation on adolescent emotion regulation and depressive symptomatology. *Child Development, 79*(5), 1415–1431. https://doi.org/10.1111/j.1467-8624.2008.01196.x

24. Bryant, F. B., & Veroff, J. (2007). *Savoring: A new model of positive experience.* Lawrence Erlbaum Associates.

25. Peters, B. J., Reis, H. T., & Gable, S. L. (2018). Making the good even better: A review and theoretical model of interpersonal capitalization. *Social and Personality Psychology Compass, 12*(7), Article e12407. https://doi.org/10.1111/spc3.12407

26. Doan, S. N., & Wang, Q. (2010). Maternal discussions of mental states and external behaviors: Relations to children's emotion situation knowledge in European American and immigrant Chinese children. *Child Development, 81*(5), 1490–1503. https://doi.org/10.1111/j.1467-8624.2010.01487.x

27. Wang, Q., Koh, J. B. K., Santacrose, D., Song, Q., Klemfuss, J. Z., & Doan, S. N. (2019). Child-centered memory conversations facilitate children's episodic thinking. *Cognitive Development, 51*, 58–66. https://doi.org/10.1016/j.cogdev.2019.05.009

28. Doan, S. N., Lee, H. Y., & Wang, Q. (2019). Maternal mental state language is associated with trajectories of Chinese immigrant children's emotion situation knowledge. *International Journal of Behavioral Development, 43*(1), 43–52. https://doi.org/10.1177/0165025418783271

29. Borelli, J. L., Hong, H., Sohn, L., Smiley, P., & Guo, Y. (2020). *Parents' depressive symptoms and reflective functioning interact to predict proficiency in relational savoring and children's physiological regulation* [Manuscript submitted for publication]. Department of Psychological Science, University of California, Irvine.

30. Burkhart, M. L., Borelli, J. L., Rasmussen, H. F., Brody, R., & Sbarra, D. A. (2017). Parental mentalizing as an indirect link between attachment anxiety and parenting satisfaction. *Journal of Family Psychology, 31*(2), 203–213. https://doi.org/10.1037/fam0000270

31. Wang, B. A., Bouche, V., Hong, K., Eriksen, D. E., Rice, R., & Borelli, J. L. (2019). Investigating the efficacy of relational savoring among male adolescents in residential treatment. *Residential Treatment for Children & Youth, 38*(3), 307–323. https://doi.org/10.1080/0886571X.2019.1707146

32. Borelli, J. L., Rasmussen, H. F., Burkhart, M. L., & Sbarra, D. A. (2015). Relational savoring in long-distance romantic relationships. *Journal of Social and Personal Relationships*, 32(8), 1083–1108. https://doi.org/10.1177/0265407514558960

33. Bond, D. K., & Borelli, J. L. (2017). Maternal attachment insecurity and poorer proficiency savoring memories with their children: The mediating role of rumination. *Journal of Social and Personal Relationships*, 34(7), 1007–1030. https://doi.org/10.1177/0265407516664995

34. Doan, S. N., Ding, M., & Smiley, P. (2021). *Capitalization and children's vagal tone* [Manuscript in preparation]. Department of Psychological Science, Claremont McKenna College.

35. Borelli, J. L., Smiley, P. A., Kerr, M. L., Hong, K., Hecht, H. K., Blackard, M. B., Falasiri, E., Cervantes, B. R., & Bond, D. K. (2020). Relational savoring: An attachment-based approach to promoting interpersonal flourishing. *Psychotherapy*, 57(3), 340–351. https://doi.org/10.1037/pst0000284

36. Burkhart, M. L., Borelli, J. L., Rasmussen, H. F., & Sbarra, D. A. (2015). Cherish the good times: Relational savoring in parents of infants and toddlers. *Personal Relationships*, 22(4), 692–711. https://doi.org/10.1111/pere.12104

37. Wang, B. A., Bouche, V., Hong, K., Eriksen, D. E., Rice, R., & Borelli, J. L. (2019). Investigating the efficacy of relational savoring among male adolescents in residential treatment. *Residential Treatment for Children & Youth*, 38(3), 307–323. https://doi.org/10.1080/0886571X.2019.1707146

38. Borelli, J. L., Bond, D. B., Fox, S., & Horn-Mallers, M. (2019). Relational savoring reduces physiological reactivity and enhances psychological agency in older adults. *Journal of Applied Gerontology*, 39(3), 332–342. https://doi.org/10.1177/0733464819866972

39. Waters, S. F., Karnilowicz, H. R., West, T. V., & Mendes, W. B. (2020). Keep it to yourself? Parent emotion suppression influences physiological linkage and interaction behavior. *Journal of Family Psychology*, 34(7), 784–793. https://doi.org/10.1037/fam0000664

40. Goldin, P. R., McRae, K., Ramel, W., & Gross, J. J. (2008). The neural bases of emotion regulation: Reappraisal and suppression of negative emotion. *Biological Psychiatry*, 63(6), 577–586. https://doi.org/10.1016/j.biopsych.2007.05.031

CHAPTER 9

1. James, W. (1890). *The principles of psychology.* H. Holt and Company.
2. Rothbart, M. K., & Derryberry, D. (1981). Development of individual differences in temperament. *Advances in Developmental Psychology, 1,* 37–86
3. Little Zen Monkey. (2015, June 25). *Baby climbing indoors* [Video]. YouTube. https://youtu.be/Oo85Bkm-Ano
4. Degnan, K. A., & Fox, N. A. (2007). Behavioral inhibition and anxiety disorders: Multiple levels of a resilience process. *Development and Psychopathology, 19*(3), 729–746. https://doi.org/10.1017/S0954579407000363
5. Kiel, E. J., & Buss, K. A. (2013). Toddler inhibited temperament, maternal cortisol reactivity and embarrassment, and intrusive parenting. *Journal of Family Psychology, 27*(3), 512–517. https://doi.org/10.1037/a0032892
6. Murray, L., Creswell, C., & Cooper, P. J. (2009). The development of anxiety disorders in childhood: An integrative review. *Psychological Medicine, 39*(9), 1413–1423. https://doi.org/10.1017/S0033291709005157
7. Ashton, M. C. (2018). Biological bases of personality. In M. C. Ashton (Ed.), *Individual differences and personality* (3rd ed., pp. 107–125). Academic Press. https://doi.org/10.1016/B978-0-12-809845-5.00005-6
8. Merenda, P. F. (1987). Toward a four-factor theory of temperament and/or personality. *Journal of Personality Assessment, 51*(3), 367–374. https://doi.org/10.1207/s15327752jpa5103_4
9. Rothbart, M. K., Ahadi, S. A., Hershey, K. L., & Fisher, P. (2001). Investigations of temperament at three to seven years: The Children's Behavior Questionnaire. *Child Development, 72*(5), 1394–1408. https://doi.org/10.1111/1467-8624.00355
10. Kagan, J. (1997). Temperament and the reactions to unfamiliarity. *Child Development, 68*(1), 139–143. https://doi.org/10.2307/1131931
11. Rothbart, M. K. (2007). Temperament, development, and personality. *Current Directions in Psychological Science, 16*(4), 207–212. https://doi.org/10.1111/j.1467-8721.2007.00505.x
12. Rothbart, M. K. (2004). Temperament and the pursuit of an integrated developmental psychology. *Merrill-Palmer Quarterly, 50*(4), 492–505. https://doi.org/10.1353/mpq.2004.0035

13. Thomas, A., & Chess, S. (1977). *Temperament and development*. Brunner/Mazel.

14. Zentner, M., & Bates, J. E. (2008). Child temperament: An integrative review of concepts, research programs, and measures. *European Journal of Developmental Science, 2*(1–2), 7–37. https://doi.org/10.3233/ DEV-2008-21203

15. Holden, G. W., & Hawk, C. K. (2002). Meta-parenting in the journey of child rearing. In L. Kuczynski (Ed.), *Handbook of dynamics in parent–child relations* (pp. 189–210). SAGE Publications.

16. McKee, L., Roland, E., Coffelt, N., Olson, A. L., Forehand, R., Massari, C., Jones, D., Gaffney, C. A., & Zens, M. S. (2007). Harsh discipline and child problem behaviors: The roles of positive parenting and gender. *Journal of Family Violence, 22*(4), 187–196. https://doi.org/ 10.1007/s10896-007-9070-6

17. Smetana, J. G., & Daddis, C. (2002). Domain-specific antecedents of parental psychological control and monitoring: The role of parenting beliefs and practices. *Child Development, 73*(2), 563–580. https:// doi.org/10.1111/1467-8624.00424

18. Maccoby, E. E. (1998). *The two sexes: Growing up apart, coming together*. The Belknap Press of Harvard University Press.

19. Kushnir, T. (1985). Israeli parents' role in emergencies. *Journal of Social Psychology, 125*(1), 75–79. https://doi.org/10.1080/00224545. 1985.9713510

20. Hildebrandt, K. A., & Cannan, T. (1985). The distribution of caregiver attention in a group program for young children. *Child Study Journal, 15*(1), 43–55.

21. Klein, M. R., Lengua, L. J., Thompson, S. F., Moran, L., Ruberry, E. J., Kiff, C., & Zalewski, M. (2018). Bidirectional relations between temperament and parenting predicting preschool-age children's adjustment. *Journal of Clinical Child & Adolescent Psychology, 47*(Suppl. 1), S113–S126. https://doi.org/10.1080/15374416.2016.1169537

22. Kiff, C. J., Lengua, L. J., & Zalewski, M. (2011). Nature and nurturing: Parenting in the context of child temperament. *Clinical Child and Family Psychology Review, 14*(3), 251–301. https://doi.org/10.1007/ s10567-011-0093-4

23. Barkley, R. A., Karlsson, J., Pollard, S., & Murphy, J. V. (1985). Developmental changes in the mother–child interactions of hyperactive boys:

Effects of two dose levels of Ritalin. *Journal of Child Psychology and Psychiatry, 26*(5), 705–715. https://doi.org/10.1111/j.1469-7610.1985. tb00585.x

24. McBride, B. A., Schoppe, S. J., & Rane, T. R. (2002). Child characteristics, parenting stress, and parental involvement: Fathers versus mothers. *Journal of Marriage and Family, 64*(4), 998–1011. https://doi.org/10.1111/j.1741-3737.2002.00998.x

25. Volling, B. L., & Belsky, J. (1991). Multiple determinants of father involvement during infancy in dual-earner and single-earner families. *Journal of Marriage and Family, 53*(2), 461–474. https://doi.org/10.2307/352912

26. Belsky, J., Bakermans-Kranenburg, M. J., & van IJzendoorn, M. H. (2007). For better and for worse: Differential susceptibility to environmental influences. *Current Directions in Psychological Science, 16*(6), 300–304. https://doi.org/10.1111/j.1467-8721.2007.00525.x

27. Dich, N., Doan, S. N., & Evans, G. W. (2015). Children's emotionality moderates the association between maternal responsiveness and allostatic load: Investigation into differential susceptibility. *Child Development, 86*(3), 936–944. https://doi.org/10.1111/cdev.12346

CHAPTER 10

1. Bois, J. E., Sarazzin, P. G., Brustad, R. J., Trouilloud, D. O., & Curry, F. (2005). Elementary school children's perceived competence and physical activity involvement: The influence of parents' role modelling behaviours and perceptions of their child's competence. *Psychology of Sports and Exercise, 6*(4), 381–397. https://doi.org/10.1016/j.psychsport.2004.03.003

2. Bowlby, J. (1973). *Attachment and loss: Vol. 2. Separation, anger and anxiety.* The Hogarth Press and the Institute of Psycho-Analysis.

3. Fincham, F. D. (1998). Child development and marital relations. *Child Development, 69*(2), 543–574. https://doi.org/10.1111/j.1467-8624.1998.tb06207.x

4. Altenburger, L. E., Schoppe-Sullivan, S. J., Lang, S. N., Bower, D. J., & Kamp Dush, C. M. (2014). Associations between prenatal coparenting behavior and observed coparenting behavior at 9-months postpartum. *Journal of Family Psychology, 28*(4), 495–504. https://doi.org/10.1037/fam0000012

5. Cohen, R. S., & Weissman, S. H. (1984). The parenting alliance. In R. S. Cohen, B. J. Cohler, & S. H. Weissman (Eds.), *Parenthood: A psychodynamic perspective* (pp. 33–49). The Guilford Press.

6. Katz, L. F., & Woodin, E. M. (2002). Hostility, hostile detachment, and conflict engagement in marriages: Effects on child and family functioning. *Child Development, 73*(2), 636–652. https://doi.org/10.1111/1467-8624.00428

7. McHale, J. P., Kazali, C., Rotman, T., Talbot, J., Carleton, M., & Lieberson, R. (2004). The transition to coparenthood: Parents' prebirth expectations and early coparental adjustment at 3 months postpartum. *Development and Psychopathology, 16*(3), 711–733. https://doi.org/10.1017/S0954579404004742

8. McHale, J., Khazan, I., Erera, P., Rotman, T., DeCourcey, W., & McConnell, M. (2002). Coparenting in diverse family systems. In M. H. Bornstein (Ed.), *Handbook of parenting: Vol. 3. Being and becoming a parent* (2nd ed., pp. 75–107). Lawrence Erlbaum Associates.

9. Van Egeren, L. A. (2003). Prebirth predictors of coparenting experiences in early infancy. *Infant Mental Health Journal, 24*(3), 278–295. https://doi.org/10.1002/imhj.10056

10. Van Egeren, L. A. (2004). The development of the coparenting relationship over the transition to parenthood. *Infant Mental Health Journal, 25*(5), 453–477. https://doi.org/10.1002/imhj.20019

11. Doss, B. D., Rhoades, G. K., Stanley, S. M., & Markman, H. J. (2009). The effect of the transition to parenthood on relationship quality: An 8-year prospective study. *Journal of Personality and Social Psychology, 96*(3), 601–619. https://doi.org/10.1037/a0013969

12. MacDermid, S. M., Huston, T. L., & McHale, S. M. (1990). Changes in marriage associated with the transition to parenthood: Individual differences as a function of sex-role attitudes and changes in the division of household labor. *Journal of Marriage and the Family, 52*(2), 475–486. https://doi.org/10.2307/353041

13. Abidin, R. R., & Brunner, J. F. (1995). Development of a parenting alliance inventory. *Journal of Clinical Child Psychology, 24*(1), 31–40. https://doi.org/10.1207/s15374424jccp2401_4

14. Bradbury, T. N., Fincham, F. D., & Beach, S. R. (2000). Research on the nature and determinants of marital satisfaction: A decade in review. *Journal of Marriage and Family, 62*(4), 964–980. https://doi.org/10.1111/j.1741-3737.2000.00964.x

15. McHale, J. P., & Rasmussen, J. L. (1998). Coparental and family group-level dynamics during infancy: Early family precursors of child and family functioning during preschool. *Development and Psychopathology, 10*(1), 39–59. https://doi.org/10.1017/S0954579498001527

16. McHale, J. P., & Irace, K. (2011). Coparenting in diverse family systems. In J. P. McHale & K. M. Lindahl (Eds.), *Coparenting: A conceptual and clinical examination of family systems* (pp. 15–37). American Psychological Association. https://doi.org/10.1037/12328-001

17. Ventura, S. J., & Bachrach, C. A. (2000). Nonmarital childbearing in the United States, 1940–99. *National Vital Statistics Reports, 48*(16), 2–46.

18. Cooper, C. E., McLanahan, S. S., Meadows, S. O., & Brooks-Gunn, J. (2009). Family structure transitions and maternal parenting stress. *Journal of Marriage and Family, 71*(3), 558–574. https://doi.org/10.1111/j.1741-3737.2009.00619.x

19. Grill, E. A. (2005). Treating single mothers by choice. In A. Rosen & J. Rosen (Eds.), *Frozen dreams: Psychodynamic dimensions of infertility and assisted reproduction* (pp. 167–196). The Analytic Press.

20. Groze, V. (1991). Adoption and single parents: A review. *Child Welfare: Journal of Policy, Practice, and Program, 70*(3), 321–332.

21. Haugaard, J. J., Palmer, M., & Wojslawowicz, J. C. (1999). Single-parent adoptions. *Adoption Quarterly, 2*(4), 65–74. https://doi.org/10.1300/J145v02n04_05

22. Patterson, C. J., Farr, R. H., & Hastings, P. D. (2007). Socialization in the context of family diversity. In J. E. Grusec & P. D. Hastings (Eds.), *Handbook of socialization: Theory and research* (pp. 328–351). The Guilford Press.

23. Atwood, J. D., & Genovese, F. (2006). *Therapy with single parents. A social constructivist approach.* The Haworth Press.

24. Kreider, R. M. (2003, October). *Adopted children and stepchildren: 2000.* U.S. Census Bureau. http://www.census.gov/prod/2003pubs/censr-6.pdf

25. Siegel, J. M. (1998). Pathways to single motherhood: Sexual intercourse, adoption, and donor insemination. *Families in Society, 79*(1), 75–82. https://doi.org/10.1606/1044-3894.1795

26. Luker, K. (1996). *Dubious conceptions: The politics of teenage pregnancy.* Harvard University Press.

27. Reece, S. M. (1995). Stress and maternal adaptation in first-time mothers more than 35 years old. *Applied Nursing Research, 8*(2), 61–66. https://doi.org/10.1016/S0897-1897(95)80490-0

28. Schoppe, S. J., Mangelsdorf, S. C., & Frosch, C. A. (2001). Coparenting, family process, and family structure: Implications for preschoolers' externalizing behavior problems. *Journal of Family Psychology, 15*(3), 526–545. https://doi.org/10.1037/0893-3200.15.3.526

29. Carlson, M. J., McLanahan, S. S., & Brooks-Gunn, J. (2008). Coparenting and nonresident fathers' involvement with young children after a nonmarital birth. *Demography, 45*(2), 461–488. https://doi.org/10.1353/dem.0.0007

30. Dorsey, S., Forehand, R., & Brody, G. (2007). Coparenting, conflict and parenting behavior in economically disadvantaged single parent African American families: The role of maternal psychological distress. *Journal of Family Violence, 22*(7), 621–630. https://doi.org/10.1007/s10896-007-9114-y

31. Fagan, J., & Palkovitz, R. (2007). Unmarried, nonresident fathers' involvement with their infants: A risk and resilience perspective. *Journal of Family Psychology, 21*(3), 479–489. https://doi.org/10.1037/0893-3200.21.3.479

32. Mincy, R., Pouncy, H., Reichert, D., & Richardson, P. (2004). *Fragile families in focus: How low-income never married parents perceive relationships and marriage* [Executive summary]. TANF Executive Office, Division of Administration, State of Louisiana.

33. Shook, S. E., Jones, D. J., Forehand, R., Dorsey, S., & Brody, G. (2010). The mother–coparent relationship and youth adjustment: A study of African American single-mother families. *Journal of Family Psychology, 24*(3), 243–251. https://doi.org/10.1037/a0019630

34. Waller, M. R. (2009). Family man in the other America: New opportunities, motivations, and supports for paternal caregiving. *Annals of the American Academy of Political and Social Science, 624*(1), 156–176. https://doi.org/10.1177/0002716209334372

35. Amato, P. R. (1998). More than money? Men's contributions to their children's lives. In A. Booth & A. C. Crouter (Eds.), *Men in families: When do they get involved? What difference does it make?* (pp. 241–278). Lawrence Erlbaum Associates.

36. Amato, P. R. (1994). Father–child relations, mother–child relations, and offspring psychological well-being in early adulthood. *Journal*

of Marriage and the Family, 56(4), 1031–1042. https://doi.org/10.2307/353611

37. Borelli, J. L., Slade, A., Pettit, C., & Shai, D. (2020). I "get" you, babe: Reflective functioning in partners transitioning to parenthood. *Journal of Social and Personal Relationships*, 37(6), 1785–1805. https://doi.org/10.1177/0265407520905641

38. Belsky, J., Crnic, K., & Gable, S. (1995). The determinants of coparenting in families with toddler boys: Spousal differences and daily hassles. *Child Development*, 66(3), 629–642. https://doi.org/10.1111/j.1467-8624.1995.tb00894.x

39. McHale, J. P. (1995). Coparenting and triadic interactions during infancy: The roles of marital distress and child gender. *Developmental Psychology*, 31(6), 985–996. https://doi.org/10.1037/0012-1649.31.6.985

40. Minuchin, S. (1974). *Families and family therapy*. Harvard University Press.

41. Feinberg, M. E., Brown, L. D., & Kan, M. L. (2012). A multi-domain self-report measure of coparenting. *Parenting*, 12(1), 1–21. https://doi.org/10.1080/15295192.2012.638870

42. Johnson, V. K., Cowan, P. A., & Cowan, C. P. (1999). Children's classroom behavior: The unique contribution of family organization. *Journal of Family Psychology*, 13(3), 355–371. https://doi.org/10.1037/0893-3200.13.3.355

43. Karreman, A., van Tuijl, C., van Aken, M. A. G., & Deković, M. (2008). Parenting, coparenting, and effortful control in preschoolers. *Journal of Family Psychology*, 22(1), 30–40. https://doi.org/10.1037/0893-3200.22.1.30

44. Kolak, A. M., & Vernon–Feagans, L. (2008). Family-level coparenting processes and child gender as moderators of family stress and toddler adjustment. *Infant and Child Development*, 17(6), 617–638. https://doi.org/10.1002/icd.577

45. Bandura, A., Ross, D., & Ross, S. A. (1961). Transmission of aggression through imitation of aggressive models. *Journal of Abnormal and Social Psychology*, 63(3), 575–582. https://doi.org/10.1037/h0045925

46. Teubert, D., & Pinquart, M. (2010). The association between coparenting and child adjustment: A meta-analysis. *Parenting*, 10(4), 286–307. https://doi.org/10.1080/15295192.2010.492040

47. Margolin, G., Gordis, E. B., & John, R. S. (2001). Coparenting: A link between marital conflict and parenting in two-parent families. *Journal of Family Psychology, 15*(1), 3–21. https://doi.org/10.1037/0893-3200.15.1.3

48. Jones, D. J., Shaffer, A., Forehand, R. Brody, G., & Armistead, L. P. (2003). Coparent conflict in single mother-headed African American families: Do parenting skills serve as a mediator or moderator of child psychosocial adjustment? *Behavior Therapy, 34*(2), 259–272. https://doi.org/10.1016/S0005-7894(03)80016-3

49. Feinberg, M. E., Kan, M. L., & Hetherington, E. M. (2007). The longitudinal influence of coparenting conflict on parental negativity and adolescent maladjustment. *Journal of Marriage and Family, 69*(3), 687–702. https://doi.org/10.1111/j.1741-3737.2007.00400.x

50. Fagan, J., & Cabrera, N. (2012). Longitudinal and reciprocal associations between coparenting conflict and father engagement. *Journal of Family Psychology, 26*(6), 1004–1011. https://doi.org/10.1037/a0029998

51. Minuchin, S., Baker, L., Rosman, B. L., Liebman, R., Milman, L., & Todd, T. C. (1975). A conceptual model of psychosomatic illness in children: Family organization and family therapy. *Archives of General Psychiatry, 32*(8), 1031–1038. https://doi.org/10.1001/archpsyc.1975.01760260095008

52. Kerig, P. K. (1995). Triangles in the family circle: Effects of family structure on marriage, parenting, and child adjustment. *Journal of Family Psychology, 9*(1), 28–43. https://doi.org/10.1037/0893-3200.9.1.28

53. McBride, B. A., Brown, G. L., Bost, K. K., Shin, N., Vaughn, B., & Korth, B. (2005). Paternal identity, maternal gatekeeping, and father involvement. *Family Relations, 54*(3), 360–372. https://doi.org/10.1111/j.1741-3729.2005.00323.x

54. Schoppe-Sullivan, S. J., Brown, G. L., Cannon, E. A., Mangelsdorf, S. C., & Sokolowski, M. S. (2008). Maternal gatekeeping, coparenting quality, and fathering behavior in families with infants. *Journal of Family Psychology, 22*(3), 389–398. https://doi.org/10.1037/0893-3200.22.3.389

55. Ängarne-Lindberg, T., & Wadsby, M. (2012). Psychiatric and somatic health in relation to experience of parental divorce in childhood. *International Journal of Social Psychiatry, 58*(1), 16–25. https://doi.org/10.1177/0020764010382372

56. Lamela, D., Figueiredo, B., Bastos, A., & Feinberg, M. (2016). Typologies of post-divorce coparenting and parental well-being, parenting quality and children's psychological adjustment. *Child Psychiatry and Human Development*, 47(5), 716–728. https://doi.org/10.1007/s10578-015-0604-5

57. Lamela, D., & Figueiredo, B. (2011). Post-divorce representations of marital negotiation during marriage predict parenting alliance in newly divorced parents. *Sexual Relationship Therapy* 26(2), 182–190. https://doi.org/10.1080/14681994.2011.563288

58. Sbarra, D. A., & Emery, R. E. (2008). Deeper into divorce: Using actor-partner analyses to explore systemic differences in coparenting conflict following custody dispute resolution. *Journal of Family Psychology*, 22(1), 144–152. https://doi.org/10.1037/0893-3200.22.1.144

INDEX

ABOUT THE AUTHORS

Stacey N. Doan, PhD, received her doctorate from Cornell University. She is an associate professor of psychological science at Claremont McKenna College in Claremont, California, and an adjunct associate professor at City of Hope National Medical Center in Duarte, California. A developmental health psychologist, she is particularly interested in understanding factors that predict resilience, emotional intelligence, and happiness in children. Her research also focuses on how early life experiences, both positive and negative, have short- and long-term effects on health and well-being. In addition, Dr. Doan has a genuine interest in helping individuals flourish through her health/life coaching work.

Her work has been published in the top developmental journals in the field and recognized, with early career awards, by the Society for Research on Child Development, the American Psychological Association, and the Western Psychological Association. Her research is funded by the National Institutes of Health, the National Science Foundation, and multiple private foundations.

In writing this book, Dr. Doan drew on her research and also on her personal experiences as a child of refugee parents raised in poverty and, just as important, as a mother of two young girls, Eliana and Samara. In her free time, she plays the piano (poorly), runs (slowly), and cooks (rather well). She is a fervent believer in the idea that love may not be sufficient, but it is necessary, as demonstrated to her so well by her amazing partner-in-crime, her husband, Daniel.

Jessica Borelli, PhD, is an associate professor of psychological science at the University of California, Irvine. Her research focuses on relationships and mental health with a particular focus on developing ways of improving relationships to improve well-being. Dr. Borelli has published more than 100 peer-reviewed journal articles and book chapters in the areas of child development, developmental psychopathology, and relationships. In addition, she is a practicing clinical psychologist and the clinical director of Compass Therapy in Newport Beach, California.

Dr. Borelli wrote this book from the parenting trenches. In between writing chapters, she was braiding hair, helping with homework, spotting handstands and bridges (how else can kids learn gymnastics?), giving baths, rehearsing songs, making dinner, and coordinating with her coparent.

Being a parent is the most challenging and rewarding journey she's had in her life, and she wouldn't trade it in for anything. She's grateful to her copilot (Dale) and her crew (Sam, Charlie, and Talia) for the help, support, input, inspiration, illustrations, and laughs they contributed along the way.